Praise for

THE UNSUBSTANTIAL AIR

"Samuel Hynes is simultaneously a great gift to his complicated country and to our English language. He vividly brings to life our earliest air warriors and does so with a seemingly effortless but exhilarating prose that soars in much the same way his aviators do. Masterful."

—Ken Burns

"This history of American airmen in the First World War conveys the fervor with which young men rushed to take part in a new form of combat. Many of them were acquainted thanks to boarding schools or the Ivy League, and illusions of glory lingered among the corps, even as pilots crashed carrying out ill-defined missions in untested machines and without parachutes. Hynes relies on contemporary letters and diaries . . . [and] captures the flyers' perspective and the rackety, exhilarating experience of flight."

—*The New Yorker*

"This year we saw a lot of books about World War I, and Samuel Hynes's *The Unsubstantial Air* is one of the best . . . [Hynes] writes in such a beautiful way, so the experiences of these men are so moving, and they were so brave . . . He does a wonderful job honoring them."

—Nancy Pearl, NPR's *Morning Edition*

"The American pilots of the early air corps did not sound the death knell of an old world like [Wilfred] Owen but instead shone with the promise of a new nation rising, asserting America's arrival as a great power. It is these voices, sometimes jejune, sometimes wise beyond their years, that Samuel Hynes evocatively documents in *The Unsubstantial Air*."

—John F. Ross, *The Wall Street Journal*

"*The Unsubstantial Air* follows multiple lives into and through the war, relating their story in part through their own letters, diaries and other accounts which, together with Hynes's own voice, are woven into a history . . . As a former Marine combat pilot himself in the Second World War, he is able to bring knowledge and a dose of nostalgia to the task."

—James Salter, *London Review of Books*

"A must-read for anyone interested in military history, *The Unsubstantial Air* is also Hynes' illuminating, heartfelt tribute to his pilot comrades of another conflict." —Chris Patsilelis, *Tampa Bay Times*

"A deeply empathetic account of the first gentlemen pilots feeling their ways in uncharted territory . . . Intimate and memorable portraits of these idealistic, daredevil young men are contained in a marvelously fluid narrative." —*Kirkus Reviews* (starred review)

"Hynes vividly re-creates the experience of flying in WWI . . . A must-read for anyone interested in aviation history, military history, and the American experience in the Great War." —*Publishers Weekly*

"Hynes deftly interweaves . . . individual stories and the larger war effort, making *The Unsubstantial Air* a joy for both history and biography readers." —Tobias Mutter, *Shelf Awareness*

"This is a magical book. With the deft wizardry we've come to expect from him, Samuel Hynes manages to take us simultaneously up into the air and back in time. No one who encounters his knowing but empathetic portraits of America's first wartime fliers will ever forget them." —Geoffrey C . Ward, author of *The Roosevelts: An Intimate History*

"A remarkable achievement. Drawing on his own experience as a Marine combat pilot in World War II and a treasure trove of little-known letters and journals, Samuel Hynes tells the story of American pilots during the Great War. He shows who these men were, what drew them to aviation, and how and when they learned to fly and fight in the air—what one of them called 'this killing business'—and does it in understated yet moving prose that reads like an extended elegy for a bygone and unrecoverable time. The result is mesmerizing from its lighthearted beginning to its often deadly end." —Robert Wohl, author of *The Spectacle of Flight: Aviation and the Western Imagination, 1920–1950*

"Drawing on meticulous research as well as the author's own experience as a combat aviator in World War II, *The Unsubstantial Air* is Samuel Hynes's intimate human history of the dawn of American aerial warfare during the Great War. Following the young pilots, many well-born gentlemen and many others not, Hynes paints a fascinating group portrait of American aviators as they are initiated into the deadly new game of aerial combat. No one I know of writes about flying, and fighting in the air, as gracefully as Hynes."

—Roger J. Spiller, author of *An Instinct for War: Scenes from the Battlefields of History*

"Samuel Hynes, who gave us the finest memoir of aerial combat in World War II, has journeyed back to the earlier global conflict and returned with the finest history of the first air war. He retrieves that long-ago struggle from the quaint half-remembered movies of faintly comical-looking planes made of cloth and wood, to put us among a generation of young Americans being fiercely tested as they learn to wage war with the most modern machines in the world. At once rich and restrained, sparkling with calm humor, full of weather and peril and wisdom and rue, and wholly engrossing from the very first page, *The Unsubstantial Air* is a monument worthy of the fliers it brings to intimate life. It is also a narrative that could only have been written by one who, under very different yet also very similar circumstances, has been there himself."

—Richard Snow, former editor in chief of *American Heritage*

"A marvelous book, which nobody but Samuel Hynes could have written. Of course he gives us the battles, the development of tactics and technique, the expansion of operations as the war goes on. But the heart of this book lies in his brilliant recovery of 'the pilot's world,' with its sense of romance and wildness, its mixture of valor and fatalism, its reticence and pride."   —Patrick Wright, author of *Tank: The Progress of a Monstrous War Machine*

Samuel Hynes

THE UNSUBSTANTIAL AIR

Samuel Hynes is the Woodrow Wilson Professor of Literature Emeritus at Princeton University and the author of *Flights of Passage*, a celebrated memoir of serving as a marine pilot in World War II. His book on soldiers' accounts of twentieth-century wars, *The Soldiers' Tale*, won a Robert F. Kennedy Book Award. He was a featured commentator on Ken Burns's documentary *The War*. He is also the author of several works of literary and cultural criticism, including *The Auden Generation* and *The Edwardian Turn of Mind*, and a second memoir, *The Growing Seasons*. He lives in Princeton, New Jersey.

THE
UNSUBSTANTIAL
AIR

American Fliers in the First World War

SAMUEL HYNES

Farrar, Straus and Giroux

New York

For Susanne McNatt,

with gratitude and affection

Farrar, Straus and Giroux
18 West 18th Street, New York 10011

Excerpts from *Over the Front* 1, no. 3 (Fall 1986), courtesy of the League of World War I Aviation Historians.

The Library of Congress has cataloged the hardcover edition as follows:
Hynes, Samuel, 1924–
    The unsubstantial air : American fliers in the First World War / Samuel Hynes. — First edition.
        pages   cm
    Includes bibliographical references (p.   ) and index.
    ISBN 978-0-374-27800-7 (cloth : alkaline paper) —
    ISBN 978-0-374-71225-9 (e-book)
    1. World War, 1914–1918—Aerial operations, American.
    2. Fighter pilots—United States—History—20th century.   3. Fighter pilots—United States—Biography.   4. World War, 1914–1918—Personal narratives, American.   I. Title.

D606. H86 2014
940.4'4973—dc23

                                                                2014008673

Paperback ISBN: 978-0-374-53558-2

Farrar, Straus and Giroux books may be purchased for educational, business, or promotional use. For information on bulk purchases, please contact the Macmillan Corporate and Premium Sales Department at 1-800-221-7945, extension 5442, or write to specialmarkets@macmillan.com.

www.fsgbooks.com
www.twitter.com/fsgbooks • www.facebook.com/fsgbooks

1   3   5   7   9   10   8   6   4   2

> Welcome, then,
> Thou unsubstantial air that I embrace:
> The wretch that thou hast blown unto the worst
> Owes nothing to thy blasts.
>
> *—King Lear*

CONTENTS

ILLUSTRATIONS

THE
UNSUBSTANTIAL
AIR

PROLOGUE: A FIRE
BEYOND THE HORIZON

A decade after the First World War ended, General William "Billy" Mitchell looked back on the fighting years and concluded that for the troops on the ground it had not been an interesting war. "There was no marching and maneuvering," he wrote, "no songs, no flying colors and bands playing while going into action. It was just grovelling in dirty mud holes and being killed and maimed by giant projectiles, or permanently incapacitated by gas. The only interest and romance in this war was in the air."

"Romance" strikes me as an odd word to come from the man who more than any other American had created the huge destructiveness of massed aerial bombing. But Mitchell was above all a *pilot*: he loved flying, and planes, and the fighting you could do with them. For him, it was *all* romantic. Once the cavalry charge with pennons flying had proved suicidal against machine guns, and cavalrymen had been dismounted and turned into infantry, aviation was the only kind of combat left in which one man, mounted on a machine now instead of a horse, could fight a personal war. If the big words of war—"glory," and "honor," and "chivalry," and "romance"—applied anywhere in this vast conflict, it would be in the air.

To young men in America who heard the news of a European war in the summer of 1914, it wasn't flying that was romantic; it was simply war itself. Some wars are like that; they have a power that draws young men to them. Not every war, not the little interventions and police actions and civil disruptions that are always breaking out somewhere in the world, but the big wars, the urgent, consequential ones. A big war is like a great fire burning far off, beyond the horizon; you can't see the flames, but you can see the reflection in the sky and smell the smoke when the wind is right, and if you're young, and especially if you're male, you want to witness that conflagration. And so you hurry off, eager to be where the danger and the excitement are and fearful that you'll arrive too late and find the fighting over, the fire only ashes.

In young imaginations, the First World War would be like that: it would be like stepping into history—romantic history, like the Civil War some of their grandfathers fought in, and back beyond that the brave War of Independence. One young Southerner, eager to enlist in the French army in 1914, announced, "I pay my part for Lafayette and Rochambeau," as though the French contribution to the American Revolution were an old personal debt he owed.

And so they went. Not to aviation, though, not at first; in the summer of 1914 there wasn't yet an air war to go to. The first American volunteers enlisted as ambulance drivers or joined the French army and wound up in the Foreign Legion. And were disappointed. And so they moved to the French Service Aéronautique, where the war would surely have the qualities that Mitchell prescribed: interest and romance.

There is a story to be told about those young men and the air war they fought. It's not military history; it's not about generals and their strategies and the movements of armies: rather, it's a story of the experience of becoming a pilot and then of flying in combat over the Western Front. It's about the men, and the planes; the French earth and sky; the flying, and killing, and dying, and surviving. That experience is new and strange, and unimaginable till you've had it. The closest a noncombatant can come to it is through the testimonies of the young men themselves, the pilots and observers and gunners who were there. We must listen to their voices as they recorded their war lives in letters and diaries and journals at the time and in the memoirs that some wrote, often long afterwards.

The stories they tell are not only about the hours they spend in the air: a flier in a combat squadron (or any other flying job, for that matter) spends more time on the ground than he spends in the air. A lot of other new experiences come to them there: They discover Abroad (most of them have never been outside their own country before). Being there is as much a learning experience as flying is. They see great European cities—Paris and London—and the foreigners who live there; they discover café life; they eat foreign food and meet foreign girls. None of it is what they imagined it would be, and they write home about that, too (though they go easy on stories about the girls). They visit towns and villages near their airfields; they take walks in the country; they swim in the rivers. They go on leave and visit Deauville or the Riviera (travel seems surprisingly easy, in a country at war); they're invited to country châteaus and meet the local gentry. It's all strange and new.

As they live these lives, in the air and on the ground, they are changed by it all and come to see that the lives of pilots compose a culture, a separate society defined by what they do together. They're different from the rest of the Army: they dress more casually than officers on the ground do; they're wilder in their behavior, with a certain unmilitary independence. A pair of wings on your chest identifies you as a different kind of soldier (the girls notice that).

Other elements, other emotions, enter their lives that they have not felt before. They grieve for dead friends; most of them have never seen someone as young as they are die. They take those losses personally and try to write home about them and, by describing them, to endure them. As they fly their missions, and the casualty lists grow, death in the air comes to seem likely, inevitable even; they become fatalistic: next time it will be me. And go on flying.

And yet, for all that, the romance that Mitchell found in war in the air remained. It wasn't quite the romance they expected in the innocence of their enlistments, but it was there—in the solitude of a single plane, high over France on a fine day, or in the excitement of an attack, two or three planes diving on a trench or a gun site and the antiaircraft fire rising.

Over time the stories of those young men and their flying war have blended into one story—a myth, you might say, of a big war that is past but remembered, like Homer's story of Greeks and Trojans, a part of our collective memory. Two decades after their war ended, when the fires of war burned once more beyond the horizon, another generation of boys—I was one of them—would look back to those earlier pilots and see them as our ancestors, and know that when the fire came closer, we, too, would go to it, and would fight, as they did, in the unsubstantial air.

ONE

AN OCCUPATION
FOR GENTLEMEN

The First World War was more than half over when the United States entered it in April 1917 and well into its last year before American troops engaged enemy forces on the Western Front. By then the terrible battles of Ypres, Verdun, and the Somme had been fought, and German troops had launched their 1917 spring offensive. That belated commitment came far too late for many young American men; from the first day, August 4, 1914, they were eager to get into this war that was not theirs.

Among those eager young men were seven who joined the French cause in the first months of the war, trained with the Service Aéronautique, and were the first to join what became the Lafayette Escadrille, the first squadron of American pilots to fly for France. They came from different places and from different lives.

Their motives for joining that far-off, foreign war were various and complex. Kiffin Rockwell was the son of an old southern family and the grandson of Confederate officers who had fought in the War Between the States. He'd been a student at Virginia Military Institute and considered himself already a trained soldier who only needed the experience of battle to fulfill himself. The war in Europe was "a great opportunity," he wrote to his mother soon after he enlisted—an opportunity, perhaps, to follow his grandfathers' example in a great charge, like the rebel charge at Chancellorsville. To that motive he added another, in a letter from France: "If I should be killed in this war I will at least die as a man should . . . I think if anything will make a man of me, it is this giving as a volunteer one's best for an ideal." Rockwell had just turned twenty-two. At that age, manhood is not a condition but a goal, and war is a training ground, a test. And death? Death is a romantic dream.

Victor Chapman, on holiday from his art studies in Paris, joined the French Foreign Legion, as Rockwell and many of the others did, but for reasons that seem quite opposite. Rockwell wanted romantic war, a war of ideals. Chapman didn't write about such abstractions; his letters home are about the hard life of a common legionnaire, and his aim seems to have been simply to submerge himself in that life. You can speculate about why he would want to do that—perhaps to escape from his father, John Jay Chapman, a well-known New York man of letters with a high opinion of himself and high expectations for his children—but you can't know. What you do know from his letters is that when he was in the Foreign Legion he was happy.

James McConnell quit his job with a railroad company and headed for war. Like Rockwell, McConnell saw the war as an opportunity—the opportunity of a lifetime, he told a friend back home. "These Sand Hills," he said, gesturing toward the North Carolina landscape he lived in, "will be here forever, but the war won't, and so I'm going." That explanation seemed to worry him, for he added, "And I'll be of some use, too, not just a sight-seer looking on; that wouldn't be fair." But clearly his deep motive wasn't service; it was curiosity. War would be memorable, something huge and strange—like seeing Africa or the South Pole. It would be history happening, bigger than anything that could possibly happen to you back home. And he'd be right there in it. Curiosity like that is a young man's itch; whatever you're doing when you're eighteen or twenty or twenty-two, it's bound to be less exciting than the war that other young men just like you are fighting, somewhere else. Your idea of what that war is like will be far from the reality—nobody can imagine war who hasn't seen and heard and touched and smelled it—but that war in your head will have a powerful attraction nonetheless. And so you'll go where it is. So McConnell went.

William Thaw and Norman Prince had both lived in France when they were children and felt a love for the country that was a motive—something like patriotism, as though they were partly French. They were also both already sportsman-pilots, and that gave them another motive. In the air above the Western Front the world's first flying war was being fought; up there they would use their flying skills in a new kind of sport, played for the highest possible stakes. Where else would you find a challenge like that?

I don't know why Elliot Cowdin, a well-off young man of no visible employment, chose to go to war: he seems to have left no records, and there are gaps in his story. And then there was Bert Hall, a Paris taxi driver. In *En l'Air!*, the book he wrote toward the end of the war, he said he enlisted two days after the war began, because "if a country is good enough to live in it is good enough to fight for." But everyone who knew Hall agreed that you couldn't believe anything he said (for example, he didn't enlist on August sixth but on the twenty-first). Would an American drifter who happened to be driving a taxi in Paris love France enough to fight for it? If he had been driving a taxi in Berlin, would he have fought for the Germans? Maybe the French army looked like a better job than taxi driving—not as well-paying (a common soldier in the French army got a penny a day in 1914), but more interesting and more exciting. Give it a try.

Here they are, all seven of them, with their two French officers.

The date of the photograph is May 1916; by now they're all trained pilots and are wearing the uniform of the Service Aéronautique. Most of them didn't set out to be fliers. Only Prince enlisted directly in the French air service; Thaw tried to, but was turned down. Four—Chapman, Rockwell, Hall, and Thaw—first joined the French Foreign Legion and fought in the trenches; two—Cowdin and McConnell—first served as drivers in the American Ambulance Field Service.

It may seem strange that six of the first seven Lafayette Escadrille pilots should have begun their war on the ground. There are practical explanations. The French flight-training program was crowded in those early days, and there were more would-be pilots than there were training planes. For foreigners, the only sure and immediate routes into the war were the Foreign Legion and the ambulance service. The Legion had always welcomed *les étrangers*, no questions asked; criminals, fugitives, and vagabonds could submerge their old selves in the anonymity of the Legion—all you had to do was remember the alias you made up. To some young men—romantic ones like Rockwell—the regiments of the Legion must have seemed to offer what they wanted, pure war, where the real soldiers were and the real battles were being fought, right now.

The American Ambulance Field Service was almost the opposite: it was staffed and financed by Americans and recruited its drivers mainly on American college campuses, and its mission was not killing but saving lives. You can see how appealing that would be to some young men: you could be a sightseer at the war, as McConnell put it, while also being useful. You wouldn't hurt anybody, and you might even persuade your mother that in an ambulance you wouldn't get hurt. College students could sign up to drive during their summer vacation and be home again in time for the fall semester. It would be sort of like summer camp or a guided tour of the Continent.

There was another explanation for the earthbound choices those future pilots made in 1914 and early 1915: in the first months of the war combat flying hadn't yet become romantic. The planes that flew above the Western Front weren't there to fight, because they couldn't: they weren't armed. They were observation planes—a superior means of looking around, nothing more. The heroic myth of the air war, in which single pilots fought each other as though they were chivalric knights, would come later.

One more thing remains to be said about those seven pilots. I can say it best in the form of a table:

Victor Chapman	St. Paul's and Harvard
Elliot Cowdin	St. Paul's and Harvard
James McConnell	Haverford School and University of Virginia
Norman Prince	Groton and Harvard
Kiffin Rockwell	VMI and Washington and Lee
William Thaw	Hill School and Yale

One of the seven is missing from that table—Bert Hall. We'll come back to him.

Those six young men were all from well-off families, the kind that can afford to educate their sons in expensive schools and colleges. They were "college men"—a phrase of the time that identified not only an educational level but a small elite class; if America had an aristocracy, they'd be in it.

It's not surprising that men of that class and background were drawn to military flying; even before the war, flying, for such young men, was a dashing, dangerous sport, like ocean sailing, motor racing, and polo. The men they knew who flew were sportsmen, who did what they did for its own sake, and for the competitiveness of it, and for the danger. If you were a sportsman-flier you entered air races and air meets, or you tried to set records—altitude records, speed records, distance records, endurance records (which would then be broken by some other gentleman sportsman)—or you flew from somewhere to somewhere else—Philadelphia to New York, Boston to Albany, New York to Washington, it didn't much matter where—and dreamed of flying coast-to-coast or even across the Atlantic.

This kind of sportsman flying was expensive; you'd have to be wealthy to afford it. Two of the first seven Lafayette fliers were rich men's sons. Norman Prince was the son of a Boston financier who expected his son to be a lawyer. Norman dutifully went to Harvard (class of 1908) and Harvard Law School (1911), passed the bar exam, and joined a Chicago law firm. It must have seemed to his father that that was that: his son was settled in what would be a prosperous upper-class career. But Norman was less interested in torts and injunctions than he was in a sportsman's life. In 1912 he began to take flying lessons (he had to do it under a pseudonym to conceal his defection from his father), and in 1913 he quit the law altogether.

William Thaw had a more indulgent rich man for a father—a Pittsburgh banker who didn't seem to mind at all when his son dropped out of Yale after his sophomore year (it was 1913) to take up flying. He even bought him a plane of his own, a Curtiss flying boat that young Thaw kept moored at the family's Newport home and used to take friends cruising over Narragansett Bay, as though a plane were simply a new kind of yacht.

The social class that Prince and Thaw belonged to would provide many of the American volunteers who first flew for the French and became the Lafayette Escadrille (including all but one of the seven in the photograph). But what about the seventh, the odd man out? Bert Hall was the son of a Missouri dirt farmer. Uneducated and poor, Bert had worked as a farmhand, a section hand on a railway, a chauffeur, a circus performer (he was the "Human Cannonball"), and a seaman before he reached Paris and took up taxi driving.

Many men like Hall—wanderers, jacks-of-all-trades, free spirits—became pilots in the European war. Some flew with the Lafayette Escadrille: the great Raoul Lufbery was one; Eddie Rickenbacker was another. (Lufbery had been an aviation mechanic before he became a pilot; Rickenbacker had been a racing driver.) The use of such men as pilots didn't bother other Allied air forces (or for that matter the Germans); they'd probably serve as enlisted men, while the gentlemen pilots became commissioned officers, but they'd fly. For the Americans, however, the social class to which military pilots would belong, and from which they should be drawn, was a question to be debated.

———

By early 1915, Kiffin Rockwell had spent enough time—some four months—in the trenches to know what war in the Foreign Legion was like. It was, he had found, a small-scale, anonymous business in which the dying was grotesque and random and without glory and the space between battles was filled with mud, lice, bad food, shell fire, and blistered feet. In a letter to his brother Paul, who had been invalided out of the trenches and sent back to Paris, he wrote, "The reason I keep writing you not to come back here is because I know that you are not able to stand it, and then there is no romance or anything to the infantry. It is not a question of bravery, it is a question of being a good day laborer. So if you don't want to leave the service, get into something that requires education and not brute strength." Kiffin will stay in the Legion for another eight months, fight in some fierce battles, and be badly wounded, but he has served without belief in the war he is fighting; as he says in that February letter, he has rejected two of the big words of war: "romance" and "bravery." Reality has revised his dream.

But to Rockwell one big word remains: "gentleman." To realize that word, he will turn to aviation. That move will be more than a change in the work he does; it will be a change of class. To switch from infantry to flying, he wrote to his mother, was to "jump from the lowest branch of the military service to the highest. It is the most interesting thing I have ever done, and is the life of a gentleman, and I am surrounded by gentlemen." The move meant, among other things, comfort: clean clothes on your back, clean sheets on your bed, a bath when you need one, a little money in your pocket. With all those comforts, you are a gentleman. And you are treated like one. Rockwell had been a day laborer at war long enough.

Victor Chapman felt differently about the Legion; he had found a kind of contentment in the ordinary life of a machine gunner. "We, the *Mitraille*, are joyous," he wrote to his father, "good chiefs, fair treatment, and sure fighting before us." But his father wanted more for his son than that; he wanted a war that would reflect glory on himself. That spring John Jay Chapman was in Paris pulling strings to transfer his son to the Service Aéronautique. "It is perfectly obvious," Victor wrote to his stepmother, "that I am not wanted [in the Air Service] and have been foisted on them by Uncle Willy and Papa." (Uncle Willy was his mother's brother, who lived in Paris and had connections.) But his father insisted, and so Victor left the Legion and became a pilot.

At the same time, Americans in the ambulance service were also beginning to look toward aviation as a better route to war. James McConnell, who had come to France as an ambulance driver, reflected in 1916 on his fellow drivers' motives for transferring to aviation: "There seems to be a fascination to aviation, particularly when it is coupled with fighting. Perhaps it's because the game is new, but more probably because nobody knows anything about it. Whatever the reason, adventurous young Americans were attracted by it in rapidly increasing numbers." The young drivers had come to France expecting excitement, adventure, danger, and the company of other young idealists, and some of them had been disappointed. They had imagined steering their ambulances full of wounded men to safety through exploding shells and whistling bullets; instead, they often found themselves driving supply trucks or simply hanging around, waiting. Even if they reached the front and drove an ambulance there, they often didn't feel altogether *in* the war. McConnell explained that feeling: "All along I had been convinced that the United States ought to aid in the struggle against Germany. With that conviction, it was plainly up to me to do more than drive an ambulance. The more I saw the splendour of the fight the French were fighting, the more I felt like an *embusqué*—what the British called a 'shirker.' So I made up my mind to go into aviation."

In December 1915 three of the Americans who were flying with French squadrons—Elliot Cowdin, Norman Prince, and William Thaw—returned to the United States. Ostensibly, they were simply home on leave, but in fact they were there to demonstrate to their fellow Americans that the war in Europe was also an American war.

When the three arrived in New York, they were photographed on the deck of their ship, and the picture was distributed among American newspapers.

The publicity point of their visit is in the accompanying headlines: "Daring Flyers . . . Brilliant Exploits." If you read the copy below the photograph, you'll find their work described more soberly; they've been doing the ordinary scouting jobs that pilots have done since the war began—observing enemy troop movements, directing artillery fire. There's no mention of air-to-air combat: that kind of fighting, which makes pilots into heroes, is still ahead. But the material for heroes is already here—three young American gentlemen, two from Harvard, one from Yale, in their gentlemen's clothes, on the first-class deck of the *Rotterdam*.

Airplanes were rare in America in the years before the country entered the European war; in 1917 many citizens would never have seen one. They were almost as rare in the armed services as they were out on

the farms: in the summer of 1913 the Army's airpower (it was called the Aviation Section of the Signal Corps) consisted of fifteen operational planes; in 1916, twenty-three; and in the spring of 1917, when the United States declared war, fifty-five, of which all but four were obsolete. The Army had used its planes in action only once, in 1916, when General John Pershing led a force into northern Mexico in search of the rebel leader Pancho Villa, who had been raiding over the border into American territory. The First Aero Squadron, with eight Curtiss JN-3s (known as Jennies), went along as part of the Signal Corps, to do Signal Corps jobs—to reconnoiter, to search, and to serve as couriers between Pershing and his separated units. The pilots were under orders not to respond to any attack by enemy forces, which they couldn't have done in any case, since they were unarmed.

The Secretary of War in those years, Newton Baker, expressed American thinking of the time on the subject of airplane use: "The aeroplane service is, of course, the scouting service." Of course. An airplane was like a balloon freed from its cable or a more powerful pair of binoculars—a device for observing the enemy from a better viewpoint than a patrol of cavalry had.

That might have been understandable in 1914, but in 1916, when Pershing marched into Mexico and Baker made his remark, it seems surprisingly ignorant. By then the British, the French, and the Germans had all been busy for two years inventing war in the air: the plane-against-plane combat, the many-plane dogfights, the bombing and strafing of troops. They had devised tactics of attack and defense, as the advantage and control of the air shifted and new models of planes were brought into action.

When the United States entered the war in 1917, American pilots couldn't do any of these air-war tricks, and neither could American planes. Furthermore, their country lacked the means to correct those shortcomings—the factories to mass-produce competitive fighting aircraft, the pilots to fly them, the instructors to train those pilots, the training fields to fly from, the staff to organize it all. All of these necessities for a modern air service would have to be created from scratch. The Air Service would enter the war in Europe two and a half years late, ill-equipped, ill-trained, and undermanned—a part of a nineteenth-century army in the world's first twentieth-century war. Belatedness would be like a second enemy: Americans would still be fighting against it when the war ended.

America was belated in every aspect of war-making in the spring of 1917: short of troops, guns, shells, rifles, uniforms, gas, tanks, tents, rations—everything. But the Aviation Section's belatedness was special, because aviation represented a new way of making war. Adding more infantry battalions would be relatively easy; you simply drafted enough men and taught them military skills that were already defined and in practice—marching and saluting and wrapping puttees, or leggings. And most American males would know how to fire a rifle already. But for an air service an entirely new military subculture would have to be created. What kinds of men do you want? What should their qualifications be? Should they all be officers? All volunteers? How should they relate to nonflying officers? To enlisted men? What should their uniforms look like? Some of these questions you could call training questions, but others are more a matter of imagination—imagining a service with no tradition, composed of young men who will not exactly be soldiers and whose war will often be fought alone, in a place where war had never been fought before, in the great vacancy of the sky.

To answer such questions, and to create a training program that would put the answers into practice, the Signal Corps might have turned to a senior officer on the Army List—some experienced old brigadier from the cavalry, say; that would have been the Army way. Instead, the Corps chose an Ivy League professor—Hiram Bingham, professor of South American history at Yale. It seems an odd decision: What could a university history professor have that an air service could use?

But Hiram Bingham wasn't your usual professor. He had learned what he knew about South America on mule-back expeditions into the mountains and jungles there, on one of which he had rediscovered the ancient Inca city of Machu Picchu. The books he wrote about those expeditions had earned him a reputation that reached far beyond New Haven and was more romantic than professorial.

Bingham certainly didn't think of himself as a professor: he preferred the term "explorer" (when he wrote his war memoir, he titled the book *An Explorer in the Air Service*). *The New York Times* went further; in an article on Machu Picchu in 2006, it called Bingham a "swashbuckling explorer." And he did look like one: tall (he was six feet two), lean and athletic-looking, and handsome in a hawk-faced way, with an intense, penetrating gaze. In 1917, forty-one years old and gray-haired, settled in New Haven with a wife and seven children, he must have felt that his swashbuckling days were over and that only years of teaching history and rearing children lay ahead. I can imagine that such a man might well have seen military aviation in a time of war as an honorable escape route from all that, a last shot at adventure.

So the Army didn't have to go looking for Bingham; he went looking for the Army. Even before the United States entered the war, he traveled all the way from Yale to Miami to enroll in the flying school that Glenn Curtiss, the aviation pioneer and plane builder, had established there. Bingham learned to fly both land and sea planes and earned his license as an "aviator pilot." It wasn't difficult, he said, a man could be taught to fly in a few days of good weather. (Actually, it took him two months.)

Bingham was still in Miami when war was declared. He applied at once for a commission in the Aviation Section of the Signal Corps and was summoned to Washington. He was appointed a major and ordered to plan a training program for thousands of new pilots. He immediately set to work, and as he interviewed and traveled and observed, a conception of what he was aiming for took shape in his mind. What he would create would not simply be a training syllabus—nothing so plain and pedagogical as that. It would be a process of selection and education that would produce ideal pilots—a swashbuckler's vision of flying heroes.

Bingham's account, in his 1920 war memoir, of how he came to imagine and define the ideal pilot candidate ends with this summarizing passage:

> It was borne in on us by all those with whom we talked that the first necessity in the Air Service was to get the right type of personnel: fellows of quick, clear intelligence, mentally acute and physically fit; that the next thing was to make soldiers of them and teach them the value of military discipline; finally, that we should eliminate the unfit as fast as possible and avoid giving them flying instruction unless they proved themselves to be morally, physically, and mentally worthy of receiving the most expensive education in the world.

When I first read the end of that long sentence, I thought it had a familiar ring: surely I had read it in my boyhood, in some important text. I went back to the Boy Scout handbook, and there it was, in the third promise of the Scout Oath: "To keep myself physically strong, mentally awake, and morally straight." So there was to be an element of the Boy Scout in the American combat pilot.

This ideal American pilot—wellborn, well educated, athletic, patriotic, and honorable in all his doings—wasn't invented by Bingham; he was simply endorsing a type that already existed in upper- and upper-middle-class American society. That ideal figure was there in the Yale men Bingham taught and took with him on his expeditions: he was Dink Stover of Yale; he was Princeton's athletic hero Hobey Baker; he was the young American gentleman, circa 1917. By accepting the assumption that such young men were the best possible material for combat pilots, the Service made a class distinction: flying—American combat flying—would be an occupation for gentlemen.

That assumption came up in Congress that summer when the Military Aviation Appropriation Bill was debated. Members of both houses were aware that they were engaged in an extraordinary process, the creation of an entirely new military force, and they struggled to explain to each other what the differences were. In the House of Representatives, Lenroot of Wisconsin tried to define an aviator: "An aviator is very different from a man in the Infantry or a man in the Cavalry. To fly requires altogether different qualifications. It requires nerve, bravery, and those things that can not be acquired, because each man has got to be his own boss and must act on his own initiative." And in the Senate, Norris of Nebraska said, "When [a pilot] flies out over the enemy or anywhere else he must necessarily in a sense be his own commander. He is really supreme."

Most of these congressmen had never flown, but they all seemed to have an idea—a romantic idea—of what a pilot should be: a solitary seeker, brave, supreme in his lonely element, self-reliant, self-commanded. Miller of Minnesota summed up this hero's qualities. "There is being attracted to the Aviation Corps," he said, "the brightest, nerviest, most efficient of our youth—what might be called the flower of our chivalry."

Congressmen worried about the implications of this idealized figure. If pilots were to be chivalric heroes, was it reasonable to *draft* them? If they were to be so independent and self-commanded, should they be college-educated? Wood of Indiana protested that "there are many men who have these diplomas who are not fit and can not be made fit to do the work required in the Aviation Service. Upon the other hand there are many men who have not college diplomas or high-school diplomas, but who have the intelligence, the nerve, and all the qualifications fitting them for this extraordinary service, who would make excellent aviators." Wood had a point: if only 3 percent of young American men were in college in 1917, was it just and sensible to exclude the other 97 percent from aviation service? In the end, Congress compromised: there would be regulations, including educational requirements, but the War Department would have the authority to waive them.

One other element from Bingham's vision of the perfect pilot made it into the final bill. "No person," it reads, "shall be . . . promoted, appointed, detailed, or attached until he shall have been found physically, mentally, and morally qualified under regulations prescribed by the Secretary of War." He'd not only be a college man and a gentleman (with perhaps some exceptions); he'd also be a Boy Scout.

These assumptions about flying and class would have consequences for the selection of pilots, but more than that, they would affect the way the young pilots thought about themselves and their pilot culture. From the beginning they would consider themselves an elite, separate from the rest of the military, and a bit superior. They'd be officers and gentlemen, but they would also be adventurers, explorers, sportsmen, romantic heroes. An aura of personal danger and possible sudden death would hang over them, and they'd absorb it. It would get into their letters home and into their conversations with one another. They'd fight their war in their own element, apart from the rest of the army, and that separateness would affect the way they lived, and the way they fought and died.

TWO

THE IVY LEAGUE AIR FORCE

In the months from the autumn of 1915 to the summer of 1916 the war in the air changed. New and faster planes came into action on the Western Front, and both sides—the Germans first and then, belatedly, the Allies—developed fixed, forward-firing machine guns that could fire through the arc of the propeller without hitting the blades, making the plane itself a weapon that the pilot aimed simply by flying. With such a weapon, pilots became hunters of planes—*chasse* pilots in French, *Jagdfliegern* in German, pursuit pilots in English. Air fighting took tactical form and became a kind of deadly sport in which a pilot might hope to meet an enemy one against one, duel with him, and win or lose by his own skills. Those who won would accumulate scores and acquire reputations like any sports star, become celebrated, and be reported in the press.

A search through files of any American newspaper of record for 1916 will turn up air heroes in the headlines. Most of them will be Frenchmen, like Georges Guynemer, Charles Nungesser, and Jean Navarre; diplomatically the United States was neutral in 1916, but emotionally the country favored the Allies, and especially the French:

FRENCH AVIATOR BAGS
HIS FIFTH ADVERSARY
Guynemer Only 21 Years Old

French Birdman, Battling Alone,
Brings Down Five Hostile Aeros

DOES MARVELS IN AIR
Nungesser, on a Dare, Looped
Loop Under Enemy's Fire

TWO FRENCH AVIATORS TIED
FOR WEST FRONT HONORS.
Guynemer and Navarre Each Bring
Down Twelve Enemy Planes

The texts of these stories stress the pilots' youth, their daring, and their solitariness. "Guynemer flies alone," *The New York Times* reports, as though that were an especially sporting thing to do.

In the spring of 1916, the French Service Aéronautique created an all-American *chasse* squadron. It was called, at first, the Escadrille Américaine, and then, when the still neutral American government protested, the Lafayette Escadrille. Once the escadrille reached the front, accounts of its actions began to appear among the French and German victories in newspaper headlines back home—like this one from *The New York Times* for May 22, 1916:

AMERICAN AVIATORS
WIN FRENCH HONORS
Rockwell of Atlanta to Get the
Military Medal for Bringing
Down an Enemy Machine

And this one, a few days later:

AMERICANS BRING DOWN
THREE GERMAN PLANES
Thaw, Rockwell and Cowdin Account
for One Each—Thaw
Slightly Wounded

These headlines aren't just reporting, either; there's national pride in them. Rockwell's victory is the first by an American volunteer. The United States may still be neutral, but its pilots have entered the game of war; they have an enemy, even if their country doesn't.

Another headline, from the following month, reminds us of the other side of that game, the human cost:

AMERICAN FLIER
DIES FOR ALLIES;
DROPS TWO FOES
Victor Chapman, Son of a New
York Lawyer, Killed as He
Goes to Aid Comrades

The essential story of Chapman's death is clear enough, though the details differ depending on whether you read it in *The New York Times* or the *Chicago Tribune*, or in Kiffin Rockwell's letter to Chapman's stepmother, or in the memoir Chapman's father wrote. Three (or there might have been four) planes of the escadrille were on patrol near Verdun when they were jumped by four (or perhaps five) Germans. Chapman was not a member of the patrol, but was flying alone nearby. He saw the attack and at once plunged into the fight. The patrol under attack, being outnumbered, prudently withdrew, but Chapman fought on alone (in one version of the story he shot down two enemy planes) until he was killed in midair (possibly by Oswald Boelcke, the German ace).

It's not surprising that stories of the fight differ in particulars; dogfights are wheeling, confusing melees, and none of the tellers was a witness. But the differences don't matter; a myth is in the making, in which a hero rushes to the aid of his comrades and fights a solitary battle against the odds, killing two of the enemy before he dies at the hands of a greater hero. Only one of his comrades adds a qualifying note: Rockwell praised Chapman's courage, but added, "He was too courageous."

By the time the class of 1920 entered college in the fall term of 1916, the myth of the air war was in place—a kind of lobbying for danger that would be part of their student lives. You can see the spread of that myth in the way Aero Clubs sprouted on American college campuses. In 1910 the Aero Club of America had only one college-based affiliate, Harvard's Aeronautical Society. In 1916, the list of American Aero Clubs published in *Jane's All the World's Aircraft* included twenty colleges and universities, most of them well-off gentlemen's schools, where you might expect to find the would-be sportsman-fliers that the air service would be pursuing a year later.

At Cambridge, in the spring of 1916, the Harvard Flying Corps, initiated by an alumnus who had flown in France, began to take shape: a meeting room was opened, a field to fly from was rented, students were enrolled and dues collected. Everything seemed ready—on paper—though nobody flew. A. Lawrence Lowell, Harvard's president, was not pleased. In April he wrote to the Corps to say firmly that the Corps had not been sanctioned by the university and wouldn't be. "A flying corps is certainly one of the things the Army needs," he wrote, "and it ought to be encouraged; but I feel that the time has not yet come for it at Harvard." Within a month the scheme had collapsed.

Lowell had got rid of the Flying Corps, but he hadn't got rid of the dream of flying at Harvard. The university's archives are full of documents from the summer of 1916 demonstrating the relentless pressure that was being put on President Lowell by the flying lobby: by students, by alumni, and—most heavily—by the Aero Club of America down in New York. No opportunity was lost to preempt the issue by announcing that what Lowell opposed already existed. A letter to Lowell from an alumnus dated June 5 reports a new scheme for a university aero training fund as a fait accompli; it was to be financed by contributions from concerned Harvard alumni, with help from the Aero Club of America, and the funds used to subsidize the flight training of Harvard's students "at some good school."

Lowell's response was a model of Bostonian good manners:

> I submitted your generous proposal to the Corporation this morning, but they felt that it was unwise for the University to undertake instruction in the practice of flying. I think you will see the many difficulties that would present themselves in such instruction at the University and feel that the members of the Corporation realize the importance of the art while thinking it should be done elsewhere.

By the time Lowell wrote his dismissive letter, ten Harvard undergraduates were already at the Curtiss Flying School at Buffalo, preparing to begin flight training subsidized by the training fund, and had sent a report of their activities to the *Boston American*, where it appeared under the headline

HARVARD AERO
CAMP GETS
BIPLANE

A clipping of the article was sent to President Lowell. He wrote at once to the alumnus-sponsor of the training fund: "As you know, we wholly approve of the training of the air men, but do not feel that any enterprise, particularly one connected with education, not conducted by the University, ought to bear the name." The students obediently changed the name of their tent community to Victor Chapman Camp, thus gathering to themselves the fame of Harvard's first air hero (who had died three weeks earlier).

Before the summer's end, other Harvard students were training at other flying schools, some at Ithaca, others at Hempstead, Long Island. In July, an article in *The New York Times* on flight training at colleges (most of it information supplied by the Aero Club of America in New York) announced what had obviously become the case:

HARVARD LEADS IN
AIR PREPAREDNESS

In the fall, *Flying*, the Aero Club's magazine, followed up with a similar headline:

THE HARVARD AERO CORPS A REALITY

Lowell and his prewar sense of the Harvard military tradition had lost, and the Aero Club and modern war had won.

In the September issue of *Flying*, the Club flaunted its victory by printing a photograph of that first group of Harvard fliers at the Buffalo camp. There they stand, gawky and uncertain in their new uniforms—campaign hats, baggy breeches, puttees—looking more like Boy Scouts at a jamboree than a new generation of pilots training for a new kind of war. The uniforms bear no insignia that might identify them as belonging to any particular branch of any particular army, and that's appropriate, since at this moment in the summer of 1916 they are neither quite military nor entirely civilian but in between, promised to the Signal Corps's

Aviation Section should that service ever need them, but expecting to go back to being Harvard undergraduates in the fall (as indeed they did). The war is still a distant foreign war toward which the United States preserves a neutral posture, and these are still college boys at summer camp, and flying is a game.

———

Yale's flying project was different from Harvard's in two respects. First of all, it was conceived and organized entirely by one Yale undergraduate— the tireless, completely confident Trubee Davison. In June 1915, Davison, then a Yale sophomore, sailed for France, to work through the summer with the American Ambulance Field Service. He was disappointed in the job he was given. He'd gone for a taste of real war; instead, he was kept in Paris, driving an ambulance between railway stations and hospitals. The closest he got to war's excitement was meeting French and American aviators who had fought in the air.

Davison returned to Yale that fall intending to organize an ambulance service unit there, but like many other college students he changed his mind. By the summer of 1916, he had decided he would rather fly than drive. Perhaps he remembered the fliers he had met in Paris; perhaps he read the newspaper accounts of their battles over the front. Or maybe there is such a thing as a spirit of the time, and for young men in 1916 that spirit was becoming airborne. Whatever the motivating force, Davison set about organizing a flying group at Yale. In August, he began flying lessons at Port Washington, near his family home on Long Island.

There was talk that summer of a need for Volunteer Aerial Coast Patrols to work with the Navy defending the American coastline: not regular Navy squadrons, but volunteer units, each with its stretch of coast to watch over and flying its own planes. Why shouldn't Yale provide such a unit? The students who joined it wouldn't be enlisting, exactly, and they'd pay for their own flying lessons, but later, if the country went to war, they could be sworn in and commissioned. At Yale, as at Harvard, flying would be a new undergraduate sport, and most of the men who took it up would be athletes—rowers, many of them, but also football players, baseball players, hurdlers, hockey players.

The role of Trubee Davison in organizing this unit was central. When someone had to get the university's approval, it was Trubee who called on the dean. When negotiations with the Navy were necessary, it was Trubee who traveled to Washington armed with a letter of introduction from the Aero Club and went straight to the Secretary of the Navy. To show the Yale community how easy flying was, he flew his own plane from his home across Long Island Sound to attend morning chapel and got to his classes on time. The energy and social poise of this twenty-year-old undergraduate were extraordinary; the First Yale Unit came together and learned to fly because he was determined that it should and that he would go to his war among the friends he chose to fly with.

A difference between Yale's flying program and Harvard's was the amount of money involved. From the beginning, Yale's program was lavishly financed. At Harvard the subsidizing money came in modest private checks from many alumni supporters; at Yale it came in dramatically large sums from a few very rich patrons. In the matter of fund-raising the managerial Trubee had one special advantage: his father was a partner of J. P. Morgan. Over the period of the group's training, the elder Davison provided his son and his son's friends with a hundred thousand dollars of his own money (roughly a million and a half in 2014 dollars), plus another hundred thousand from his firm. He also gave them free use of both his yachts. Later he bought the unit a cedar-hulled flying boat. (His brother-in-law trumped that grand gift with a grander one—a new flying boat with a hull of solid mahogany.)

Other rich men added their contributions: the father of Bill Rockefeller, one of the Yale pilots, gave the unit another plane; a vice president of the National City Bank gave yet another; Harry Payne Whitney lent them his luxurious cruising houseboat. The atmosphere of conspicuous affluence extended to the places where the Yale unit flew: Rodman Wanamaker offered his waterfront properties on Long Island Sound and at Palm Beach for use as training bases—Long Island for the summer months, Palm Beach for the winter. Their lodgings while they trained were the homes of the wealthy and the kinds of resort hotels where the wealthy stayed; the parties they went to were society events. If the Harvard flight program was like a Boy Scout camp, the Yale locations were like rich people's house parties. *The New York Tribune* called them "the 'millionaire unit.'"

In that good-time atmosphere, it's not surprising that the First Yale Unit didn't live a very military existence: after all, they weren't yet formally the Navy, had no ranks, wore no uniforms, and drew no pay. They didn't salute senior officers when they turned up, they didn't fall in for muster, they didn't drill. They were flying college men, still civilians at heart.

You can see that relaxed unmilitary spirit in the photographs that survive from the unit's training days. Collectively, their clothing doesn't represent any possible military organization. They're simply a number of young men on a beach having their picture taken. The pilots in the unit would remain like that right through the war—part naval officers, and part college men on a long party. The distinct, independent culture of pilots that made them different from military officers on the ground and on ships at sea took form, in part, in groups like the First Yale Unit.

As the war came nearer, the unit moved toward a more complete and formal connection with the Navy, but even as the pilots acquired naval rank and uniforms, their costs continued to be paid by their wealthy sponsors. Those sponsors must have felt a good deal of patriotic satisfaction with what they had accomplished. They had provided the money, and they had used their considerable influence to move the government to action. You'll get a sense of where the power was in this operation if

you consider the chain of command by which the unit's move from the student world of New Haven into full-time active duty was accomplished. First, Trubee Davison polled the members of the unit: Did they really want to be full-time Navy pilots? When he had their positive vote, he asked his father for his permission. Mr. Davison approved and notified the president of the Aero Club of America, who advised the Secretary of the Navy of the decision.

Once the transfer of the unit to the Navy had been arranged, the group's supporters, being businessmen, began to think about compensation for their expenses. Letters were written to the Secretary of the Navy and to Rear Admiral Robert Peary (who was in charge of naval aviation)—including a very stern one from Trubee. Various sums of money were mentioned: $100,000 for planes and equipment, $10,000 for four engines, $200,000 for their "total disbursement." The Navy Department responded with a check—for $1.

———

Flying didn't come to Princeton until after it had become a part of student life at Harvard and Yale, but when it did, it arrived in style. The occasion was the Yale-Princeton football game, November 18, 1916. The Yale game is always a big event on the Princeton campus, but this one was made bigger by what else happened. Here is the account from *The Daily Princetonian*, the university's student newspaper:

> A fleet of twelve aeroplanes which is the largest that ever took flight at one time on the American continent flew from New York to Princeton Saturday. Ten of the aeroplanes left the government aviation camp at Mineola at 9 in the morning and were joined by two privately owned biplanes from the Governors Island camp as they were flying over the Narrows in regular formation . . . The squadron circled around the town and finally landed in a large field east of the Stadium.

You can feel the student reporter's excitement in that account—the largest flight *ever*! All the way from New York! And in regular formation! The numbers, the distance, and the military order of the planes were all new to the watching crowd on the ground.

In fact, the flight to Princeton wasn't quite as choreographed as the *Princetonian* reported; one plane had engine trouble and had to land in Flushing, another got lost and wound up in Atlantic City, and another smashed a wheel landing at Princeton. Still, for witnesses on the ground (and according to the Aero Club's *Flying*, "their flight in battle formation was watched by thousands"), it was a stirring spectacle.

For Princeton students and alumni, the most thrilling thing about the flight must have been that the lead plane was flown by H.A.H. Baker, class of 1914. Hobey Baker, Princeton's greatest athlete, the most famous of college football players, the handsomest, blondest, straightest, and most gentlemanly of them all, had chosen the Yale game as the time and place to demonstrate his latest athletic skill. He wasn't the only college man in the flight: the *Princetonian* reported that of the other eleven pilots, three were from Yale, three from Harvard, and one from Princeton. Flying had become an Ivy League sport.

That was the fall of 1916. The following spring the United States entered the war. And Princeton University began, belatedly, to organize its own flying corps. Like the Harvard and Yale programs, this one was a private enterprise, financed by wealthy alumni. Planes were ordered (Jennies, of course) from Glenn Curtiss's factory and paid for by Old Princetonians; a pasture south of town was leased as a flying field, hangars were built, and an instructor was hired. Stationery was printed: "Aviation Corps of Princeton University." The planes began to arrive in crates at the university railroad station (for the benefit of Old Princetonians, the station was then at Blair Arch) and were carried by truck from there to a field on Princeton Pike, where they were put together. The preparations took the entire spring semester.

Finally, late in May, flying began. By the end of June, most of the students had flown with an instructor and had been shown how to get a plane off the ground and back down again without breaking anything and perhaps how to make a cautious, flat turn. A few had advanced enough to be allowed to solo. Having done so, they were considered to have graduated. There wasn't time for more than that.

Spring semester of 1917 had been a disrupted, uncertain time for colleges. As winter turned into spring, the war came closer to America, and the need to confront it became more urgent. Military advisers appeared on campuses, and military science courses were added to class lists. Some students joined reserve units, wore their uniforms to class, and practiced marching on playing fields while they waited to be called up. In faculty meetings and committee rooms professors and administrators groped for ways of serving the nation's war need while protecting students' interests and maintaining a male population on their campuses.

In the middle of that spring semester, when the United States declared war on Germany, the attentions of colleges turned further toward military matters. What had been college life—the sports, the clubs, the lectures, the exams, the grades—seemed to fade and become irrelevant. "The colleges all closed around the end of April," one student recalled, "and gave the seniors easy examinations." Some colleges gave no final exams at all but simply passed everyone. At Yale, one of the Yale Naval Unit seniors assured his family in April, "We did not join without ascertaining at New Haven whether or not we would be given diplomas. My record was looked up. Everything was above passing and I was guaranteed a diploma, which will be sent to me on Class Day, provided I do good work in aviation up to that time." At Princeton the faculty voted that any senior who left college and was accepted for active service would be given his degree if his work for the previous term was complete.

You can imagine the conversation in men's dormitories that spring: not about books or girls or the Yale game, but about the game of war and what position one should play in it. But you don't have to imagine it; Scott Fitzgerald wrote it down in *This Side of Paradise*:

> "What are you going to do, Amory?"
> "Infantry or aviation, I can't make up my mind—I hate mechanics, but then of course aviation's the thing for me—"
> "I feel as Amory does," said Tom. "Infantry or aviation— aviation sounds like the romantic side of the war, of course— like cavalry used to be, you know."

Tom was right: by the time the United States entered the war, aviation had become the romantic choice of undergraduates. That's not surprising; the air war had produced the best stories, the ones that got into newspapers and magazines and stirred the hearts of college men: *personal* stories, with heroes.

———

In January 1917, two firsthand accounts of war in the air were published in the United States: Carroll Dana Winslow's *With the French Flying Corps* and James McConnell's *Flying for France*. They were the first such books to be written by Americans and addressed to Americans. Both were written in a hurry; you feel that in the writing: Winslow wrote his while he was on leave back in the States, where his child was ill; McConnell wrote his while he lay in a French hospital recovering from injuries suffered in a crash. Before the books were published, both men were back in the air over France.

The two men had almost identical service records—up to a point. Both joined the American Ambulance Field Service in 1915; both transferred to the French air service in October of that year; both completed their preliminary training and were brevetted (in the States you'd say they "got their wings") early in 1916. But then their careers diverged. Winslow was sent to the front to fly Maurice Farmans—the slow, cumbersome pusher planes that were used for observation work. It was a disappointment to him, as it would have been for almost any new pilot; by then, Nieuport fighter planes (*avions de chasse*, the French called them) were what the young pilots wanted. After two months in Farmans he talked his way back into training in Nieuports, but before he'd finished, his daughter's illness (it was diphtheria) called him home.

When Winslow returned to France a year later, he hoped to join a *chasse* squadron, and eventually he did. But he didn't write that story. The story he did write is nearly all training. It wasn't his fault—a father goes to his sick child—but it left his book unfinished, all preparation and no climactic action, like *Henry the Fifth* without Agincourt.

In *With the French Flying Corps*, Winslow recalls a visit he made in the spring of 1916 to the American Escadrille at Bar-le-Duc. He was invited to stay for dinner. It was a meal, he wrote, that he would never forget. As a visiting pilot he was seated beside the squadron commander, Captain Georges Thenault. On the other side of the table were

Victor Chapman, Norman Prince, and Kiffin Rockwell, and at the end were Elliot Cowdin and Jim McConnell. There they all sat—the first American flying heroes. And on this side sat Winslow, unknown and unheroic, a mere observation pilot, a stranger in their brave world.

By the time Winslow wrote his book, three of those heroes had been killed. Reflecting on that dinner with the dead, Winslow thinks, "The places of the three pilots killed have since been taken by other volunteers, but in the minds and memories of the Americans dining at the camp that night their places can never be filled. We know that they did not die in vain, and that what they did will live in history." A trite way of putting it, perhaps; "in vain" was a tired, empty phrase even then. But sometimes trite is true. Winslow knew that night that he was in the presence of heroes and that he would never achieve what they had achieved; he had come too late to the table.

McConnell was luckier than Winslow, in one way. He trained in France in Nieuports, and he was sent straight to the front to join the new Escadrille Américaine and to fly into combat and a place in the air-war myth. Unlike Winslow's book, McConnell's is full of action— the flying, the fighting, and, inevitably, the dying. Where Winslow simply notes that some of the men at the table will be killed, McConnell describes their deaths as a witnessing pilot would—how in a fight a Nieuport's wings buckled and tore away, fluttering to the ground like falling leaves, how the broken plane dropped like a stone, the sound of the crash—"I know of no sound more horrible than that made by an airplane crashing to earth." He knew about crashes; it was while he was convalescing from one that he wrote his book.

As McConnell moves to the heart of his story, his plain style gathers emotion, and description becomes eulogy. He remembers his dead friends: Rockwell, "the best and bravest of us all," in whom "the old flame of chivalry burned brightly"; Prince, who didn't mind dying, so long as he did his part before he was killed; Chapman, "too brave if anything." Naming those dead comrades, he mythologized them and the squadron they flew with. By the time *Flying for France* was published, McConnell would be one of them—the mythical dead.

These two books, so hasty and so convincing, must have been popular reading in college dormitories where students like Fitzgerald's Amory Blaine talked together and tried to decide between war on the ground and war in the air. Here were two young men much like themselves, both college men (Winslow had been at Yale, McConnell at the University of Virginia) who had actually flown over France. Their stories would have changed the dormitory conversations, made the aviation option seem less vaguely romantic and more actual, and so made the choice of flying imaginable.

We have one testimony that that did happen. Stuart Walcott, a Princeton classmate of Fitzgerald's, was thinking about going to the war after he graduated in the spring but couldn't decide between ambulance driving and flying. Early in January 1917, his parents sent him a copy of Winslow's book. Two days later he responded:

> Many, many thanks for sending me the book on the French Flying Corps by Winslow. I read half of it the night that it came and stayed up late last night to finish it. He gives a very straight, interesting and apparently not exaggerated account of the work over there, which has made it somewhat clearer to me, just what it is that I want to get into. Now I am even more anxious than I was before to join the service over there. The more that I think about it and the more that I hear of it, the more desirous I am of getting into the Flying Corps. If a man like Winslow with a wife and daughter dependent on him is willing to take the risk involved, I see no reason why I should not.

Walcott's letter is dated January 26, 1917. On that date the United States was not at war, and Walcott was not threatened with military conscription; he was simply a Princeton senior one term short of his degree. Yet he writes as though his commitment to the war were fixed and irrevocable; he must go, and he must go as a pilot. By then many college men like Walcott had committed themselves to one flying service or another. These young men would enter the Army's air service, or the Navy's or the Royal Flying Corps, or the Service Aéronautique, confident that wherever they served they would find young men like themselves, men from a common background of sufficient money and good schools and universities. Some of those young men would surely be old friends from back home. They'd meet at airfields, or in the Crillon Bar or the University Club in Paris, and would report their meetings in letters home: I saw X from Groton, or Y from the Hill School, or Z who played hockey with me at Harvard. It must have seemed certain to them (and to their parents, too) that in the air, at least, this would be a college man's war and that they were the gentlemen who would fight it. There'd have been a certain security in that.

THREE

GOING

None of the martial bustle on American campuses that spring
was really urgent: the country was not at war, Congress had not
yet passed selective service legislation, students were still civilians. But if it wasn't wartime, it wasn't exactly peacetime, either; "War is
practically inevitable," one Princeton student wrote to his parents in
March 1917. There's fatalism in that sentence, but there's eagerness, too.
War is coming; it will reach him and his classmates eventually, and when
it does, they'll go.

For some of them, eventually wasn't soon enough; in those months
before the United States entered the war, students began to leave their
campuses, singly or in groups, to join one service or another—the Army,
the Navy, the French Foreign Legion, the ambulances, some air service
(French or English or Canadian, it didn't seem to matter)—whoever
would take them. The volunteers didn't only come from East Coast campuses, where the war excitement was the greatest; they came from Illinois and Texas and Idaho and California, too. It was as though the
continent had tilted, tipping its young males eastward toward the Atlantic coast, and the broad ocean, and the European war beyond.

In February 1917, a contingent of Stanford University undergraduates sets out to join the American Ambulance Field Service. They are
the first university group to join the service as a complete unit, and
their send-off is a celebration: *The Daily Palo Alto Times* headlines their

departure, and a crowd gathers at the San Francisco train station to see them off. A camera crew films the scene, and the film is shown in San Francisco and in Paris.

One of the Stanford boys, Alan Nichols, is a dutiful son who writes letters home all along the way, so we know a good deal about what that long journey toward the war is like: it is a traveling fraternity-house party. The Southern Pacific and Union Pacific Railroads have provided the group with their own Pullman car, and they are free to do what they like there. Someone has brought along his banjo, and others play harmonicas; they serenade one another and the folks in the dining car. Somebody has a typewriter, and on it they compose a newspaper, "The Ambulance Tattler." In it they tease the leader of the group, a student named Joe Eastman; they say he wears three suits of long underwear to protect his delicate constitution from the high-mountain cold. (Eastman is a nervous, anxious young man, the kind who anticipates problems and shrinks from new experiences. He will keep a diary of his war that will tell a less exuberant story.)

The mood of the journey as Nichols tells it, so playful and careless, reminds us of how young they are: college kids, eighteen or nineteen or maybe twenty, away from their parents and adult supervision for the first time in their lives. For most of them this must be their first journey across their own country, and they look with astonishment at the scenes as they pass.

In all this two-week telling of their journey from San Francisco to New York, there is scarcely a word about the war they're going to. The journey itself is the reality: mountains are real, and plains, and towns, but the war isn't real—not yet. Nor is there anything in Nichols's letters about their motives for going to war: no patriotism (of course not, it's not their country's war), but also no expressions of sympathy for France, or poor little Belgium, and no hostility toward the Germans. These boys are not moved by a cause, or at least not by any they can articulate; they're going to war for the excitement of it, for the adventure.

Nor is there anything about the greatest adventure—flying. Yet by the end of that year four of them, including Nichols and the nervous Eastman, will have left the ambulance corps to become pilots—too eager for a total immersion in the game of war to settle for mere driving.

All that winter and early spring the war pulled young Americans toward France, and they responded, eagerly but uncertainly. At Princeton, Stuart Walcott applied to American representatives of the Lafayette Flying Corps in January, was accepted in February, chose the U.S. Army in April instead, resigned from the Army in May to take private flying lessons, and sailed for France later that month to join the Service Aéronautique. At Harvard, Briggs Adams, a student who had driven an ambulance in France the summer before, was back in Cambridge for his senior year. When he graduated in June, he didn't go back to ambulance service but chose aviation instead; when he found that U.S. Air Service training would take too long, he hurried to Toronto and joined the Royal Flying Corps. At Yale, George Moseley joined the New York Naval Militia when war was declared in April, got himself discharged from the Navy in June, and signed up instead with the French air service. At Princeton, Zenos Miller, a freshman, joined the National Guard in the fall of 1916. He was called to active duty in the spring and was set to guarding German prisoners in Trenton. But what kind of a war was that? He quit the Guard, joined the U.S. Army Air Service, and was sent to Toronto to train with the Canadians.

This kind of service jumping had gone on from the war's beginning, but in the months just before and just after the American entry into the war it seemed to increase, as more and more young Americans succumbed to the eager need to be there and joined whatever service was open to them; any uniform was better than no uniform, and you could always change your mind later. In the confusion of the time, it was sometimes difficult to get into a service, but it was apparently easy to get out again and try another. Every service, it seemed, had a revolving door.

Once in, the volunteers looked around for what they really wanted, and more and more often their choice was aviation. Even after the United States became a belligerent, American volunteers continued to head for the British and French flying services rather than their own (all the eager young men whose impatient moves I just described joined either the British or the French flying service *after* the American declaration of war). If you were eager to fly in combat, those forces were already doing it and had been for more than two years. Their flight schools were well established and were turning out pilots in substantial numbers.

Compared with such immediate opportunities for action, the belated U.S. Air Service had little to offer applicants. The will to build an
air force was certainly present from the beginning: young men in their
thousands swarmed to the recruiting offices ("there were at least 50,000
young Americans," Bingham recalled, "all eager to become pilots").
Members of Congress were just as eager to give them the chance; in
May, when the French premier, Alexandre Ribot, sent a cable asking
(*demanding*, really) that the Americans provide five thousand pilots and
forty-five hundred planes within a year, Congress agreed at once and appropriated $640 million—an unheard-of budget sum in those days—to
pay for an "Air Program."

But though enthusiasm for the Air Program was there, and Colonel
Bingham's plan was complete, there was not yet an actual working system turning out pilots. "The situation at that time, as to aviation," General Pershing later wrote, "was such that every American ought to feel
mortified to hear it mentioned." Of the sixty-five officers and one thousand enlisted men in the Air Service when the United States declared
war, only thirty-five knew how to fly, and except for five or six none was
ready for combat flying or knew anything about antiaircraft guns, or
bombs, or bombsights, or bomb racks. As for planes, the entire Air Service stock consisted of fifty-five trainers, unarmed and useless for combat; of those, fifty-one were obsolete, and the other four were obsolescent.
When Pershing concluded, "We could not have put a single squadron in
the field," he was understating the situation; the air service could not
have flown a single combat-ready plane into the war in the air.

Virtually no planes, then, and almost no pilots. And Pershing might
have added: nowhere near enough training fields, or flight instructors,
and no ground schools in which to teach eager young civilians how to
be military as well as the principles of aeronautics; enlisting in the Air
Service would be like joining the American League if the League had
no bats, or balls, or ballparks, or anybody who knew how to play the
game. Belatedness would always be part of the American story of the
war; none of the brave promises to the French would be kept, and even
at the Armistice Americans back home would still be constructing
training fields to train more pilots who were no longer necessary, and no
fighting plane of American design would have yet been built. Eagerness
plus belatedness equals muddle, and muddle would be the condition of

the U.S. Air Service, its training program and its squadrons, throughout the war.

The muddle began with enlistment. Even if you wanted to join the Air Service, it wasn't at all clear, in those early months, how you did it. Douglas Campbell was a senior at Harvard in the spring of 1917. Like many other students, he had planned to join the ambulance service when he graduated, but once war was declared, he decided that he must play a more combatant role, and he turned toward aviation. It wasn't easy, he later recalled: "Two or three of us were very interested in getting into the flying game, but we had a very difficult time for the first couple of weeks just trying to find out how to get into it. One weekend shortly after that, two other fellows and myself went to Washington to find out how to get into the air service." What they found was a one-room office in a Washington building, manned by one captain and his secretary; it was here that the initial organization of the flying service was taking place. The captain told the young volunteers what was planned, took their names and addresses, and told them they'd be contacted. It all sounds so drab and bureaucratic, like applying for a tax return or a job in the post office. Where was the dream of being young and marching off to war? Where was the immediate action? Eagerness cried, "Take us now!" And the system answered, "We'll be in touch."

Finding out how to do it was only the beginning of the enlistment muddle. What were the rules and qualifications? To the candidates, they seemed to vary from place to place and day to day. How young was too young? How old was too old? What about a college education? Did you need a degree or only part of one? You had to take a physical, of course, but what would the necessary tests be? Eyes, surely, and your hearing, and weight and height and bend-over-and-spread-your-cheeks, but what else? They found that there was also the whirling chair. One candidate described that test in a letter home: "He [the examining doctor] gave us about ten minutes each of that most unpleasant testing. Whirled in the chair, then told to look at his finger, here and there. Whirled again, head down; told to sit up, but unable to do so. It turned out O.K. for us all, as we all reacted favorably and were duly dizzy." He was proud to report that the semicircular canals in his ears had "proven of good quality"; in this new flier's world, dizzy was good, and he had passed into that whirling world. A trick roller skater who took the test failed because he *didn't* get dizzy; he was used to spinning, he did it all the time. Eventually, he was recognized as an exception and passed with the rest.

The new would-be pilots heard stories of older men already flying in the war who would never have passed the tests the young men were taking. Mick Mannock, the British ace, was said to have only one eye; another British flier named Carlin had only one leg (he tied his foot to the rudder pedal); Frank Alberty, an Australian, lost a leg on the Somme and learned to fly without it—well enough to shoot down seven German planes; William Thaw had a 20/80 left eye, defective hearing, and a bad knee, yet by the end of the war he was a lieutenant colonel in the Air Service commanding the Third Air Group. The *Air Service Medical Manual* of 1918 acknowledged that service doctors had been aware of the existence of such rickety pilots when they planned the standard flight physical: "It was known that men had been able to fly in spite of one or more physical handicaps, such as having only one leg, having one eye, having tuberculosis, or being cross-eyed, or having one collapsed lung, or being well over 50 years of age. Instances were at hand of those so handicapped who had been able to learn to fly and to fly well." Such men were already on active duty, and the Air Service needed all the pilots it could find. But in the future, when it selected the next batch of fliers, it would choose only those who were intact: one eye good, two eyes better.

The manual also worried about keeping the tests uniform. And well it might. Candidates knew, or at least believed, that the rules differed from one recruiting officer to another. If you failed the tests in Boston, you could go down to Hartford and try again.

What if you failed, and kept failing—in the eye test, say? Well, in those cases you could cheat; in the middle of enlistment, who would know? You could memorize the eye chart, or at the point in the test where you were asked to cover your good eye and test your bad one, you could peep between your fingers and test the good eye twice. Dudley Hill did that and passed into the Lafayette Flying Corps, where he had a distinguished one-eyed career. James Norman Hall, the Lafayette's historian, praised Hill for his deception, as though cheating in the cause of flying were in itself heroic. (Hall himself had lied his way into the British army at the war's beginning, presenting himself as a Canadian citizen when in fact he was American.) Other men lied on other subjects; John Grider claimed a college education he didn't have, and nobody noticed.

If you were a young gentleman with family influence and money, you could use those advantages to bypass the muddle. Quentin Roosevelt was the youngest son of Theodore Roosevelt. In 1917 the former president was surely the most influential man in America, and he was determined to use his influence and the force of his belligerent personality to thrust his four sons into the heart of the war that he was too old to fight in. He got what he wanted; within a few months all four were in uniform, commissioned, and headed for war zones: Archie became a captain in the infantry; Kermit was a captain first in the British and then in the American field artillery; Ted rose to the rank of lieutenant colonel in the infantry. And Quentin? With his weak eyes and his bad back (bad enough that he couldn't take part in athletics at Harvard) he seemed an unlikely candidate for any fighting role, yet he, too, was commissioned—as a first lieutenant in the U.S. Air Service. (He was said to have memorized the eye chart.) Their father was very pleased. "I don't believe in all the United States," he wrote in a letter at the time, "there is any father who has quite the same right that I have to be proud of his four sons." One can't help feeling that his pride was not so much in his sons for being brave as in himself for having begotten such men.

The muddle about qualifications and recruitment is perfectly understandable; military flying was a new kind of warfare, and especially in the United States. Air Service officers like Colonel Bingham simply had to guess what attributes and skills would make the ideal combat pilot. Two Harvard students offered themselves to the Air Service as specially desirable candidates on the grounds that they had driven both automobiles and motorcycles—as though these were unusual and valuable skills for a pilot to have in 1917. And maybe they were; maybe a young man who couldn't drive a car would be hopeless as a pilot, and one who could would be an ace. Nobody knew. British medical officers took the opposite view; they considered that it might be better to seek out as prospective pilots men with no mechanical knowledge at all, on the grounds that when they got into combat, they wouldn't always be listening to the engine for sinister noises. Other authorities argued that driving a machine along the ground simply wasn't comparable to flying. "Many people," a British flight commander wrote, "imagine that motoring or motor cycling forms an excellent apprenticeship to flying; but beyond the fact that these pastimes provide the learner with useful mechanical knowledge, they will not be found to be of particular value to the aviator. It is the man who has been accustomed to riding and outdoor games who proves quickest at picking up the feel of an aeroplane." The American plane builder Glenn Curtiss agreed with that: he told Colonel Bingham that anyone who could ride horseback and sail a boat could learn to fly. It's the country gentleman's argument: flying is a field sport, and military aviation is simply the cavalry with a different mount under you.

The War Department agreed: it sent out letters to college and university presidents offering "Air Service Information for College Students" that began: "There has been a decided demand among college men of athletic attainments, particularly those in or nearing the draft age, for information about the Aviation Service." The idea was to send information, including application forms, to "a selected list of the football players in your educational institution, as men of this class have not only exhibited a pronounced preference for the flying branch of the service, but have proven to be excellent material for training as aviators."

Harvard's president, Lowell, replied politely that he thought it very likely that his students might be interested in such materials. But two weeks later, when the same Air Service officers sent Lowell a set of articles for publication in the Harvard newspaper, Lowell frostily refused them. Harvard had already lost two-fifths of its undergraduate body, he wrote, and most of the rest were in military training on the campus. He thought it undesirable that more students should be taken out of college for aviation, "a service which can be recruited by selection from the conscript army." That last clause must have rankled the brass hats down at Air Service headquarters. Lowell was saying, in his superior Cambridge way, that he didn't want to waste his young men in flying jobs that any draftee could do; for him, pilots were truck drivers.

Still, the Air Service was right about what college athletes wanted; they enlisted in aviation in substantial numbers that spring. When ordinary students in flight schools wrote home, they mentioned the college sport stars who were among them: I'm flying, they said proudly, with Al Weatherhead, the Harvard quarterback, or Buck Church, the Yale end, or with George Moseley or Steve Philbin, both All-Americans at Yale, or Spuddy Pishon, the Dartmouth quarterback, or Mowatt Mitchell, captain of the Stanford football team, or Jimmy Vidal, captain of the University of Minnesota team, or Rabbit Curry, Vanderbilt's All-American quarterback. It was as though by becoming the flying companions of such campus heroes, they had somehow made the first team.

These new recruits were young. Until this point in their lives the challenges they'd faced had been the kinds that college boys face: the big game, exams, the first drink, girls. War is going to be different: it will confront them with a series of grown-up tests requiring skill and quick judgment and above all physical courage. A boy who passes these tests will be a man. They think a lot about manhood and write home about it. Jack Wright, an ambulance driver from Phillips Andover, still only eighteen years old, leaves the ambulance service for aviation and writes to his mother: "I think, en plus, that I have at last a right to call myself a *Man.*"

All these tests will rank order them, like the A-to-F tests back in school—from exceptional at the top down through mere ordinariness, which would be like getting a C, to of no use at all, which would be flunking. Nobody wants to fail; nobody wants to be ordinary. And so, as they move through the test and the flight checks, each young man begins to form a conception of himself: I'm healthy. I have twenty-twenty eyes. I'm coordinated (some fellows aren't). Maybe I'm one of the special ones; maybe I belong among pilots! Though, along with the exuberance of success, there must always be the companion fear: What if I'm *not* special? What if I fail the next test? Fear of failing isn't a condition that Army doctors can examine, but it's there, when you're young. So George Moseley, the All-American, the perfect athlete-candidate, explains to his parents that he is going to take the tests for the Lafayette Escadrille because he feels that he should know whether he can be a flier or not. The tests, he explains,

consert of a severe physical exam on your nerves, heart, lungs, and eyes. Then a flying exam. You are taken up in an aeroplane for 100 minutes, so I understand; at first you are a passenger; then you are given the controls and the instructor or examiner tells you to fly the machine yourself. He sits beside you and corrects any mistakes which you may make. Then he takes the controls and does fancy things, to see if you can stand it.

As that last clause makes clear, Moseley is not simply describing a flight physical; this is a test of something more. In another letter of the same time he writes, "I am going to take these tests . . . because then I will be able to find out the truth about myself as far as flying is concerned." *The truth about myself*, that's what they're all after: myself as a man.

Stuart Walcott is another would-be pilot who had to test himself in the air before he committed himself to flying. In May 1917 he went to the private flight school at Newport News, Virginia, to find out about himself. After his first flight there he wrote to his family with a kind of relief: "Flying from my first impression is a very fascinating game and the one I want to stay with for a while. I have signed up for 100 minutes in the air. While this hundred minutes will not make me a flier by any means I think it is well worth the while in that it gives me a little element of certainty in going abroad. I will know if all goes well that I am not unable to fly."

There's another, deeper fear that young men facing war feel: the fear of being afraid. What will I do when the bullets fly and the shells burst? Will I turn and run? Will I cower? Or will I act and not tremble? That fear must be especially present in a flying war, where the airplane itself, the instrument of war, is new and strange and dangerous. Unreflective flight candidates might regard the challenges of flight as simply a grander kind of sporting contest, the biggest big game, but for others, the sensitive, imaginative ones, it will be more than that.

Alan Winslow was a Yale junior in the spring of 1917 who was thinking about becoming a pilot. But he felt he had to test himself first. His own account of that testing, written fifteen years later, begins abruptly. He's on a visit to New York with his friend Phil: "I was lying full length, face down, on a narrow window ledge of the Hotel Biltmore in New York. My fingers clutched the cold stone. I peered, terrified, at the street twenty-six stories below. I was fascinated. I wanted to hurl myself over the edge." Phil has to drag him back into the hotel room by his legs. "What a hell of an aviator I'll make!" Winslow thinks. "If I'm frightened with a solid window ledge beneath me . . . what will happen when I'm actually up in the air?"

Phil suggests that maybe it will be different in a plane. The next day they travel to Newport News, where Winslow hires a flight instructor to take him up. As the Jenny takes off, he clutches the cockpit cowling, not daring to look over the side. But then he does and sees houses and fields sweeping past below him and feels no giddiness. He's two thousand feet in the air, many times higher than the Biltmore ledge, why isn't he scared? "Soon I had the answer," he writes. "In an airplane there was nothing between me and the earth. There was no side of a building, no wall of a cliff to give me a relative sense of height—nothing to make me dizzy. Perhaps I could be a pilot after all." His eagerness restored, Winslow returns to New York and sets about entering the muddle of flight training with all the other young men.

All war is a muddle; anyone who's been touched by it knows that. For governments, war is confusion on a national and international scale: too many people trying to do things they don't know how to do, too much matériel to be shifted from here to way over there, too many obstacles that nobody anticipated. On battlefields unpredictable things predictably happen: the weather changes, weapons don't function, reinforcements don't arrive, the enemy doesn't behave the way he's supposed to. Delays occur and throw the plan of attack off schedule. Commanders improvise or do nothing. It's surprising anybody ever wins.

The muddle is worst at the start, as a nation accustomed to the conditions of peace tries to make a hasty transition to a state of war. Certainly that was true in the United States in 1917. Huge and complicated arrangements had to be made, right now. Arms factories and training camps had to be built, workers had to be recruited and war materials gathered, citizens had to be turned into soldiers. Promises to allies had to be kept, as in the case of the telegram that Ribot sent to the American government in May.

The confusions of becoming a belligerent nation might have been inevitable, but to a young man in Brooklyn or Chicago (or Idaho or Arkansas or Boston), eager for war and impatient to be flying over the Western Front, muddle was what was happening to *you*, keeping you hanging around at home while in France other guys your age were fighting the air war without you. Muddle was being moved from one base to another for no reason that you could see. Muddle was hearing that your orders had been lost. Muddle was waiting: waiting to be sent to ground school. And then waiting to finish the course. And then waiting to be sent on to a flight school. And then waiting there for a plane, and an instructor, and decent flying weather. "Hurry up and wait!" the old-timers said. "That's all the Army is, just hurry up and wait."

The ground schools were the easiest part of flight training to organize. Most universities already had the staff for a School of Military Education (as they were called)—someone in engineering or physics who could teach the theory of flight, and a bit of meteorology, and how aircraft engines work; an Army reserve officer from the ROTC who knew the commands for close-order drill and could lecture on Army regulations; and plenty of athletics coaches for the physical exercise part. The Army would send specialists to teach the rest. And every university had housing space for the cadets: they'd all lost a fifth or a quarter of their male students to the war already, and men's dormitories were sitting empty. By the end of May 1917 ground schools had been established at state universities in California, Illinois, Ohio, and Texas, and at Cornell and MIT, and were ready to take in their first classes. (Princeton and Georgia were added later.) Their first classes graduated in July—on the fourteenth, Bastille Day, as it turned out.

Colonel Bingham describes in his memoir what the cadets were taught in ground school. First, three weeks of intensive military training and instruction in military topics: how to be a soldier and an obedient one. Then five weeks of the really serious stuff: signaling with a radio buzzer, lamp, and paneled shutter and care of the radio apparatus; care of machine guns and practice clearing jams; lectures on bombs, theory of flight, cross-country flying, meteorology, and night flying; explanation of instruments and compasses; practical work in map reading; lectures on types of airplanes; classroom work in aerodynamics; practical work in rigging and repairing planes; lectures on the principles of internal combustion engines and on the care of engines and tools; practical work with various types of engines; practice in troubleshooting; lectures on the theory of aerial observation and artillery ranging; a few lectures on liaison with infantry and the latest tactics of fighting in the air.

In their letters and diaries the young would-be pilots didn't have much to say about what they were learning in ground school. They wrote instead about what they were enduring during those eight weeks. At the University of Illinois school John Grider, the Arkansas boy who had lied about his education to get into the Air Service, struggled to prove that he was as good as any college boy. Halfway through the course he wrote home, "This place is getting harder and harder, a boy is shipped [that is, dismissed from the program] almost every day." There's nothing here about the subjects he's studying; what matters is working hard and obeying orders. And not getting shipped, which would turn you back into nobody.

To students like Grider, ground school was a ritual test; you did it because it stood between you and the flying life and because it was tough. If you did what you were told to do (or didn't, and got away with it), at the end you'd move on to flight school, and the presence of airplanes, where you belonged.

If the students saw ground school as a trial inserted in their training to test their endurance and waste their time, the men who had designed the program saw practical reasons for its existence: it delayed the flow of cadets into flight training; what was time lost for the impatient students was time gained for the builders of barracks and runways and airplanes. There would be delays, and many moves, and many disappointments.

For this problem of numbers the ground schools offered another kind of relief; they provided opportunities to "weed out those who were mentally, morally, or physically unfitted to become flying officers." A quarter of the young men who entered the ground schools would not graduate. The cadets were very aware of the relentless weeding process. John Grider wrote to his family, "It's going to be Hell for the next four weeks, but they can't Cull you unless you do something and I am not going to weaken."

When cadets had finished ground school, they'd be scattered around the country to such flying schools as existed: to Kelly Field in Texas, to Wright Field in Ohio, to Camp Borden at Toronto. Smaller groups traveled even greater distances. Five cadets from the Princeton ground school went all the way to San Diego to learn to fly at North Island.

The Navy scattered its cadets, too; the first draft of Navy cadets to reach Pensacola arrived just after the declaration of war in April 1917. They were surprised to learn that they hadn't come there to fly. "There were more than 200 of us there," one of the students recalled. "For a month and a half we drilled in deep sand under a hot sun. We attended aviation ground-school classes and tried to learn Navy regulations. We strove to persuade ourselves that sometime we'd fly, sometime we'd get to France."

At about the same time, the first wartime draft of college men arrived at the Army flying school at Mineola. The Hughes brothers, Gerard and George, came down from Harvard in that draft, expecting to begin flying at once. They found that "the men who have been here all winter are using the machines all the time to finish up as soon as possible" and the new men would have to wait. They were put to work drilling, doing guard duty, and learning wireless, semaphore, military customs and courtesies, and military law—"military junk," George called it in a grumpy letter home. Ground school stuff.

These local muddles were all parts of the one great muddle that creating an American flight program out of nothing was bound to produce. But the eager cadets, out there drilling in the sun, were bound to take it personally; for them, the service life must have seemed designed to keep them waiting on the ground, when all they wanted to do was fly.

As 1917 passed from spring to summer to autumn, the tilt of the country eastward seemed to steepen, tipping more and more young men toward the East Coast and the ports of embarkation there. They came singly and in groups, converging mainly on New York, where they reported to holding camps at Mineola or Garden City or Bedloe's Island (if they were Air Service men) or found rooms in Manhattan hotels, if they were Navy, or in Alan Nichols's case put up at the Harvard Club.

While they waited for a ship, they wrote to their folks, letters full of jittery exhilaration; the prospect of actually going "across" is exciting, but it's also daunting. Most of them have never been out of the United States or on an oceangoing ship; they don't speak any foreign language, or not well enough to say anything useful; they don't know anything about foreigners and the lives they live. They've never lived the disciplined, confined life of a combat unit. They've never commanded other men. They've never been anywhere near a war. What lies ahead of them will be strange and confusing, and frightening, too. They acknowledge these feelings to the home folks—all but the fear. They admit that only to themselves.

One young man's diary will give you a sense of what it was like for them, waiting *there* in that impatient time. Josiah Rowe was a student at Virginia Polytechnic Institute when the country entered the war. He enlisted in the Air Service and was sent to the School of Military Aeronautics at Princeton. Rowe began to keep a diary in October 1917, at the end of his ground school training, and continued it through his crossing to Europe.

It begins in haste and confusion: Rowe's Princeton unit is ordered to report to Mineola the next day. They travel through rain and cold and find that Mineola has no room for them; they spend the night in New York. The next day they return to Mineola, expecting to leave immediately, and are left to hang around and watch other units leave, and listen to rumors: they're all going to Italy; no, they're headed for France, to the biggest flying school in the world; no, they'll get off the ship at England and train with the RFC. Nobody *knows* anything. On their fourth day at Mineola they're told to pack up and leave in fifteen minutes. They do and are trucked across Long Island and through New York to a pier, where they board the steamer *Adriatic*. At 3:00 p.m. they steam out from the dock—but not for England or France, not directly. Two days later they are at anchor in Halifax harbor in Nova Scotia, where they are held on board for two days. On the third day, without warning, the *Adriatic* lifts anchor and steams off, followed by all the other ships in its convoy.

There's none of the romance of a first ocean crossing in Rowe's terse account: no ceremonial raising of the gangplank, no band playing, no waving crowd growing smaller on the dock. Only ship's names are still romantic: the *Adriatic*, the *Carmania*, the *Orduna*, the *Rochambeau*, the *Espagne*—all passenger liners in peacetime. And the *Leviathan*, the world's largest liner, confiscated from the Germans (who called it the *Vaterland*).

If you were lucky, you'd board one of the luxury liners and find that the luxury was still there, in spite of the war, and that you were entitled to share it. Rowe describes what it was like for the hundred student aviators aboard the *Adriatic*:

> The *Adriatic* is a wonderful ship—a perfect monster of wood and steel—about ten years old but quite modern in every respect. We have first-class passage, and the accommodations are magnificent—every possible comfort and convenience—elevators, Turkish bath, swimming pool, gymnasium, spacious

lounge and saloon, and a peach of a bar and smoking room. The
bar is an unhoped for luxury, and everyone patronizes it liberally.
Oh! What a joy to sit in your stateroom and have the steward
bring down the most delicious drinks!

And, he adds, "there are four pianos on board and about every other
person plays, so we have an abundance of music." And an abundance of
drinking (the bars were always open). And of gambling: poker, craps,
even bridge at half a cent a point (these were college men, remember).

On some crossings there were women aboard: nurses, or Red Cross
workers, or, on one memorable voyage, a female musical group. On the
Leviathan three bands played, one after the other, and there was dancing all afternoon and into the evening. Percival Gates, a Baptist preacher's
son who neither drank nor gambled, met a Red Cross nurse from Wisconsin named Bernadine and danced with her every night until the
lights went out. Aboard the *Espagne*, Dick Blodgett, on his way to join
an ambulance unit in the spring of 1917, had a romantic adventure on
his crossing and reported it in a letter to his little sister, and because he
was proud of his linguistic skills, or maybe because he thought French
was the appropriate language for romance, he wrote in French:

> Dear Ruthie:
>   . . . The first day I was sick, three times. Now je me porte
> bien. Pas plus de mal de mer. Hier et aujourd'hui il fait très
> beau. Hier nuit la pleine lune sur l'eau était magnifique. J'étais
> assis sur le pons avec une très jolie femme. Elle est la plus belle
> femme qui soit sur le bateau, et tous les garcons essayaient à lui
> faire connaissance, mai c'était moi qui avait diné avec lui, et
> après cela qui avait regardé la lune. Elle s'appelle B. Nous se-
> rons dans la même bateau de vie (life boat). Je l'ai puit sur moi-
> meme de la protégée en case de danger. Mais n'aie pas de peur.
> Elle est mariée. Elle n'a que vingt-deux ans. Son mari est
> malade. Probablement je le verrai beaucoup à Paris.

And then, just to be sure Ruthie got the point, he said it again in English at the end of the letter: "Don't worry. There's no cause for it. I am
assigned to the best lifeboat on board, with the prettiest girl. How could

I be safer?" It all sounds like one more college house party—like Alan Nichols's cross-country train journey or the First Yale Unit's days in Miami.

That's if you were lucky. If you weren't, you were hustled aboard a troopship or a former liner that had been converted to maximum payload: stacked-up bunks in the third-class cabins, partitions removed from the first-class staterooms to crowd more men in. On such ships you might be treated as roughly as the enlisted men were, crammed into the lower decks, and fed two meals a day. The newly formed 104th Squadron crossed on such a ship in the fall of 1917. Here's the first day aboard, as recorded by Jack Coffin, one of the 104th's pilots:

> *Thursday, October 18, 1917*: On board the *U.S.S. Covington*—an interned German liner—We came on at 1:00 p.m. Assigned to bunks and kept below until the ship sailed. Hell of a hole. Steerage. Waited two hours for mess.

And his entry for the last day of the voyage:

> *Sat., Nov. 3*: Still on board. Our Colonel apologized for our treatment during the voyage. He might well do so!

The inequalities were more apparent when men who had been close companions at Harvard or Dartmouth or St. Paul's found themselves separated on shipboard, like gentlefolk from immigrants. If anyone belonged with the gentlefolk it was Hamilton Coolidge. Ham was the son of an old New England family that claimed descent from Thomas Jefferson; he'd been at school at Groton and then Harvard. Yet when he sailed on the *Orduna* in July 1917, he was assigned to a berth in steerage. In a last letter to his mother before he went on board he wrote, "Q. [Quentin Roosevelt, his friend at Harvard] sails on the same boat, and he is a first Lieutenant! [and presumably in a first-class cabin]. I travel steerage (because the old commission hasn't arrived) with the contingents from the six Government schools: Tech., Cornell, Ohio, Berkeley, Cal., Texas and Illinois."

Coolidge doesn't seem much troubled by the inequality of the assignments. But then, he wasn't really stuck in steerage; he moved into a second-class cabin with another old Harvard friend, Doug Campbell.

Rowe, ever the careful diarist, remarks on the frivolous goings-on of his shipmates in the first-class bars and lounges:

> The attitude of the men and officers on board certainly presents an interesting study in psychology. With few exceptions, they seem to look upon this expedition as a frolic—more of a sight-seeing tour than, as it really is, a fight to the death with the Germans. Some appear to think more of matters of dress and plans for joy parties in Paris than they do of the more grim aspects of war.

The grim aspects were present, though; out there beneath the surface of the sea German U-boats hunted. The cadets stood submarine watches, and at night all external lights were extinguished, and the darkness on deck was absolute. Seven days out of Halifax, Rowe described the ship's two moods:

> It is funny to observe the contrast between the inside and outside of the ship—the lounge and smoker are ablaze with light; pianos, guitars and ukes are making merry music; the smoker is crowded with men drinking, smoking, and gambling, and having the best of fun, apparently oblivious to the dangers of the present and those of the immediate future. One could easily imagine himself in a club or hotel in New York. Then, just step outside on deck, and there isn't a gleam of light nor a sound except the blowing of the wind and the splashing of the waves.

The gaiety in the lounge may seem strange, Rowe thinks, but he decides it's all right: "There isn't any use putting on a long face and bemoaning the fact that a torpedo may strike at any moment, blasting away the side of the ship—all the worry in the world will not prevent it."

Still, at the bar and the poker tables much of the talk is of subs and torpedoes. What are the odds of being attacked? Houston Woodward, crossing in March 1917 to drive an ambulance, estimates they are one in fifteen, though he adds that others started out figuring one in fifty or a hundred but lowered them to one in ten, even one in five. If they're attacked, what are the chances of surviving? Of even managing to reach the deck before the ship goes down? They speculate and scare one another.

They trade rumors. A sub has just hit a transport returning from New York; somewhere in the Atlantic the *Glendavid* has been sunk; the radio operator says New York papers have reported that the ship they're on has been torpedoed. In the letters the young men write to the folks at home—journals, really, to be mailed when they reach port—they repeat the rumors, along with day-by-day accounts of the ship's gunnery practice, and lifeboat drills, and mysterious lights seen on the horizon, and trails of foam along the surface of the sea that could mean periscopes. It all makes real the presence of possible death in their lives where none was before.

A week out of New York and four days from Liverpool, Rowe noticed a change in his shipmates: "Fellows are getting the flying fever again—the events of the voyage made us forget aeroplanes for a while but the spell is gripping us stronger than ever as we near the place where we are to begin work."

They were surely close to their war in the air now.

FOUR

ABROAD I:
FIRST IMPRESSIONS

Although the young men who sailed on those passenger liners turned troopships were college men from well-off families, the grand tour of Europe was not a part of their culture, and for most of them their possible destinations—England, France, Italy, London, Paris, Rome—were only words on a map. When they stepped ashore—at Liverpool, or Le Havre, or Bordeaux—they looked around with innocent American eyes and judged what they saw by American values: back home, big was good; so was modern, and clean; so was progress and comfort. This Old World they'd landed in seemed the opposite of all that.

Because it is so different, they write home about it and offer first impressions that are like snapshots a tourist might take. Josiah Rowe, on his way to flight training in Italy, lands in Liverpool and snaps its picture: "The principal streets of the town were quite clean and orderly, but the side streets were narrow, dirty and crowded just like the ideas you get from Dickens' stories. The houses were all of brick about a thousand years old and two stories high and practically all just alike."

Other pilot-travelers reach England and are shocked by the differences they find in ordinary things. The English trains they board are dinky, they say, and the English landscape is all wrong: it's green in November, and trees are conspicuously absent, and every inch of ground is under cultivation. London, too, disappoints them; under the weight of war the city is gloomy and quiet, the streets are unlit, and the hotels are dark. They witness that weight on the people they see. At railway stations, Bogart Rogers writes, "you see Tommies coming in covered with Flanders mud, rifles over their shoulders and iron hats strapped to their backs, and you realize that maybe less than twenty-four hours ago they were in the front line trenches."

But it's not only the soldiers who bear that weight; everyone has been hit and hit hard. "I had no idea," Rogers goes on, "what a tremendous affair the war is, how terrible it is, and how the English people have worked and sacrificed."

Surely France will be different; surely they'll see it—and especially Paris—with more joyful eyes. Josiah Rowe, continuing on his long journey to Italy, crosses the Channel from Southampton to Le Havre and boards a train, thinking as he goes that he's headed "for Paris—even the mention of that name gave us a thrill."

The countryside they roll through is interesting, Rowe writes, though it's "not nearly so attractive as England." But the real interest for him and his companions is not the landscape but the people they see at stations along the way. Soldiers and civilians alike greet them with cheers, and the young pilots respond with such French phrases as they have— "Bonjour," and "À la carte," and "Bon amis"—and the French folks shout back phrases that the Americans don't understand. For most of these innocents abroad, the language problem will remain a barrier. But the French will forgive them.

To Rowe, Paris is the thrilling city he expected, and he responds to its beauty and its history with due reverence: "For real beauty Paris is absolutely unsurpassed. Everything that you have ever read about Paris— and some that you haven't—is true. I was deeply impressed when we went to see the Bastille and more so at the tomb of Napoleon." But he's most touched by the French people he sees in the streets and cafés:

> While everything was greatly subdued there was gaiety in abundance and crowds and crowds of people. Some of the cafes were going full blast and life there was anything but serious . . . The people are certainly fascinating. White uniforms for men [perhaps hospital convalescents?] and black for women [in mourning] were almost universally worn and you could see that

though the weight of war bore heavily upon them, they didn't take matters so seriously as the English. Their gaiety and frivolity were only on the surface and you could tell that under it all they were hiding untold suffering.

It's the paradox that strikes him: the frivolity and the suffering, the gay crowds and the black clothes of the mourning women. So French, he thinks, so unlike the always-serious English.

Other pilots have other first impressions. They see French women for the first time—not individually, but in crowds, in cafés, and on street corners. In their young men's minds women collectively are divided into two types: nice girls, like the ones they know back home, and the others, for whom they have many terms, such as "easy women," "bad women," "chips," "painted ladies," "street women." Such women, confronted en masse, are frightening, or tempting, or both (remember how young the pilots are, and how innocent). Waldo Heinrichs, on his first day in Paris, writes in his journal: "Women are wild & loose in this city. Many offers for 'Voulez vous coucher avec moi.' They grab a person on the streets in their effort. It all looks so loose."

Roland Richardson, also on his first visit to Paris, goes out for a good time with two friends. They run into "all the unattached girls in the place." The girls pester them to buy them drinks. On their way home the three meet more girls hanging around on all the corners; girls take them by the arms and try to start conversations. "Thank goodness we got out safely," Richardson writes. "Some of them were good looking, but they were all too anxious . . . Paris is *some* city."

Some pilots react to the swarming young women of Paris differently. The exuberant Kenneth MacLeish reached Paris in November 1917 and wrote home at once: "Here I am, and my little bells are tinkling. And Paris! Oh, it's far better than even the wildest tales picture it. It's as much as your life is worth to go out to dinner here. There are literally *thousands* of girls who say they will show you around Paris, and it's a two-fisted fight to shake them off!"

And there are the others, the very shy and the very young, for whom the French women, and the Americans who get involved with them, and Paris itself are just too much to cope with. Dick Blodgett, nineteen years old and fresh off the boat, passes through Paris and writes plaintively to his mother, "I am very much disappointed in French women. They are not nearly so much of a good thing as at college or in Boston." And a few months later, on his first visit there: "This city is the rottenest morally I've ever seen. It seems to degenerate everyone. The boys that go to seed over here are almost beyond figures . . . I don't see why they can't take a girl to supper and let it go at that."

Whatever the reactions, it is clear that there are a lot of young women around the cafés and on the streets of Paris and that, as Harvey Conover exclaimed, they are "wild and full of pep." They're different from the girls back home.

George Moseley arrived in Paris in July 1917, just in time for the Fourth of July parade, and put his impressions and emotions in a letter home:

> During the morning of "The Fourth," American troops paraded in Paris. They were preceded by a company of French soldiers in their blue uniforms which showed signs of hard wear in the trenches. When our troops passed, every Frenchman cheered, old soldiers with the medals across their chests stood at attention saluting, flowers were thrown at our boys by the thousands, people rushed out from the crowd and stuck flowers in their guns, in their hats and all over.

Most Americans traveling to Europe for the first time expect a place where history is everywhere, in castles and cathedrals and battle-fields and great old cities, waiting to be stared at, and where the people are either quainter or more sophisticated than Americans are. There's some of that tourists' vision in the first impressions of the young pilots, but it's colored by the fact that what they are witnessing is Europe at war: many soldiers, some wounded, some still intact, none of them heroes in the romantic sense; and many civilians, some grieving, some frivolous, some hungry; and the darkness that war imposes on nations under its shadow. They share the difficulties and inconveniences that all naive visitors meet: the languages they can't speak, the food they don't like, the shabby age of things, and the dirt that goes with it.

It's a complex beginning for the lives they will live here. They see it all with newcomers' eyes that are innocent but alert to its strange particulars. Their first impressions will change: London and Paris will become familiar places that they'll grow fond of and comfortable in, and the French and British people will cease to be strangers with peculiar customs and become familiar company. They'll go home after their war changed by Abroad and will find that their world back home has become a different place.

Not all of them are innocents abroad. Quentin Roosevelt arrived in Paris in August 1917 already familiar with the city, remembering it as he had known it in the years before the war and seeing the wartime city in that nostalgic light:

> It is not the Paris that we used to love, the Paris of five years past. The streets are there, but the crowds are different. There are no more young men in the crowds unless in uniform. Everywhere you see women in black, and there is no more cheerful shouting and laughing. Many, many of the women have a haunted look in their eyes, as if they had seen something too terrible for forgetfulness. They make one realise the weight that lies on all alike now.

It's the same Paris Rowe will see a few months later, but darker, because Roosevelt had known it when it was the City of Light. Still, he's at ease in Paris: he speaks the language, and he has connections there; his sister-in-law has a house in the avenue du Bois de Boulogne that she has opened to visiting American officers, and he stays with her when he's in town. He knows Paris the way a frequent visitor does—the shops, the bars, and the restaurants.

———

Ham Coolidge arrived in Paris in the same detachment as Roosevelt. Like his friend, he speaks some French, though less well; he's just able, he says, to get what he needs at stores and restaurants and inquire his way around the city, but he's improving! Also like Roosevelt, he has connections in the city; his uncle John is in the American Embassy, and his aunt Helen invites him to dinner, where the other guests include Colonel Raynal Bolling (then Assistant Chief of Air Service, Lines of

Communication), Major and Mrs. Scott, his cousin Colonel Kean, and "a Marquise de something, but not much!"

As for Coolidge's first impressions of Paris, he exclaims in a letter that "Paris is wonderful," but the only wonderful detail he offers is "one of the incomparable little patisseries," where he stops to gorge on cakes. Then he turns to what really excites him—the prospect of working with the group of young officers (Roosevelt is one of them) who will be in complete charge of organizing the vast new American flying school at Issoudun, down in the middle of France a hundred miles south of Paris. "It is a job so overwhelming," he writes, "and we are so inexperienced that I can hardly believe it all." It will mean he won't be able to fly, or only occasionally, and it will look as if he were avoiding combat by taking an *embusqué* job, but he thinks it's important. He advises his mother just to tell the folks at home that he is "on special duty connected with the organization of new schools in France." That will make it sound better—like some secret mission and not just a job.

Students who reached France in late 1917 and after were generally sent to Issoudun. They arrived there with high expectations; they'd heard of this brand-new American Aviation Center, built just for them. Here they'd begin flight training at once and would quickly move up to the front, long before the students still back in the States even got to France.

The reality wasn't like that. When the first students arrived at Issoudun, in August 1917, not only was there no flying school ready for them; there was no airfield at all—only farmers' fields and a few tents. Before the cadets could fly there, they'd have to build the facilities they'd fly from—the landing fields, the roads, the barracks, the hangars. That would take the whole of the autumn and winter, and the first impressions of students who reached the field during that time would be of a huge building project, and of the rain and the mud. Jack Coffin disembarked from the *Covington* at St. Nazaire in November and recorded his impressions of his new life in his diary. Here are his entries for his first ten days at the aviation center:

Mon., Nov. 5: took train at 4:30 for flying school.

Wed., Nov. 7: Reached Issoudun about eight o'clock. Trucks took us to camp. Time on train 44 hours; time traveling 16 hours. Camp only partly built. It is a sea of mud.

Thurs., Nov. 8: No immediate hope of flying. Fatigue duty getting barracks into shape. Hell of a hole [he'd said the same about his steerage quarters on the SS *Covington*]. Rains every day. Mess poor.

Sat., Nov. 10: More fatigue duty . . . Men in this camp seem to have been forgotten. There are cadets here who have been digging for months.

Sun., Nov. 11: K.P. duty today. My kingdom for a good shower bath.

Nov. 13: Shoveled and hauled cinders, fixing ground in front of hangars.

Nov. 14 and 15: More cinders.

It was troopship steerage all over again: partly the discomfort and partly outrage at the gross indignity of it—would-be pilots doing day laborers' jobs. Not only did the work they were doing have nothing to do with flying, but it was antithetical to what they wanted and had expected— not up in the clouds, but down in the mud, and not free, but regimented. Morale among the students sank.

That rapid drop in student morale wasn't only an Army problem. In the summer of 1917 the Navy began a training program in collaboration with the French to teach American seaplane pilots at Moutchic, on the coast north of Bordeaux. The arrangement was that the French would teach the students to fly, supply the necessary planes, engines, instruments, and armament, and construct three new training stations. All the American Navy had to do was provide the students.

It was a fine plan [one of the students recalled] except that it didn't work out . . . From French flying schools we bounded right into the construction gang. We built the navy's school of aeronautics at Moutchic, roads, hangars, shops, barracks, and schoolrooms . . . We who had enlisted to fly shoveled sand, toted supplies, broke rocks—and our hearts, backs, and spirits. Morale suffered. There were fights, mutinies, desertions. Courts-martial began to sit.

All the rottenness in every one came out.

I was near rebellion—and trouble—many times.

"Mutiny," "desertion," "rebellion"—those are strong words for strong feelings.

There were no actual riots, because there was too much at stake—the chance to fly, a commission, and a war ahead. But the anger and bitterness the young pilots felt was deep and long-lasting. They had learned a tough old soldier's lesson: once the Army (or the Navy) has you, it can do what it wants with you. For these would-be pilots, that meant it could keep you on the ground, working and waiting, while at the front other guys flew your war.

For early volunteers who signed up with the French Service Aéronautique and were ordered to French flying schools, what struck them most forcibly wasn't usually the fields (which were functioning well), or the planes, or the training they faced; it was the company they'd be keeping. Stuart Walcott had just arrived at the field at Avord in July 1917 when he wrote his impressions:

> There are some 150 Americans learning to fly now in France, besides the ones the Government may have sent over—more than a hundred at this one school, and the oddest combination I've ever been thrown with: chauffeurs, second-story men, ex–college athletes, racing drivers, salesmen, young bums of leisure, a colored prizefighter, ex–Foreign Légionnaires, ball players, millionaires and tramps. Not too good a crowd according to most standards, but the worst bums may make the best aviators.

Some of these types would have been familiar to Walcott—the athletes and the millionaires and maybe the playboy bums belonged to the world he'd left behind at Princeton—young men from families of some substance, with social positions, connections, and confidence, who knew the rules by which their part of American society lived, played the same sports, drove the same cars, married each other's sisters.

The others—the chauffeurs and the second-story men—would have been strange to him, as different in the lives they'd lived as Bedouins or Eskimos. They came from all over the place in that vast expanse of America that wasn't the East Coast—from farms and ranches and small towns and from all kinds of jobs. They hadn't gone to college, or if they had, not to Yale or Harvard, but to some crossroads college out

West somewhere. Their families didn't have old money or connections with people who mattered; they weren't, that is to say, *gentlemen.*

Walcott put a label on that other kind of pilot later, when he met the members of the Lafayette Escadrille for the first time: "They are a very odd crowd—the members of the Lafayette Escadrille, a few nice ones and a bunch of rather roughnecks. Their conversation is an eye opener for a new arrival. Mostly about Paris, permissions, and the rue de Braye, but occasionally about work and that *is* interesting. Nonchalant doesn't express it."

They're "roughnecks"—rough in conversation, rough in experience (what happened, I wonder, in the rue de Braye?)—and interesting. Walcott's reaction to them isn't snobbish and superior; its tone isn't one of class disdain; it simply expresses surprise and delight that the flying world includes such people. They aren't what he expected. It isn't only the flying world that he's discovering to be so various and strange; it's the whole world of war. College men like him would have lived their entire lives among people like themselves, had it not been for the war; they'd never have come across a second-story man, or a colored prize-fighter, or a tramp. And here they all were. They'd be the men he would fly with.

That's what big wars do: they bring together young men who would never meet in ordinary civilian life, dump them together in barracks and tents, and in foxholes and airplanes, set them marching to the same drum, fighting in the same war. It was like that in my war, too; until I went to flight school, I had never met anyone who went to Yale, or came from Texas, or pitched in the International League, or drove an MG. Or a girl who drank Southern Comfort. I met them all before I was done. War is a broadening experience.

FIVE

DRIVING THE MACHINE

July 1917: on the edge of a field in the middle of France, Stuart Walcott sits alone in a contraption made of wood and wire. It looks like a box kite with an ironing board stuck on crosswise and an engine and propeller attached on the front. The whole thing rests on a pair of what look like bicycle wheels. On the grass beside this curious machine a French officer stands shouting instructions in rapid French. "Tout droit!" he says, making a chopping motion with his hand. "Tout droit!" Walcott doesn't have much French, but he gets the idea; he's to drive the contraption across the field in a straight line.

That sounds easy enough; after all, he knows how to drive an automobile: you just grab the steering wheel and step on the gas. He opens the throttle, and the machine begins to move, slowly and bumpily at first, then faster as the back end lifts from the grass. He tries to keep it moving in a straight line, but that isn't as easy as it would be in a car, since he has no steering wheel and no brakes. As the machine accelerates, the rotation of the propeller pulls it away from a straight-ahead course (an action that's called torque, though Walcott may not know that).

Wind is another problem: if a gust blows hard across the path of the machine, it will strike the vertical rudder on the plane's tail and swing the whole thing like a weather vane into the wind. Either force, torque or wind, can throw a plane that's rolling along the ground into a violent skidding turn that American pilots call a ground loop and Frenchmen (who are more poetic about flying) call a *cheval de bois*—a wooden horse, like the horses that go round and round on a carousel. The young man will try to keep his course straight, but he will learn that a plane sometimes has a mind of its own.

Walcott makes it to the far side of the field, where other students rush out and turn his machine around, point him back to where he started. He rolls back across the field, but more slowly. The *moniteur* is waiting. "Plus encore!" he shouts. "Et plus vite!" and turns him round again.

What happened next is told in a letter Walcott wrote home:

My first sortie or trip went O.K. with a considerable breeze on the tail, but on the second there was too much wind and after I got going pretty fast—around she went. The wind caught under the inside wing and up it went. Smash went the outside wheel, and a crackle of busting wood. All the front framework of wood that holds the motor was smashed—a pretty bad break. The monitor was a bit mad and talked to me a bit in French.

The plane that Walcott has just wrecked is a Blériot XI, the standard plane for primary training in the French air service. Its design is archaic by 1917: it looks like the plane that Louis Blériot first flew across the English Channel in 1909 and quite unlike those that are in combat over the Western Front. For one thing, it's a monoplane: most combat planes in 1917 had upper and lower wings—some had three. The Blériot's fuselage is not covered in painted canvas, except around the cockpit where the pilot sits; the rest is just a bare wooden framework. The single wing is braced with many wires attached to posts above and below, which add to the box-kite effect.

Most of the control surfaces of the Blériot are fairly standard: the elevator (which controls vertical movement) and the rudder (which controls the horizontal) are at the back end of the plane; that's where they are on all planes now, but in the early days of flying they might be at the front, and the propeller might be at the rear, facing backward, which must have given the odd impression that the plane was *backing* through the air. There are no ailerons (ailerons are the movable panels on the rear edges of the wings of a modern plane that control rolling, tilting movements); in a Blériot you tilted the plane by warping the wings— that is, twisting them by means of wires. The cockpit is located in the middle; the pilot sits there on a wicker seat, not so much *in* the plane as *on* it, with most of his body up in the air above the cockpit rim. Since the Blériot has no windshield, he's exposed to the buffeting slipstream of the propeller and will be sprayed with the castor oil that lubricates the engine.

One other thing about Walcott's Blériot: it can't fly. Its wings have been cropped, like the wings of a barnyard turkey, to keep it on the ground. All you can do with it is drive it across the field. Students call these earthbound machines Penguins, after another bird that can't fly.

Nobody seems bothered that Walcott has busted his plane; it happens all the time. Mechanics simply haul the wreckage off the field and bring him another one. (Being mostly wood and wire, the Blériot is easily repaired; it will be back in service in a couple of days.) Walcott continues with his taxiing practice. When he's mastered the Penguin, he's promoted to another Blériot with uncropped wings, which can rise a few feet off the ground; now he practices getting it up and down again. When he can do that without crashing, he gets another model with larger wings, and a bit more horsepower, in which he learns to take off, fly a circuit of the field, and land.

In all these exercises, Walcott is alone in the plane. Before he takes off, his *moniteur* will stand beside him and tell him what to do in the air, but the *moniteur* will never go along on the flight to take over if his student gets into trouble and to demonstrate the right way to do it. (How could he? This Blériot model has only one seat.)

The teaching language is primarily French, which isn't surprising, since the *moniteurs* are Frenchmen and the country they're flying in is France. The students learn to speak Pilot French, a language of French metaphors for the parts and movements of planes. Their letters home are full of its terms: *cheval du bois* and *tour de piste*, *panne* and *vrille* and *pique*, some of which they spell phonetically—*vree* and *peek*—since they've never seen the words written. Some of this language fades when the young pilots go on to fly in English-speaking squadrons, but some remains and becomes the standard English terminology for airplane parts: "aileron" (from the French term for a spindle); "empennage," the vertical and horizontal tail surfaces from the French term for the feathers on an arrow.

The Blériot way is the one Walcott chose, back at Princeton, when he wrote to his father about "being sent to France to learn to fly according to French methods."

At least one senior American aviator fully endorsed the Blériot method. When Colonel Billy Mitchell, then Chief of Air Service, First Army, visited the Avord flying school in the spring of 1917, he concluded that the system in use there produced excellent pilots, though he admitted it took a great deal of time. "I went through this same sort of instruction myself," he recalled, "and know it taught me more about flying than any other system could possibly have done." In this system, he said, the student really taught himself to fly. Mitchell thought that was the right way to learn—perhaps because he had begun his military career as a cavalryman; you learn to ride a horse by climbing on its back, giving it a kick in the ribs, and hanging on until you fall off. And if you think about it, the great Louis Blériot himself must have learned to fly by the Blériot method (who was there to teach him?), as did the Wright brothers, and no doubt many another backyard tinkerer, in the early days of flying.

As Stuart Walcott moved on through the stages of his training, he continued to write letters home. All the young pilots did; they were well-bred young men; they'd always written to their parents when they were away from home—at private school, at summer camp, at college. Their letters from flight training are much like the ones they'd have written from school: I'm learning this and then that; if I pass the tests, I'll be promoted, and then I'll graduate—the usual narratives of the hurdle race that education is. And because their families were the sorts of people who save such mementos of their children's growing, they preserved the letters and sometimes published them in small editions for the family. So we know a lot about how American flight students learned to fly during the First World War. They explain what they're doing in planes in careful detail, knowing that the folks back home have never been in a plane, or maybe even seen one.

Charles Biddle, a young Philadelphia lawyer turned aviator, describes the first stages of the Blériot method to his parents. Biddle arrived in France knowing something of how to fly; he had had dual-control training at the Curtiss Flying School at Newport News. The French took no note of his experience; they simply started him at the beginning of the process that Biddle calls "driving the machine"—as though a plane were a tractor or a dump truck.

You might expect that Biddle would be angry at the delay in his progress on the front and perhaps surprised at the teach-yourself method the French used. But there's none of that in the letters he wrote home in the spring of 1917; he simply describes the stages of the process, step by step: the Penguins, the *rouleur* (that's the straight-ahead-on-the-ground stage), and the *décolleur* (three feet up and down again), and eventually a little higher, and regular, sure-enough landings.

There is no criticism of the method in Biddle's account, but there is a kind of patient impatience; this isn't really flying. Other beginners feel that impatience, too; Sidney Drew called those early exercises "inconsequential flying" and was eager to move on to the next stage, the *tour de piste* (the *piste* is the airfield), where real, consequential flying would begin. Drew explains what the tour amounted to in a letter to his father: "All one has to do is to mount into the air to the height of a hundred and fifty metres, follow the course closely [it's a rectangle], making your turns at the right angle and, when you come back to your starting point, *pique* and make a good landing."

The course is only two and a half miles around, and the plane is still just a Blériot (though with a more powerful engine), but Drew calls these flights "absolute flying classes"—still classes, but no longer beginners' exercises; "at last," he writes, "I can say that I have flown an aeroplane."

There will be other, more challenging tests: the *petit voyage*, a trip from here to somewhere else and back; two triangular cross-country flights; an hour spent at two thousand meters altitude; precision landings. Real flights, all of them, flown by a young man who was beginning to think of himself as a real pilot.

Simply describing the flight-training syllabus won't be enough to give the folks back home that sense of real flight; the young pilots will try to express the *feeling* of flying—what it's like to be up there, airborne and alone, how the air is another country with a different geography, a different sense of space, different emotions, different physical responses.

Their efforts at description begin with the first flight and continue through the whole training period. They're not all gifted writers (though some—Quentin Roosevelt, Ham Coolidge, Drew, Walcott—are), but they are telling personal stories that are absolutely new to their experience, and the newness lifts their imaginations and makes the telling immediate and alive. Here is Drew on his first flight: "Well, father, at last I have been in the air. The class I am in now is the first real air class, and it is quite interesting to be up in the air all by yourself."

He's barely off the ground, but something absolutely new has happened to him. He tries to put it into words, first general, abstract terms: it's "interesting," he says, it's "exciting," this learning to fly. But such words aren't good enough; he tries again with similes: learning to fly in the Blériot school is like trying to paddle a canoe straight (that's the Penguin stage); then it's like trying to ride a bicycle for the first time (that's the *décolleur* stage). But the flying, the actual flying? He turns to pure imagination: flying, when he has mastered it, will be "like trying to drive a light cloud."

A month later Drew has advanced to the *tour de piste* class. In a long letter he tells his stepmother what it's like. "One gets into the machine," he writes,

> makes himself as comfortable as possible, pulls on the "gaz" and with the assistance of a few slight-of-hand tricks (the point to the trick being that the hand must be as slight as possible) mounts into the air.
>
> One then flutters about, being impressed on the head by the weight of one's helmet, and in the stomach by the tightness of one's belt, while the propeller whizzes about in one's face, causing the eyes to water and the perspective to become ethereal.
>
> One then fiddles about with the controls, twitching nervously and with "slight hands" at them as the wings rise and fall and the whole aeroplane jumps up and down answering obediently to the demands of the air currents.

I quote this passage at such length for the sake of the self-portrait in it— the comically fuddled young man who sits in the wicker seat, fluttering and fiddling, while the plane obeys not the incompetent new pilot but the insistent currents of the air. That it's a comic portrait is not surprising; Drew had been a rising comic actor in his civilian days. But any old pilot who remembers his early flying days will recognize its truth, the bouncing up and down in space while the plane and the air decide what to do.

Once Drew has gained a little altitude and the plane is flying itself, he looks around for the first time and sees the world around him, not fields and woods, not from up here, but yellow and green patches, a distant pattern far below.

Then it's time to turn, and he's back in the plane, twitching at the controls while the machine whirls around and he feels, he says, like someone "clinging to a waving flag that is suspended from the eighteenth story window of a sky-scraper"—once more the helpless comedian in the wicker seat. But he has introduced his reader to some of the complex feelings of flying: the sense you have that a plane has a will of its own; and that other feeling, of three-dimensional freedom, that comes when you're alone in a plane, separated in space from the patchwork world below, supported only by the unsubstantial air.

The altitude test that followed added another emotion to that feeling of distance from the earth: not loneliness, or fear, but an exhilarating solitude. As you rise farther and farther from the land below, it looks more and more like a map, a diagram of itself, and less like the land you live on. Walcott, on his altitude test, took his Blériot to two thousand meters (the assigned altitude for the test) in fourteen minutes but went on up, to thirty-five hundred meters, about as high as a Blériot could go (it took him another forty minutes). By the time he leveled off, clouds had formed, and he was shut off from the earth—"nothing but a beautiful sea of clouds below me, a very beautiful sight."

Every pilot shares that feeling of the sheer beauty of clouds when he flies among them. On fair-weather days cumulus clouds saunter like sailing ships on favorable winds, sliding their shadows across the green landscape below. On gray days you climb first past trailing wisps, like hems torn from the cloud above you, into the overcast; you call it "solid" when you talk with other pilots—"a solid overcast today"—but it's not, it's a luminous wetness, a shining dimness with nothing inside it. And then you come out on top, into impossible brightness, and climb on in perfect light, and look around.

Above the clouds you enter another landscape, white hills and valleys and wide plains stretching to the horizon. And thunderheads, shining mountains that tower above you, their tops like great anvils, taller than you can fly. You can play on their soft sides, slide up along their whiteness, and stall, and let your plane slide down again like a sled on a snowy hill, and when you do, a halo of light will form around you. This isn't simply more of the earth's variety; it's another, separate world made of mist and space and light, containing nothing substantial—only the white clouds and the high, empty bluer-than-blue sky.

And then the letting down, into the cloud layer where the light dims again to gray and there's nothing to see until you come out below, back in the overcast world.

After the altitude test, the *petit voyage* or *ligne droite*—a solitary flight to a town sixty kilometers or so away, where you must land, and then fly back to your home field. It's an exhilarating and slightly scary thing for a beginner, flying away from the place you know and landing where you've never landed before. More than simply another exercise, it's a little voyage to elsewhere, a liberation from the familiar.

On your first trip the world you fly over will be strange, but navigating is easy (or so Walcott assured his parents): "Nothing to do but climb two or three thousand feet and just sit there and watch the country unfold, comparing the maplike surface of the earth spread out below with the map in the machine. In good weather it is very easy to follow, spot roads, towns, woods, rivers and bridges." When it's like that—the weather good and the engine purring—you'll fly your flight happily and return home at day's end contented, pleased with yourself and your plane. Here's Walcott at the end of his first *petit voyage*: "Coming back yesterday evening, the sun was pretty low and the air absolutely calm, nothing but the drone of the motor and the wind; the only movements necessary an occasional slight pressure on the joy stick to one side or the other to keep the proper direction. I came very nearly going to sleep, it was so peaceful up there."

There's nothing about war here, no heroism, no danger, no enemy: it's pure flying. I remember that feeling.

Once he could fly in a straight line from A to B and find his way home again, the student moved on to the next challenge: a triangular cross-country journey, A to B to C and back to A. Each leg would be some forty miles long; in a Blériot that would take most of an hour. With the time you'd spend landing and refueling, the whole circuit would take you half a day—if nothing happened on the way.

To find your way around this three-cornered course, you'd have to rely on the map you carried and the look of the land below you; Blériots carried no navigational instruments, only engine gauges. If you wanted to fly by compass, you'd have to bring one with you. Alan Nichols remembered a student who tried to fly from Tours to Châteaudun on compass headings alone and wound up at Orléans and then crashed trying to find his way back.

On these triangle flights they'd discover France *profonde*, France as it has always been—the ancient forests and the farms, the rivers that water the green fields, and in the towns monuments of the French past: at Bourges, on a hill above the Yèvre, the cathedral of St. Étienne with its two tall towers; at Romorantin an island in the river with an old church on it; at Châteaudun a castle on a promontory above the Loir, at Vendôme another castle, another tall church. With such landmarks, it would be hard to get lost, as long as the weather was good.

The weather wouldn't always be good, though. In the autumn and early winter of 1917 entire weeks passed when no flying was done, and many other days when clouds lowered and contrary winds blew, when distances were blurred and hazy, and the map of the earth was hard to read. On days like that you'd fly anyway, but if the weather worsened, you might have to land somewhere, just to find out where you were. Or you might get to one of the corners of your triangle and decide to get on the ground and stay there until it cleared. Harvey Conover, flying out of Tours in December, got as far as the Pontlevoy stop by mid-afternoon. He could have flown on back to Tours, but the ceiling had dropped to six hundred meters, and darkness comes early in December, so he decided to stay overnight where he was. Eight other pilots had made the same decision. Their stay lasted three days before the weather cleared. Conover wrote home from Pontlevoy about the visit: "There are nine of us in this village awaiting favorable weather that will permit our flying back to camp. We are quartered in a small épicerie run by a Frenchman by the name of Benoist. He was chef of the Savoy Hotel in London before the war and sure can cook. We are living like kings and have nothing in the world to do but eat and sleep in big feather beds."

One evening a traveling cinema came to town, and they all went to the theater, along with the entire population of the community, to watch a movie that broke and sputtered its way through two reels, until the lack of ventilation and the smell of garlic drove the young pilots out into fresh air.

If the weather was good, your engine might not be. The rotary engines in Blériots were unreliable even when they were new, and the planes students flew were old, tired, and over-flown. The engine might fail any time, lose power, stop altogether. A prudent pilot looked around continually for a flat open space big enough to *panne* in. (*Panne* is the French word for a breakdown or mishap; in flying, an emergency landing.) Charlie Biddle, flying out of Avord in June 1917, was on a triangle flight under an overcast at 450 meters when his engine quit. He picked out a fine field, but at 300 meters the engine picked up again, so he flew on, just far enough to be out of range of the field when it stopped suddenly and irretrievably. On one side of him was a large wood; on the other the country was cut up with hills, hedges, and trees—impossible to land in. In the middle was what looked like a good narrow field full of wildflowers, but with a suspicious stream along the edge. Still, Biddle reckoned a marsh was better than a woods any day, and there was nothing to do but try it. As the Blériot settled closer to the earth, he could see that the ground was soft near the stream; his wheels would sink into the mud, and the plane would flip over. His only chance was to put the tail down first and lose all the speed possible before the wheels touched down. He did that, and the plane rolled about fifteen feet along the ground and came to rest right side up.

The inevitable crowd of peasants soon gathered. Biddle changed a couple of spark plugs and after taking some pictures of the locals gaping at the plane got them to pull it to drier ground, taught one of them how to swing the prop to start the engine, and flew off and back to Romorantin.

A clever young cross-country pilot would watch out not only for flat open fields but for châteaus. Stuart Walcott proposed this as a triangle principle: "The proper thing to do on a triangle or *petit voyage* is to have something bust directly over a nice château; make a skilful landing on the front lawn under the eyes of the admiring household and then be an enforced guest for a few days until one is rescued by a truck and mechanics."

Walcott recounts the story of a fellow student named Ed Loughran, who flew his triangles shortly before Walcott flew his. Loughran was quite a ways along on his journey when he ran into a storm, climbed above it, got caught in a cloud, drifted on in a strong crosswind, and finally let down through the overcast to find himself beneath a four-hundred-foot ceiling and lost. He found a place to land, went to the nearest farmhouse, and got the plane tied down and guarded.

> In the meantime [this is Walcott's version] word had spread over the countryside that an aviator had come down there and the entire population came out to look him over. A grand equipage drove up with a Count who lived in a nearby château. He insisted that Eddie come to the château and accept their hospitality. There the fortunate Ed stayed five days; the Countess talked English, and also some house guests. He hadn't brought a trunk so borrowed razor, etc., from the Count; went down to see the machine every day in the baronial barouche. Whenever he went to the little town in the vicinity all the kids followed him around the streets and when at last he left, he was presented with a multitude of bouquets and had to kiss each and every donor. He brought back pictures of the château—a delightful looking old place—and numerous addresses.

If you were flying from Avord and couldn't find a château, you might make a detour to Issoudun. It was a bit off the route, but not far in a plane. If you landed there, you'd be sure to see fellows you knew—from college, or ground school, or flight training back home: Quentin Roosevelt was there, and Cord Meyer (former captain of the Yale crew), and Ham Coolidge, still constructing the fields and facilities in what Roosevelt called "a sea of gumbo mud." According to Walcott, every American student who flew his triangles while he was at Avord had stopped at Issoudun, though it was against orders. This sociable touring made the French *moniteur* cross. "*Alors*," he said, "all you Americans stop off there, I don't like it." But he didn't punish anyone for doing it; he seemed to take for granted that of course pilots would break the rules, that's what pilots did.

There's a spirit in these stories of *panning* and detouring that was a part of the pilot culture of that war. It was composed of youthful high spirits, a joy in mastering a difficult skill, and a sense of life as an independent adventure. Being a pilot was something like being a college athlete, something like being a fraternity man at a house party that never ended, a bit like being a young tourist in an interesting foreign country with a few of your friends. Flying was *fun*—it was the only kind of war-making that was—and flying around France on your own in a Blériot was the most fun of all.

———

The Blériot teach-yourself method wasn't the only way of learning to fly, not even in France. By the end of the summer of 1917 the French students at Tours were being sent to other fields, and American students were replacing them (though the *moniteurs* remained French). Since Americans back in the States were learning to fly in dual-control planes, the Americans at Tours were taught that way, too—in big, slow, reliable Caudrons, which looked like a box kite with a bathtub in the middle where the student and his instructor sat, one behind the other.

They had their first flights there, and of course they wrote home about the experience. It was a very different story from what the Blériot students told. There's none of the "what do I do now?" anxiety when the plane leaves the ground; this was only a joyride, such as you might get for a dollar from some barnstorming flier at a county fair back home, with a *moniteur* in the other cockpit doing all the flying. The *moniteurs* were very firm about that: Don't touch the controls! When Alan Nichols asked if he might at least just rest his hand lightly on them, to feel what a pilot does, his *moniteur* reluctantly agreed, but he wasn't to exert any pressure, *jamais*! Nichols gingerly touched them and was surprised at how slightly they moved. He could scarcely detect any movement at all. The plane seemed to be flying itself.

With nothing to do up there, no instruction going on, he was free to concentrate on the experience—the feeling of flying, and the world outside the plane: the rising sun casting long shadows on the landscape, the smoke rising from early morning fires, a Farman plane below him that seemed to be sliding along the ground. It all looked unreal, as if it were an optical illusion. The view from the air, he wrote, is absolutely unique, and different from anything else, even a view from a cliff or a mountain, because it is all around and even straight below you. There is absolutely none of the sensation that one gets from a high building, a cliff in Yosemite, or a bridge. There is a feeling of absolute security, as if it were an absurd thing to think of falling. You have no idea how high you are, and there is no way of seeing that you are suspended there on apparently nothing. It seems natural.

That gets the feeling of flying as well as a twenty-year-old beginner could: Nichols was clearly a born writer. Other young pilots who were less gifted with words also tried, piling sentence on sentence, image on image, as though if they piled them high enough the folks back home would feel what it was like to be in a plane, apart from the earth, in that other world of the air. But parents wouldn't really be able to feel it, because they couldn't; their sons have been where their parents will never go. Out of that sense of having entered a new, young man's world comes a new tone of voice that you can hear in the letters—a little superior, a little condescending. "If you ever get a chance to take a ride, by all means take it," Nichols counsels his father. The old man can't be a pilot, of course—he's too old; but he can be a passenger, once. That tone must have had a bitter ring for fortyish fathers back home.

Dual-control instruction seems the sensible and economic way to learn to fly: first have someone show you how to do it, then try it yourself. It's the way most of us learned to drive. Having an instructor aboard didn't mean that the student got much advice while they were in the air. There was no intercommunication system in those planes, only hand signals, or a tap on the shoulder, and if all else failed, a sharp jerk on the controls. In France and Italy there was also the language problem. At Tours, Walter Avery complained that his *moniteur*, Jaudoin, spoke no English at all (and Avery, it appears, spoke no French). Rowe wrote home from Foggia that his instructor spoke only Italian. Before they flew, the instructor told a mechanic what he wanted to say in Italian; the mechanic put it into Spanish, which one of the Americans understood, and he translated it into English for the student. "But really," Rowe wrote, "these Italians don't need more than eight or ten words for a language—you can understand them almost perfectly by watching their facial expressions and the gestures of their arms."

With an instructor in the other cockpit, dual-control students feel secure and comfortable on their first training flights. "The air work is very easy," Houston Woodward assures his parents, "so is leaving the ground and using the throttle . . . it is surprising how easy single flying is." (Though he admits he doesn't know how to get the plane back down on the ground yet.) They're already confident that they'll be fliers, and they're happy in the air. More than happy. "It's like the way a fellow feels when he's in love," Alan Nichols writes, "for I am in love—with the air!"

The joy of flying is certainly real; most pilots feel it, or they wouldn't be flying. But there is also the other side of the experience, the fear. Or rather, fears, for there is more than one, all primal, built into our human natures. There's the fear that seizes some people the moment they leave the ground and feel space beneath them where there should be solidity: you might call that fear the Antaeus complex. And the fear of falling out; these are open-cockpit planes, remember, part of you is always outside the comforting embrace of the plane's fuselage, out there in empty air. If you look to your right and left and above your head, you see nothing but space; if you can bear to look over the side, you see the earth far below, with only emptiness in between. At that moment, for some would-be pilots, the stomach turns and the brain spins, and they want only one thing—to be back down there with their feet touching the ground. And the fear that comes when the plane stops in mid-space (as it does, sometimes, in aerobatics). You have been supported by the air that flows over and under the wings and holds your plane aloft. When that flow stops, the plane is no more than a material object in space—like a thrown rock or a high fly to the outfield that stops in its arc and falls like a stone. And the heart of the beginner in the plane falls with it.

Not all beginner pilots feel these fears. The natural pilots apparently don't; they seem at ease in the air from the start. Others feel them, but learn to control them and go on flying, and become nervous, worrying fliers. Some never come to terms with their fears; they drop out of flight school and become ground officers. Pilots report these failures in their letters. George Moseley writes from the flight school at Avord in November 1917, "Curtis Munson, one of the fellows who came over with us, could not stand the game. It made him very nervous; he lost weight and finally decided to stop before he hurt himself. We felt very sorry to lose him, but it is not everyone who can stand the strain." There's no judgment there; it has nothing to do with courage; the will to fly is in you, or it isn't.

Some of the would-be pilots felt a different kind of fear that had nothing to do with the way their guts feel in the air—the fear of failure, of not being good enough at flying to be a real pilot. Sidney Drew, who was usually high-spirited and confident, mentions this fear in a letter to his father, in the midst of his account of the excitement of his first flights:

> If you break a machine you get the devil and when your accidents reach the number of three, you are thrown out of the school and back to civilian life.
>
> I am hoping and praying that no such horrible thing will happen to me.

No young man attempts a serious adult action for the first time without a certain apprehension that he will fail, and so reveal that he isn't really an adult but only pretending to be one. And when he does fail, he'll be thrown out of the adult world. The French term for that rejection was *radiation*—to be obliterated, erased, struck out. A student could be radiated for busting up planes or simply because his *moniteurs* didn't think he'd make a good pilot. Or it could be a disciplinary *radiation*; Alan Nichols tells of two students who went to Paris without leave and were sent back, not to civilian life, but to the Foreign Legion. Another, who overstayed a *permission*—that is, an allowed period of free time away from the camp—in order to stay in Tours and see the moonlight on the Loire got eight days in jail. French discipline was tough.

Flying is dangerous, especially when beginners are doing the flying. Accidents happen, and students write home about them, because broken airplanes are a part of their new life, like the weather. The first accidents they report tend to be minor ones, with more damage to the plane than to the pilot. Training planes were breakaway objects, like the props in Western movies; everything might shatter, but the pilot would walk away. Briggs Adams writes home from Camp Rathbun, Ontario, on the first day of his primary training:

Smashes are of hourly occurrence on the aerodrome, but they all occur either in landing or getting off, so there is no fall, and the men get out without a scratch every time. Yesterday the fellow in the next bunk to mine went right over upside down and crawled out from underneath with nothing more than *a bump on his nose!* The machine was taken in and before night it was out and being used again. It is remarkable the way they can be banged round and stand it. Every time a fellow crashes, he has so much more confidence; for he sees he cannot be hurt. You see, you have a belt to hold you in and so cannot be thrown out and break your neck . . . The closer I get to flying the less I am afraid of it.

It's a letter written to reassure the folks at home but also, perhaps, to reassure the beginning pilot (Adams has just had his first flight, his "joy ride").

John Grider, flying with the RFC at St. Albans, tells the story of a boy named Hamilton whose engine stops while he's flying over a wood. The plane goes down into the trees; one wing is ripped away, and the fuselage is broken off just behind the cockpit. Hamilton is scared stiff. But it's a comic story in the end; when the ambulance crew arrive, they find the pilot standing under a tree "cussing like a blue streak because he had torn his new fur-lined flying coat while climbing down!"

Such reassuring stories turn up again and again among the pilots' letters. The message is the same: Don't worry, I'll be all right; accidents happen, but nobody gets hurt. And anyway, they don't happen if you're careful (as I am). "There has not been an accident at this field," Percival Gates writes soothingly to his sister, "that has not been due to first carelessness or second boneheadedness."

There are lots of ways of demolishing a plane, and the students find them all: they taxi into each other or into a hangar wall; they land on each other; they take off at the same time in opposite directions and meet in midfield; they stall on takeoff; they go into "wing-slips"; they fall out of steep turns into *vrilles*; they run into power lines at the end of the landing field and somersault to the ground. They're beginners, and these are beginners' accidents; but they haven't ventured very high, and they haven't yet tried the difficult, dangerous maneuvers that will make them combat pilots; though they break up a lot of planes, they mostly escape serious injury. "It's marvelous," Quentin Roosevelt tells his family,

> the amount you get away with in these planes. Two fellows in the last week have gone straight into the ground in vrilles, totally wrecking the plane,—and yet neither one is seriously hurt. The worst one of the two came down about three hundred feet, hit the ground so hard that he pushed the engine back where the rudder bar should be and the rudder bar under the seat,— and yet didn't break any bones. He will be out of the hospital in three weeks they think. All he got is a couple of bad cuts on his face from the wind shield and a stove-in chest. I've decided that nothing short of shooting a man or breaking a control is fatal!

It's all very lighthearted, as though crashing were a part of the fun of flying.

———

Because the students took off and landed at the same field and did their flying nearby, those on the ground often saw accidents that were be-yond laughter—a solitary plane spinning down, two planes colliding— and heard the crash and saw the smoke rising. And they must have thought, "Someone has just died over there beyond those trees," and felt the reality of death-by-flying.

There were many deaths and many funerals—at Issoudun, one ev-ery day but Monday, and the day after a rainy day, according to Temple Joyce, who was there. Not all of them were flying deaths: the young fliers were as prone to ordinary illnesses as the rest of their species; they caught pneumonia, meningitis, measles, mumps, scarlet fever, influenza—which was as epidemic among the military as it was among civilians in those years—and some of them died. But most of the deaths were death by air, in flying accidents. Any old service pilot will tell you that far more military fliers die in accidents than in combat. A book I've been looking at, *War Record of Dartmouth College, 1917–1918*, confirms that proposition. The book includes a Roll of Honor of 111 former Dartmouth students who died during the war or as a result of the war. Nineteen of those dead young men were pilots, and of the nineteen, fourteen died in accidents—on training flights, or while ferrying planes, or just fooling around in the air playing the flying game; only five were killed in action. If this sample is representative, and I think it is, the odds were three to one that if you joined an air service and died in a plane, it would be your own fault, or the fault of some other pilot in your vicinity (most accidents are caused by pilot error, either yours or the other guy's), or mechanical failure.

Some pilots seemed accident-prone, or maybe just very unlucky. Zenos Miller was a likable Princeton man who eventually flew with the Twenty-Seventh Pursuit Squadron, where he compiled a respectable score of two planes and two balloons; but his score of Air Service planes destroyed was even more impressive (the Commanding Officer of the Twenty-Seventh called him "hard luck's favorite child").

Miller destroyed his first plane during flight training at Toronto when his engine failed on takeoff, depositing him and the plane in a tree. The plane was completely wrecked, but Miller emerged unhurt. Later, in France, he wrecked two more planes in forced landings over the lines (in one, he managed to land in a trench).

Even taxiing could be dangerous when Miller was at the controls. On one occasion he had landed at his home field and was headed for the squadron's canvas hangar, when his ignition switch stuck open; the plane ran into the hangar, which caught fire, consuming both the hangar and Miller's plane. Another time he was approaching the field for a landing and didn't notice a worker on a mower cutting the runway grass. He landed on top of the mower, wrecking both machines. In this case you'd have to call it pilot error; otherwise, Miller was simply a guy who was present when accidents happened. He wasn't even safe standing on the ground. One day at Toronto he attempted to start a parked plane by swinging its propeller (the standard starting method in those days). The engine caught with a roar and the plane lunged forward, jumping its chocks, and the spinning propeller struck Miller, breaking both his arms.

In spite of the accidents students remained eager to fly and were restless when they weren't in the air. But progress was slow. The French training program was systematic in principle—first this field for this skill, then another field for the more difficult next one—but in practice it must have seemed extemporized and disorderly. Fields that should have been built and ready by the autumn of 1917 (for example, the eight outlying fields at Issoudun) were still under muddy construction at the end of the year. New drafts of Americans arrived to find there was no room for them, or no planes to fly, or not enough of them (the daily breakage sometimes reduced the number of available planes at a field to one or two).

All that and the foul autumn weather made the students bored and ill-tempered. They were eager to fly, and they weren't flying. After two months at Tours, Harvey Conover grumbled that he'd only logged twelve hours—less than twelve minutes a day. Autumn became winter, and the year ran out, and the war at the front went on without them. It might be over before they even got there.

SIX

THE PLEASURABLE SENSATION
OF FLYING

By the end of their primary training, students have learned to fly alone—not simply to get a plane off the ground and down again, but to take it from here to there and back again, to fly at high altitude, to land precisely on a spot. They've grown familiar with their planes, as a horseman grows familiar with his horse. They know what the plane will do in different circumstances: how it feels in a stall, in a dive, in a steep turn. Man and plane move together now in a kind of cooperation, both leaning into a bank, slowing as they reach for the ground in a landing; they act with a common will, centered. It's the furthest thing possible from "driving a machine."

Having come this far, they think of themselves as aviators. So do the services they're flying for. If they're with the French, they have been "brevetted"—certified, licensed as pilots, and promoted to *caporal*. There's more to this change than advancement: up to this point the student has been a mere *élève pilote*; now he's a *pilote élève*. Stuart Walcott explains the difference:

> There's a great if subtle difference when the words are reversed. An *élève pilote* is the scum of the earth, looked down on by mechanics, pilots, monitors, and everyone else; a *pilote élève* can wear wings on his collar and is as good as anyone else. He is permitted to fly in rough weather, to take chances and is not in so much danger of getting radiated if he gets in trouble.

Students in the U.S. Air Service who reach this stage are transformed in more flamboyant American ways: they become commissioned officers (usually, though not always, first lieutenants) and wear wings on their chests. RFC students in Canadian flight schools become lieutenant-pilots. In the U.S. Navy they get their Navy pilot's license and become ensigns. Whatever they're called, a change has occurred: they're *pilots* now. It's partly the wings and the bars and the uniforms: they care about these visible signs of their new condition. These are young men who a few months earlier were college boys; now they're officers. Of course the young men write home about their new glory. Not content with that, they dress up in their new finery, and have their pictures taken. Here is Lance Holden, twenty-one years old and newly commissioned a first lieutenant in the Air Service, in a Paris photographer's studio. His uniform includes a Sam Browne belt and spurs—the aviator's inheritance from the previous century's most romantic figure, the cavalry officer. Notice also the attempt at a dashing cavalryman's mustache.

They may be complacent and self-satisfied with their new status, but they shouldn't be; they aren't fully trained yet, not by any means; they still lack the skills that will make them combat pilots fit for squadrons at the front. To learn those skills, they'll be sent to other flight schools for what the Americans and English call advanced training, and the French, more grandiloquently, *perfectionnement*.

At these new fields they'll learn aerobatics—all those radical maneuvers in space that your neurological self tells you aren't natural to your species: how to pull the nose up and up and over until you are hanging upside down, suspended by your seat belt with the earth above your head and the sky under your feet, and go on flying, falling nose down now, until earth and sky return to their proper places; how to stall, kick a rudder, and go into a twisting, nose-down spin, and how to make the right moves to get yourself out of it; how to turn by pulling up until you're on your back and then doing a half roll; how to turn in a vertical bank, in which the elevator becomes the rudder and the rudder becomes the elevator.

These weren't old familiar skills in 1917, like the tricks trapeze artists performed in the circuses of childhood. They were unreasonable, extreme maneuvers: What would a Caudron do if you rolled it round its longitudinal axis? Would the wings come off? If you put a Nieuport into a vertical dive, would the wing fabric peel away? If you fell into a spin, could you get out of it? "Acrobacy used to be considered an occupation for fools and suicides," Ham Coolidge wrote to his sister as he began his advanced training, "now it is an essential part of the training of a war pilot." Many a new pilot must have entered aerobatic instruction with those fools and suicides in his mind.

As they engaged in this new upside-down-and-sideways kind of flying, the students tried to explain it in their letters, as they had explained the mechanics of planes and the feeling of flying: how you did a maneuver, movement by movement, and how it felt to be in such improbable gymnastics in a fragile machine in the middle of the air. Straight-and-level flying had been new and strange enough; aerobatics was a good deal stranger.

Looping a plane was a special challenge, a test that everyone had to pass before he could think of himself as a real pilot. It hadn't been long—only a few years—since a flier first managed to inscribe a vertical circle on the sky with a plane, and pilots argued over who did it first:

Billy Mitchell thought it was the French pilot Roland Garros; Fiorello La Guardia said, in a speech in Congress, that it was another Frenchman, Adolphe Pégoud; the Russians claimed the honor for their captain Pyotr Nesterov; some Americans argued for the American Lincoln Beachey. Whoever did it first, it was an extreme test of flying skill—or of foolhardy courage. The tolerances of those early planes hadn't been charted—you tested them by flying them; nobody knew what would happen if you stalled upside down or came out in too fast a dive. So if you did a loop—even one—you felt different, and you tried to explain it all to your parents or your sweetheart.

Learning how to loop began on the ground, in the fuselage of a wrecked Nieuport, with the student in the cockpit and a *moniteur* hanging over the side, explaining the moves by the numbers: (1) dive to gain speed; (2) pull back on the stick, and add full power; (3) when past the vertical, reduce power; (4) as you approach straight and level, slow down, and add a little power.

That's the mechanics of flying a loop. Actually doing it was sometimes quite different. Curtis Kinney tries one in a Jenny at an RFC field at Toronto:

> After a great many figure eights my confidence suddenly tempted me to try a loop. I took the Jenny up to fifteen hundred feet and dipped into a steep dive with the engine full on. When I thought I had enough airspeed I pulled the stick back abruptly. The plane shot up into the air and flopped abruptly over on its back. That was the top of the loop. I had turned the engine off too soon and the plane hung on its back, almost motionless. Although it did not pause there for more than three seconds it seemed more like three minutes—three terrifying minutes. I felt myself leaving the seat and hanging into the seat belt. I grabbed the sides of the cockpit. Dangling head down, I hoped my seat belt would hold. Then the plane completed the other side of the loop and straightened out. It was a good loop, but I decided not to do another one right away.

Kinney wasn't the only young pilot who felt that way about gravity: Ham Coolidge had special handles installed in his plane "to cling to in such emergencies" after he almost fell out in the middle of a loop.

Letters written home during this stage of the students' training speak in two quite different tones. One is an excited curiosity about what is possible in a plane, a reminder that aerobatic flying in 1917 was still a new, experimental activity—a matter of "tricks" and "stunts." What would happen, the young pilot wonders, if I . . . ? Kenneth MacLeish, a Navy pilot training with the RFC at Gosport, tells Priscilla, his back-home sweetheart, how he got up enough nerve to roll the Avro he's flying:

Well, I got around once beautifully, but I didn't know they would only roll once. The result was that I got into a spin with my motor full on, and before I could cut it, it went "dud." I was 2,500 feet up and quite a distance from the aerodrome with a stiff breeze in my face. I nearly had a fever before I got down. I just skimmed over some telegraph poles and wires and fell into the field.

It sounds scary, and was clearly meant to, but he isn't scared. "Gee," he winds up, "it was fun for a while!" Or he *is* scared, and that's part of the fun—the rush of adrenaline that comes when you put yourself in danger and get away with it.

The other tone has no such exhilaration in it; it isn't frightened, exactly, but it's cautious—the voice of common sense in an *un*-sensible situation. Briggs Adams writes to his mother from Camp Borden, in Ontario. He's just been trying his first "stunts," and now that he's done them, telling her won't make her anxious, because he'll do no more of them. "I did not expect to do any when I first came here," he writes, "but finally decided I must, for I was afraid to." And so he has tried them all: a loop, a tailslide, an Immelmann turn, a vertical bank, and a new one he has just invented—an inverted tailslide.

And now, he tells his mother, "I feel that I have banished every single atom of fear of this new element, air . . . I can't be killed in flying now." There's no exhilaration here, only relief. He's passed a test.

As the students learn to do the stunts that aces can do, their spirits rise. They're flying real combat planes now—Nieuports if they're in France, SE-5s or Camels if they're in England—and the fact that they feel at ease with such planes makes them confident. John Grider writes to his aunt Emma: "I can fly any damned thing they build over here now.

I am at last a pilot, an aviator and an airman. I admit it myself." Harvey Conover tells the folks that he feels perfectly at home in a Nieuport (though he's only just begun to fly them). Even the cautious Percival Gates is confident. "The driving of the plane comes perfectly naturally now," he writes. I suppose there's a point in every combat pilot's training when he thinks proudly, "I can do this!" And because he can, he is somebody else, somebody adult: a pilot, an aviator, an airman.

They're not finished with their training, though; there are other skills to be learned: formation flying (*vol de groupe*, the French say); the tricks for fighting plane against plane (the French call this *vol de combat*); gunnery. These aren't flying lessons, exactly; you wouldn't need to learn them to fly a private plane back home. They're extreme skills, to give your flying what Charlie Biddle calls the "necessary rashness" for war in the air.

Formation. It doesn't sound difficult; it's simply, as Moseley explains, a matter of "flying a certain distance from another machine and following it wherever it goes." Quentin Roosevelt tells the folks why that isn't so easy:

> In formation you fly rather the way geese do, in V shape, with the second men just higher than the leader and so on. At first it's rather scary, for you have to stick close together, but once you get over that it begins to be amusing, for you have to watch your plane and motor all the time without looking at them,—a rather Irish statement. What I mean is that you have to be able to watch the other men so as to keep your place in line, and at the same time manage your plane.

There's more to it than the hard work. Conover added an aesthetic element: "I led a formation of five this a.m. with a triangle of three well above us for protection, as beautiful a sight as you could see." He's not talking about the beauty of the surroundings, the clouds and the landscape (though if you were flying at Pau, as he was, close to the snow-covered Pyrenees, that must have been a fine sight), but of the formation itself, the choreography of planes flying together. If a single aerobatic performer is like a ballerina, a good formation is like a corps de ballet—many dancers moving as one—harmonious and graceful.

Vol de Combat. At this stage the student simulates the varieties of shooting—war in the air. He releases a balloon at altitude and then pursues it; or he "chases madly about the air after a parachute, pretending that one has a machine gun and that the parachute is a Boche to be shot down if caught in the line of sight"; he attacks the image of a plane painted on the ground; he tail-chases after other planes, with a gun-camera to prove that he got his opponent in his sights; he fights a pretend fight with another student and for his final exam fights his *moniteur.* Or he flies on a patrol with other student pilots and is attacked by another student patrol, the "enemy," and there is a general mix-up, and everybody comes home to say "you're dead" to the other guys, which is what they said in their childhood games of Cops and Robbers and Cowboys and Indians, back home.

Gunnery. By the time they'd finished mock-combat training, the students were assumed to know the skills they'd need to fly with a squadron at the front. Except for the most important one—the shooting. Not that they hadn't fired many kinds of weapons at many kinds of targets at different training fields: at Pau, back in 1916, a former ambulance driver named Harold Willis was firing rockets from a Nieuport at ground targets; at Plessis-Belleville, north of Paris, in July 1917, Charlie Biddle got four fifteen-minute chances to fire a machine gun from a Nieuport at a round spot of sand on the ground; George Moseley shot rifles and carbines at a rifle range and fired a machine gun at ground targets from a plane; Alan Nichols sat in a mock-up of the rear cockpit of a plane, complete with a machine-gun mounting, and shot at targets that rolled past on rails; at Issoudun, in the summer of 1918, Percival Gates flew over targets painted on the ground and shot them with a gun-camera.

Nichols wrote home excitedly that the mock-up plane he fired from was "a fair approximation of what shooting from a machine in the air will be." Maybe that was true if you were training to be a rear-cockpit observer/gunner, but it wasn't what a *chasse* pilot needed. When Charlie Biddle asked to be assigned to the new gunnery school at Cazaux, his superior officer refused:

An order came down from the colonel in command of the schools, directing that no more pilots were to go to Cazaux. His reason was that the school is intended for the training of aeroplane mitrailleurs [machine gunners] who shoot from the two-seater machines with movable guns, and is only amusing, but not beneficial, for pilots who are to use a fixed gun on a one-seater.

When Biddle was sent to the front in July 1917, he recalled, "the French were so in need of fighter pilots that we were sent out without any aerial-gunnery training at all, so that our first shooting practice was in combat over the lines."

———

In the whirling hubbub of advanced training the air is full of planes, climbing, diving, flying wing to wing, rushing at one another, the pilots focusing their attention on the target, or their engines, or where the horizon is, and not on the other planes. They're flying frontline planes now—Nieuports and Spads, SE-5s and Sopwith Pups—planes that are faster and more responsive than the trainers they're used to but also less stable and less forgiving. And less airworthy: the planes they get are tired discards from squadrons at the front. The students complain in their letters home or grumble into their diaries. "The only unpleasant part of flying at Cazaux," Quentin Roosevelt writes, "is that the machines here are the most awful old crocks. They have been in service for ages, and have old motors and fuselages and wings that are all warped and bent out of shape."

There are many accidents: a student doing combat work at fifteen hundred feet pulls out of a dive, and the wings of his plane fold up; planes simply collapse in flight and fall from the air like dead birds, or catch fire and fall burning. And many midair collisions, so many that the RFC School of Aerial Fighting at Ayr stops staging mock battles between students.

Many accidents, and many deaths. The young pilots record them sometimes in their letters and more often in private diaries and journals that will not upset the folks back home. The dead they name aren't simply random casualties: they're friends and acquaintances, fellows they've flown with. In the weeks and months of training together they've become a community of fliers—"our old bunch," young men linked by their common flying life.

When they name their dead, they usually add the cause of the death: "Leach went into a *vrille* at 50 m. out of a stall and was so badly mangled he died in ten minutes"; "Hagadorn pulled out of a dive too quickly and pulled off both left wings. He fell about 800 meters"; "Hopkins went into a *vrille* on his first *tour de piste* and collided with Turner at about 100 m. Both were killed instantly"; "Yesterday Philippauteaux fell and was killed. Another Tours pal finished. The day before O. H. Wilson fell at the same field and was killed"; "Cadet Whyte, one of the Tours bunch, was killed at Cazaux yesterday, when his wings came off at 300 meters"; "Bieglow, of our old Tours bunch, was killed in a *vrille* at Orly yesterday."

These sentences are all from the diary of Walter Avery, written while he was at Issoudun and then at Le Bourget, but you could find similar remarks in the writings of almost any young pilot in training—at Issoudun or Tours or Cazaux, or in England at Stamford, or up in Scotland at Ayr, or at Foggia, down in Italy; wherever young men are learning to fly, some of them are dying, and the others, the survivors, are recording their deaths. Their accounts are part eulogies for old pals, part cautionary tales (don't stall at fifty meters, don't pull out of a dive too fast, don't collide with another plane—a kind of Pilot's Decalogue), and part acknowledgment of the continual presence of possible death in every flying life. "Who will be next?" Avery asks himself (or perhaps God). "Me?—Possibly yes, possibly no. I hope to get to the front. Not croak here." They all feel that hope, though they don't all confess it.

What shakes the young pilots, I think, is not simply the violence of the deaths—the wreckage, the mangled bodies—it's the abruptness. If any of these young men ever witnessed the death of another young person back in their schoolboy lives, it probably came slowly, in an illness; you saw death approaching like a summer storm and had time to prepare for it. But in this flying world, death comes suddenly: a friend who was alive beside you yesterday is dead today.

George Vaughn describes his close friendship with his old Princeton friend Harold Bulkley in a series of letters home from England:

Jan. (?) 1918: Harold Bulkley and I are still leading our life of ease [they're in primary flight training at Stamford].

Jan. 1918: Harold and I are the only ones posted here [to Hounslow for advanced training], and we are very much pleased to be able to stick together.

> *Feb. 1918*: You have undoubtedly received my cable by now
> about Harold Bulkley's accident. It certainly was an awful blow
> to have him taken away so suddenly and tragically. Since we
> left the States we have been the closest of friends, and had
> stuck together all the way through, and since we came to Houns-
> low together we have been almost inseparable.

The message is terse, and the language is the conventional language of
grief, but Vaughn is shaken. He clips newspaper accounts of his friend's
death and saves them. That's because Bulkley was his friend. But it's also
because he needs to know the cause of the crash. A pilot always wants
to know what happened, to identify the exact pilot error that led to
another man's death, so that he can think, "I'll never do that." What
Bulkley did is described in one of the press cuttings Vaughn saved:

> Last Monday, he passed one of his first tests in the air, and
> later, after flying for twenty minutes, was gliding towards a
> landing place with his engine cut off. Another machine was
> also gliding down; and apparently thinking that he had not
> room enough, Bulkley put his engine on. This led his machine
> to rise suddenly and strike the under-carriage of the other ma-
> chine, causing the wings of his own aeroplane to buckle up and
> fold. He fell sixty or seventy feet.

Poor Harold (Vaughn must have thought), he didn't know what a Camel
does when you add power in an approach. I'll never do that.

Pilots who kept journals could go into more detail about the deaths
of friends. At his first training field, back in Millington, Tennessee, Percival Gates wrote this account of the first fatal crash he ever saw:

> *Saturday* it was foggy at first so nobody flew much until after-
> noon. Then the dualists went up and some cross country men.
> About four in the afternoon I went out on the field. Just as I got
> there someone pointed over the hangars. There was a terrible
> crash and I looked around just in time to see two planes disap-
> pear nose down behind the hangars. I went to the entrance of
> the field and the two planes were wrecked out in the field be-

yond. We could not go out there so we went to the hospital to find out who was killed. They took three men out of the ambulance and put them in a little house behind the hospital. Hancock and I went over to ask who the fellows were. As the officer did not know, they asked us in to see if we could recognize them. We went in and there was Jimmy Webb the first one. His face was not cut much but it was very badly bruised. I did not know the other two men . . . All three of the bodies were badly mangled. Just held together by their clothes. That accident certainly took the pep out of us all for a while.

The corpse that Gates sees there in the building behind the hospital isn't what you'd see at a viewing in a funeral parlor back home; it isn't your grandfather, dressed in his Sunday best and touched up with cosmetics, looking as though he were alive; it's mangled and bruised, the causes of death are visible all over it. And it isn't just anybody; it's Jimmy Webb.

Many deaths, many funerals—ceremonial military funerals with a color guard, sometimes a band, marching men, and formations of planes above. Quentin Roosevelt describes one at Issoudun in early 1918, not of anyone he knew, just "two fellows that were killed":

The coffins were escorted by a platoon of American soldiers, and one of French sent out from the French post. Then, flying just above, were two of the French pilots, in the larger machines. They are marvelous pilots, and it was really beautiful to watch them crossing and recrossing over the cortège in beautiful smooth right-angled S turns. Then, just as they were lowering the coffins, another Frenchman dropped down in a long swoop, his motor almost dead,—dropped a wreath on them, and then swung off. All the time we were up above, flying at about five hundred meters, in formation. We had a ten formation, two "V's" of five, circling round and round till it was over. They say that from the ground it was very impressive.

It's a ceremony that belongs to the romance of war—a funeral for heroes—even though these two fellows did not die fighting the enemy.

But the tribute is not really for them; it's for the living, for the young men who carry the coffins, or march behind the hearse, or fly overhead—a formal gesture that gives dignity to the chance they all share of sudden death. Roosevelt explains, "It takes away some of the bare horror that the two little twisted heaps of wrecked planes and twisted motors leaves," and offers instead planes in flight, beautiful, in the air where they belong, in disciplined, formal movement.

Funerals became a part of any training field routine, like the weather. But when they came too often, when there were flurries of fatal crashes, the morale of the camp suffered:

> The spirits in camp are exceedingly low [Conover wrote early in 1918], two of the fellows were killed in a collision today. This brings up the total to five in three weeks and there is a mighty big epidemic of nerves among the flyers. To see men killed is one thing, and to see your friends, fellows with whom you have been eating, singing and living, is another. Such cases as these bring a man up with a jerk to the bitter realities of war.

He wakes in the morning thinking of the tremendous casualties among Allied airmen and how few have lasted more than a few months at the front. But then reveille sounds, and he banishes such gloomy thoughts, "and I think no more of the gloom for perhaps a month when I am again brought face to face with the rosy future by the death of a friend or a similar incident." The peculiar part of it all, he continues, "is that when I fly these planes that are doing so much damage to so many students, I enjoy every minute of it and think of nothing but the pleasurable sensation of flying a high-powered, delicately-built scout aeroplane." The joy of flying trumps the gloom of the crashes and the funerals.

But they're not the same young men who left their colleges and families a few months earlier; the contrary feelings of flying have changed them—given them delight in their new and challenging skills, but also acquainted them with their own mortality. They're twenty-one-year-olds now who have many pilot friends, some of whom are dead. When they think about their immediate futures, they think about the exhilaration of what they do in planes, but they also think about the odds, about fate and luck. Kenneth MacLeish was still in training at Palm

Beach, back in the summer of 1917, when he wrote, for the comfort of his family, his version of the Laws of Chance: "I believe that a man has only a certain number of chances to take before he fails to 'get away with it.' If he takes them in rapid succession and gets into trouble, he is said to be reckless or unlucky. If he uses them slowly, he's all safe. There surely seems to be a well defined and infallible formula connected with all chances." Getting away with it: it's the philosophy of adventurous boys and young men; take a chance—drive too fast, take a drink, kiss a girl, dive from the high board—you'll get away with it, and you'll feel exuberant and free because you did it.

In their private journals the reflective ones write about their sense of living with possible death. As long as they're pilots, they can't avoid that possibility or choose the occasion; they can only tell themselves how they hope it will happen, if it does. So Lance Holden hears of the death of Wally Winter, shot down by two Boche biplanes, and remembers that he'd seen Winter play football against the Hill School. He's a part of a shared schoolboy past, and Holden is moved to write in his journal, "That's the way I want to go. I have no dread of that. It is the greatest thing in the world. Just let me get to the front. I don't want to die in an accident and so many of us seem to be playing in hard luck."

Harvey Conover, in his journal, says much the same thing: "As far as being killed is concerned, I can surely expect that everyone, who stays in the game without taking a kee wee job, gets his sooner or later, but all I ask for is a chasse plane, and I will be perfectly satisfied to play the losing game against fate and old man gravity."

No doubt infantry lieutenants in the trenches had their own dark fatalisms. But aviation was different: every flying day was potentially your last, wherever you were, and the machine you flew in was a part of the odds.

Being separate from the other services bound them more closely to one another, in a comradeship that was closer than ordinary friendship. Pilots in training or in a squadron lived continuously in one another's presence, slept in the same quarters, ate in the same mess (and drank there, shot craps and played poker there, sang there—there was always some pilot who could play the piano). And when they had a weekend off, they partied together, in whatever city was near: London, or Paris, or Dunkerque, or Nancy.

In the air they flew together, pilot bound to pilot by a sense of mutual responsibility, but with a kind of freedom that was different from what ground troops felt. In a *chasse* plane a pilot was alone—empty space on every side—and his movements were under his own control; even in formation he maintained his position by his own individual skills and decisions. If another plane made a forced landing, he landed too, to see what was wrong. But landing was an individual choice; he was still free.

And there was the joy factor. Among military occupations, flying was the only one (now that the cavalry had been dismounted) that gave personal pleasure to the individual who was doing it. With that factor came a certain recklessness—the behavior that MacLeish called getting away with it. You see that recklessness in the displays that aces back from the front gave for new pilots at the training fields. It's showing off, of course it is; it's something you do in a plane because you *can* (how would an infantry officer show off, supposing he had a mind to?). And maybe because in aviation there was always the possibility of personal glory up ahead somewhere, if your flying was "just reckless enough," the chance that someday the folks back home might read about you in their newspapers, the way the young pilots had once read about Chapman and Thaw and Rockwell.

The word the pilots used for this kind of behavior was "wildness." George Moseley, writing home from Paris to tell his parents that he has just enlisted in the Service Aéronautique, explained why: "The aviators are supposed to be the wildest lot of men in the army. They are a wild bunch of Indians. On the Fourth of July there was an aviator doing all kinds of banks, wing slips, spirals, etc. almost touching the trees, he was so low. If anything had happened he would have killed a great many of the crowd which had gathered to see the parade." What young man in a time of war wouldn't want to be that aviator, taking chances for the fun of it above a Paris crowd?

Wildness is more than simply the opportunity flying offers to show off in public (though it is certainly that); it's a necessary element in the game of combat flying, as these young men, who have not yet flown in combat, see it. Charlie Biddle, still in training at Avord in June 1917, explains to his mother, "You speak in your letter about not being rash. Taking chances to no purpose is of course foolish, but in a game of this kind one must act on the judgment of a second and snap and dash are, I think, essential to success. The nature of the work makes necessary what to many people would seem rashness."

Later, when he has fought in some battles and thought about them, he will take a somewhat different view of rash acts in the air, but for now they seem necessary—and exhilarating, too.

SEVEN

WAITING FOR THE WAR

Among military services the field of aviation is unique in that the professional quality of its fighting men is measured in hours; a pilot is more or less experienced, more or less skillful, more or less ready for the serious business of combat, depending on the number of hours he has spent in the air. The more hours you've flown, the easier you'll be in a plane, the quicker and surer your reactions will be, and the more likely you'll be to perform well and get yourself back to your field in one piece. You could put a number on a pilot's readiness. You couldn't do that with an artillery officer: What would you count? The number of shells he'd fired? Or with an infantryman: Would you count the miles he'd marched? Or the days he'd spent in a trench? But a pilot knows how much time he has: his air time is recorded hour by hour, flight by flight, in his logbook. That book becomes a sort of autobiography of the life he lives as a pilot.

If he's a young man learning to fly, he reports the growing sum of his flight time in his letters home—proudly, as though he were adding inches to his stature, or pounds to his weight, becoming a larger, more substantial person: "4 hours 15 minutes in the air since arriving here" (that's Walter Avery at Tours in October 1917); "have done thirty hours or more solo" (that's George Vaughn at Stamford in December); "I have had about 40 hours in the air now including everything" (that's Roland Richardson at Issoudun in March 1918). Sometimes they write impatiently of how little time they're logging: "I have now been in the spiral class for a week and although the weather has been perfect, I have not been inside of a machine" (Conover, November 1917, at Tours). And sometimes they worry that all the other guys have more flight time than they have: "The number of hours I have had in the air solo is approximately 10. None of the men here have had less than 40 or 50. Some have had as high as 100 or 150" (Lance Holden, January 2, 1918, at Issoudun). They're impatient and anxious: they want to be commissioned and wear the wings that will tell the world they're ready for their war. And the measure of that readiness will be the record in their logbooks.

In the mythology of First World War flying, young pilots were sent to the front too soon, with too few hours, because casualty rates were high and fighting squadrons needed replacements. It's the doomed-young-men story—good for popular fiction and a few dramatic old movies, but not in fact generally true, and certainly not among American pilots. The number of hours varied from pilot to pilot, but it was never as small as the myth would have it. The French and the British might have sent untrained young pilots into combat out of necessity, in periods when the Germans controlled the air over the front; maybe the Germans did, too. But the Americans didn't. Here are a few examples where the flight-time record is clear:

Percival Gates. He logged some 30 hours in primary training back in Tennessee, then was shipped to Issoudun, where he flew just over 100 hours more. When he pinned on his wings, he had about 140 hours.

Edgar Taylor. He flew 30 hours with the RFC at Toronto, moved on to England, where he logged another 30 hours at Chattis Hill, went to gunnery school at Ayr, but after only a few hours was ordered to France for duty with 79 Squadron. There he was given three or four practice gunnery flights—a little over 6 hours in all—and was sent on his first combat mission, with around 70 total hours.

Roland Richardson. During his primary training at Issoudun and gunnery at Cazaux he logged 71 hours, then he returned to Issoudun for final training, where he flew 23 hours: total, 94 hours.

Whatever the number, it didn't in itself mean that these pilots were all ready to fight. Most of them had little if any flight time in the service planes they'd fly in combat. According to George Vaughn, "In 1918 an R.F.C. trainee was considered ready for combat duty when he had accumulated at least twelve hours of flying time in his 'service type' aircraft." But some didn't log nearly that much. Livingston Irving was sent to the French GDE (Groupe des Divisions d'Entraînement) to be trained in Spads. "We were given one tour de piste in a 180 h.p. SPAD and one tour de piste in a 220 h.p. SPAD and we were SPAD pilots, ready to go to the front."

As they come nearer to the day when they'll be sent into combat over the front, the brash confidence with which they began their training seems to fade a bit; they see how little they've learned of the important combat skills, and a note of reluctance slips into their letters. Alan Nichols, near to finishing his training at Tours, writes that after one more class he'll be brevetted, but adds, "Really I'm in no hurry at that. I'm not wild to rush this air fighting any more than is necessary"; and Stuart Walcott, after a week at the front with SPA 84, confesses that the wily Hun "need not worry about my bothering him if he doesn't keep fooling around under my nose till I'm ashamed not to go after him. I'm not blood-thirsty a bit, especially till I learn to fly, and the lack of combats isn't going to keep me awake nights for a while yet."

On the other side of the lines were pilots who had been fighting air battles for a year, two years, even three years. The young Americans, with their seventy or eighty hours, must have been aware of the experience of those German veterans. By the end of 1917, Boelcke and Max Immelmann were dead, but Manfred von Richthofen was still flying his red Fokker. How many hours did *he* have?

Still, Colonel Edgar Gorrell, who was in command of flight training in France, was confident that a pilot with ninety hours was "fit for the front." The young pilots might be less certain, but they were still eager to join a fighting squadron, to be part of the real thing, to have a crack at the Huns. "Everyone's idea of heaven on earth," Holden wrote in his journal, "is to get some Boches and a few decorations, maybe a wound, and get back home." Often that goal is put more simply: it's to get just one Boche, "*my* Boche"; such phrases turn up in many letters and journals. When Sidney Drew writes to his actor-father, expressing his happiness at the old man's success in a new play, he adds,

> But I must confess that I will be nearly as happy if I can get a Boche. As much for your sake as for mine and above all because I want to be worthy of your belief in me and your pride.

So far, I have done nothing that the merest fool could not have done, but if I can make my mark I will feel that I have, at least, confirmed your conviction in my ability "to come across."

For young pilots like Drew, that first victory will be the final test, the coming-of-age ritual they've trained for. When they've done it, when they've got their Boche, they'll be different: they'll be *men* (there's a lot about manhood and doing a man's work in their letters).

It will be more than that, though; it will be the chivalric contest they've dreamed about all through their training—two men fighting, one against one, like knights in a tournament. Stuart Walcott, one week short of joining an escadrille at the front, writes, "I'm beginning to hear that it's nothing but a lot of routine work, few combats and pretty soon a frightful bore: I refuse to believe it and hang on to romance for all I'm worth."

To fly that romantic war, they'll have to become *chasse* pilots, in a *chasse* squadron. The very term *chasse* explains why: in French it means the hunt, the chase—the traditional act of pursuing some wild animal in order to kill it. The German word for a fighting pilot means much the same thing: *Jagd*, the hunt, *Jagdflieger*, a flier who hunts. The English at first called their little planes "scouts," because, like cavalry scouts, they went looking for the enemy, and that term continued in some pilots' vocabularies, but more and more they became "pursuit" planes, hunters like the others. In whatever language you use, one special kind of flier has appeared, whose job (perhaps one should say vocation) is to hunt enemy planes and destroy them—individually. A biplace observation plane with a pilot and a gunner in it might get the odd Boche (Frederick Libby, a cowboy from California who first flew as an RFC gunner in an FE2b, shot down five Germans and was an ace before he moved on to flight training and eventually got nine more as a pilot), but it wasn't the same: a gunner wasn't a hunter; he was simply defending himself. The real hunters were the *chasse* pilots.

The young men who came to flight school knew from the beginning that there were two classes of military pilots: the *chasse* pilots, and all the rest, who flew the observation, bombing, and artillery-spotting planes. Sidney Drew explained it all early in his training at Avord, in a letter to his father:

There are two schools or courses here. One is called *Caudron* which develops flyers for observation machines, used for the purpose of taking photographs while flying low over the enemy's lines and for directing artillery fire.

Caudron pilots also fly the big bombing machines. This work is terrifically important and very useful, but a brevetted *Caudron* pilot . . . does not rank as a flyer and as a splendid fellow with the pilot turned out by the *Bleriot* school.

The Bleriot school is the training given to men who ultimately drive *Avion de Chasse*, that is fighting planes.

The men who graduate from the Bleriot are supposed to be the cream of the flyers.

Of course Drew wants to fly *chasse* planes and be one of the "splendid fellows"; almost all the students he's with do. But most of them will be disappointed. According to Percival Gates, "Only about 20% of the men who come here to this school [Issoudun] finish up as Chasse men." "Chasse men" will be a small, select group; being chosen will be like making the first team in college or being elected to the best fraternity—you'll be one of the elite.

Those who are promoted to *chasse* training write home about the fast new planes they now fly in words of praise that might seem more appropriate to a new girlfriend: Nieuports are "delightful . . . so quick to act," "so fast and sensitive," "delicate on the controls . . . I was not used to being so gentle," "small and graceful as a maiden—and, like a maiden, dangerous to her enemies and treacherous to her friends." (That last quotation is from little Jack Wright. I wonder how much he knew about maidens when he wrote it—nineteen years old and not long out of Andover.) And always, the new *chasse* pilots compare their planes with the clumsier aircraft that less fortunate pilots fly: a Nieuport makes a Curtiss Jenny seem "lumbering," a Caudron "like a freighter."

To be sent to a squadron that flew reconnaissance, artillery-ranging, or bombing missions would be a judgment of failure in a crucial test. "If a man is training in the Bleriot school," Drew explains to his father, "and he is found wanting, he is radiated to the *Caudron*. If he fails in the *Caudron* he is radiated to civilian life." As they work through the training program, students worry about whether they'll fail, though they assure themselves that if they do, they won't really mind. Percival Gates writes in his diary, "I will probably get sent to bombing before I get through here. But I would not mind if I did as that is an awfully good way to start regular line work." And in a letter to his mother: "There is a chance that I will flunk the exams, of course, in which case I will go bombing, or something like that." They understand, they say, that such work is important and necessary, and even interesting, but they make it sound menial.

Students who suspected that they might pass the tests and still not "make *chasse*" felt angry and betrayed; Alan Nichols, at Tours in the fall of 1917, saw Farman bombing planes (the old-fashioned pusher type, with the engine behind the pilot and the propeller facing backward) arriving at the field and wondered if the authorities might make him fly one of those clunkers into the war. "I'll bomb the place myself if they do!" he exclaimed in a letter. "I came here to fly a fighting plane, and dropping bombs on people is not to my taste." And Dick Blodgett worried that because he knew something about wireless telegraphy he'd be sent to an observation squadron. "I want to fly a fighting plane," he said, "and not some slow, heavy mudscow."

Morale problems worsened as they waited, and their anger overflowed into other problems, other injustices: the honor students had been promised commissions as first lieutenants when they graduated, and now they were offered second lieutenancies while the guys who'd been left behind back home, the less-than-honor students, were arriving in France as first lieutenants, who had to be saluted! You might think the rank wouldn't matter, so long as you were commissioned and flying, but injustice does matter when you're twenty-one and in search of your manhood. Add to that the pay problem: some students were being paid only thirty dollars a month, while others got a hundred dollars. To be a student and broke, when you should be an officer with money in your pockets, was hard to bear. They wouldn't put up with it! They'd apply for discharges from the U.S. Army; they'd fly for the French or the RFC— the U.S. Army was hopeless.

Some did change air services. Some vented their frustrations by staging demonstrations (like the near riot at Tours in November over delayed commissions), by confronting their officers with demands for justice, by getting someone with influence to intervene with the Higher

Ups (Quentin Roosevelt, for example), or by writing letters to generals and telegrams back to the States—behaving more like outraged taxpayers than like cadets training for a war. But most of them did what idle, discontented soldiers do: they hung around their quarters, they drank, they played poker, they shot craps, and they bitched.

As 1917 ran toward its end, the delays and confusions multiplied; new students arrived at French training fields in ever greater numbers, and were taught to fly, and added to the pileup of pilots at the end of the production line, like factory-made widgets that nobody wanted—"awaiting assignment," the Air Service told them. Quentin Roosevelt, stuck that fall in an administrative job at Issoudun, witnessed the muddle at close range:

> Some lunatic got the idea that there was a crying need for pilots over here, that we were ready for six hundred students a month . . . so they started shipping over untrained cadets by the hundred to France. Of course we have no earthly means of coping with them, and never wanted them in the first place . . . Consequently, we have now about six hundred non-flying cadets here with nothing in the world for them to do, and apparently no chance of their flying in the next couple of months.

Student discontent was so great by the end of 1917 that the Air Service ordered Colonel Bingham to France to investigate: not, apparently, to correct the problems, but to discover who was responsible for them. His account of what he found, as set down in his postwar memoir, is a sad catalog of military muddle: there was the Army's red tape—the need for certificates of typhoid inoculations, and the clumsy way service records were shipped; there was the weather, too, which prevented the Air Service both from building airfields and from flying from them when they were built; and the failure to keep General George Squier informed back in Washington (there just weren't enough transatlantic cables, Bingham explained); and the complete breakdown of the French plan for training the Americans once they reached France; and the Army's promotion system.

Bingham was sympathetic to the students' loss of morale and to the sense of injustice they felt at their government's failure to keep its promises. It had all been a "terrific disappointment," he wrote, a "hideous mistake." But when he came to draw the conclusion from his investigation, he could find no one to blame. "So far as I could learn then," he wrote in his memoir, "no one person, but rather a series of events, was at the bottom of the trouble." He had found the classic Army explanation: in a war, stuff happens.

You have to feel some sympathy for the high brass of the Air Service training program. They had started out, back when the United States entered the war in April, with nothing: no program and practically no facilities, only Congress's airy promise to its allies that America would provide five thousand pilots by the middle of the next year. They had found fields for their student pilots (most of them in other countries); they had moved those students around from one field to another, and they had managed to get some of them trained—or partly trained—not as many as Congress had promised, but some. It was a kind of miracle that they'd accomplished as much as they had, considering the natural lethargy of institutions and the inherent confusion of war.

Miracle or not, it wasn't enough for some Americans in flight training in France. When officials at the French school at Tours announced at roll call one morning in November 1917 that the school had been taken over by the U.S. Army and would from that day be run by the Air Service, the students responded with a chorus of groans and catcalls. "Some change in the patriotic enthusiasm that brought us over here to fight for the U.S.!" Walter Avery wrote in his journal. "Most of the fellows would join the French army if they could today, and so hate to see the French management leave." Their reasoning was simple: the French system worked.

By the end of 1917 the Air Service had a growing stockpile of new pilots, with some coming along every day. What was to be done with them? There were no American combat squadrons at the front to assign them to—no squadrons, no seasoned pilots to command them, no planes, not even machine guns to arm the planes if they had them. Some pilots were offered whatever flying jobs there were behind the lines: ferrying planes, flight-testing, instructing, or some administrative job at one of the training fields.

American pilots stuck in England might find themselves ferrying planes across the English Channel to France. Frank Dixon, who was in

London waiting for his American commission to arrive, remembered what ferrying was like there. He was sent to the Sopwith factory in Lincoln, in the middle of the country; it was his first ferry assignment. A little WAC at the desk handed him a logbook. "Take this plane to Marquise," she said.

"Where's Marquise?"

"France."

He said he'd never been to France.

"Oh, as you go south from here, there are two railroads, one with green engines and the other with black engines. Stay between them. The first river you see with boats in it is the Thames, the large city is London."

He said he knew the south coast. He'd trained there, partly.

She said, "Then you go to Folkestone and land at Lympne, where they inspect the plane to see that it meets the King's Regulations for overseas. At Folkestone a pier juts out with a crook at the end. Set your compass on the crook and the first thing you see that looks like an airfield is Marquise."

With those instructions, he nevertheless found Marquise and delivered the plane. Given the choice of flying back to England or taking a boat, he decided to fly, and picked a plane with dihedral wings and a stationary engine (clearly he'd never seen such a plane before). Over the Channel, he looked out at the wings and saw one of them vibrating more than he liked. The next time he took the boat. On another ferrying flight his Camel "chewed up its engine," and he had to make a forced landing in a farmer's field. While he was away from the plane seeking help, a cow started licking the castor oil that had overflowed the engine and put her foot through a wing. All in a day's work, if you were a ferry pilot. The accidents weren't all comical; six ferry pilots flying out of Orly were killed before the war ended.

Testing was another way of waiting around. You might be sent to Orly to test planes because your commission hadn't arrived, and without it you couldn't join a squadron, or you might be ordered there because there was nothing else to do with you.

None of the pilots liked test-flying much: "It's as dangerous as going to the front," Richardson wrote, "and not near as interesting." But the point wasn't that test-flying was dangerous; it's that it was the wrong danger. "I came here to get a squint at some planes with black crosses on them and not to be a tester," Holden wrote in his diary, "so if they don't kick me out of this job I shall drop it of my own accord."

It took him two months to get transferred to the only alternative, a French "Defense of Paris" squadron. That sounds like a better, altogether more belligerent line of work; you'd be assigned to a French escadrille somewhere between Paris and the front, where you'd be responsible for protecting the capital from enemy air attacks. In the spring of 1918 there were ten such escadrilles in place: seven flying large "night battle" planes (mostly French Voisins), the other three flying Spads or Nieuports.

German attacks usually came at night, so the defenders' job would be first to find the Gotha bombers in the dark and then to destroy them. When you consider the night-flying equipment they had, both in the planes and on the ground, it sounds like a scary way to fight a war. They had minimal cockpit instruments—an altimeter, a compass, a tachometer, maybe a clock (and in earlier models of the planes they wouldn't have been illuminated)—and no permanent landing lights on the ground. Airfields would light up the runway when a plane approached using flares (a bucket with half a gallon of gasoline in it), or bonfires, or the headlights of trucks. Some night-flying planes carried wing flares, which would light up the surface of the ground if you were low enough, and bombers might have a parachute flare aboard, to be dropped from higher up (though that was intended to light a bombing target). There were, of course, no radio ranges and no rotating beacons to home in on, and no warning lights on obstacles on the ground—water towers, or power lines like the one that Norman Prince flew into in the dark, back in 1916. There were many groping emergency landings and many crashes. Still, to eager new pilots in the waiting pool at Issoudun, a Defense of Paris squadron would at least be a move in the right direction, toward action. Surely they would be excited to get such an assignment.

In fact, they weren't. Two of those waiting pilots kept journals that are almost day-to-day accounts of what Defense of Paris duty was like. Walter Avery and Lance Holden were Ivy Leaguers—Avery from Harvard, Holden from Princeton—who met at their port of embarkation, traveled to France together, and became close friends. They were assigned to the same Defense of Paris squadron at Le Bourget and flew together. And wrote about it. Here is Avery on the new assignment:

April 7, 1918: Came out to Le Bourget field to join one of the French *Escadrilles* in the defense of Paris . . . We are to have Nieuports and Spads and would be all to the merry if it were not for the disappointment of getting sidetracked from the real war work.

Here's Holden, reporting how a rumor that "some of us were to be sent out" became a reality:

The rumor turned out to be 15 men for the defense of Paris, and here we are—stationed at Le Bourget attached to French escadrilles with a Nieuport a piece . . . They asked for volunteers for the job and not a soul responded. Yes it is more or less an embusque job, but we are to be broken in as night flyers. Flying a chasse plane at night and attacking raiders is something new. No one knows the possibilities.

Neither Avery nor Holden mentions flying a single night flight. Instead, they fly daylight patrols. The rules are very clear: "we are not supposed to fly outside of a small area around Paris"—like children sent out to play but told not to cross the street. They fly around over the nearby countryside, admiring the great châteaus at Chantilly and Senlis and Compiègne and Pierrefonds. Avery spends a day flying over Paris, seeing all the famous sights—Sacré Coeur, the Eiffel Tower, the Arc de Triomphe, the Place de la Concorde, Les Invalides, Notre Dame—like any college boy on his first trip abroad. On a flight over the sixteenth arrondissement Holden runs out of gas and has to *panne* on Longchamp racetrack.

But the sight they most want to see is none of these landmarks; it's the front. Up there to the north and east of Paris, where the war is being fought—that's the magnetic north that pulls their compasses. The two friends fly together northeast, toward Soissons (it's strictly against the rules) to take a look at the lines and are disappointed when clouds obscure the earth. Holden slips away again, and this time reaches his goal and records the moment: "There, just north of Soissons—about 10 kils—was that dirty shell torn strip of Mi Maus Land between the trenches. I had seen it at last." He's seen it, but he isn't really there, not as a combat pilot. He's just a tourist.

Holden meets a French lieutenant named Hirsch on a train. Hirsch is a seasoned *chasse* pilot, an ace; he invites Holden to visit him at his squadron's airfield, near the front at Clermont. Holden and Avery fly there together, and Hirsch invites them to join him in the afternoon patrol, as though he were a country gentleman going out to shoot pheasants. Avery's account of the visit is simple: they were invited to fly with the squadron, and they flew. But for Holden the visit is memorable for another reason that he tries to express in his journal:

> I hope some really great writer and flyer gets through this war to thrill the lives of small boys hereafter. The wildest tales of Romance are stupid to what could be written about this game. For instance this lieut. Hirsch I saw was leaving for Paris that afternoon. He drops down from 2 hours over the lines packed with fights and escapes. The thing he rides isn't a truck horse they used in King Arthur's time (and I thought those tales exciting). But a thing that flies. His escadrille insignia, his escadre colors, his own design and the big number make his machine a gaudy sight. The eyes painted on the hood and the teeth on the radiator with those two black machine gun muzzles add to the general effect also. His plane is wheeled into its own little tent. His three mechanics sleep beside it. One of them pulls off his "combination" [his flight suit] and we walk down to the officer's mess shack. The captain joins us for tea. One of the lieutenants sits down at the piano. Then a beautiful Renault car appears at the door. Hirsch, meanwhile has turned into as swell an officer as you would see on the boulevards. Someone joshes him with "au allez vous comme ça?" In an hour he will be strolling with his friends along the Champs Elysées on a beautiful spring evening. Would it take much fiction to make such facts into hair-raising tales of love, sorrow, and adventure? To live among such things is thrilling. To be part of it, sublime.

Before the war is over, Holden will be an ace, but in this journal passage he is nobody—a twenty-two-year-old *embusqué* in a Defense of Paris squadron, a hero-worshipper in the presence of a hero.

Not all the pilots who were stockpiled back in rear areas spent their time flying *embusqué* jobs or just hanging around being idle. Some were assigned to administrative jobs—desk jobs, running the flight-training program.

Quentin Roosevelt was nineteen years old when he arrived at Issoudun, but in spite of his age he was made supply officer of the base (with Cord Meyer as his "running partner"). Roosevelt was modest about his qualifications—it was a job, he wrote home, "for which I am as little gifted as possible"—but in fact he was very good at it. The work consisted mainly of riding around on a motorcycle, hunting down scarce building materials and seeing that cargo ships were unloaded faster. He spoke French—not well, he said, but well enough to persuade French builders to part with their supplies, and French bureaucrats to cut their red tape. He wasn't so successful with the motorcycle: he had two accidents early in his supply-officer career—one when he was driving, the other in the sidecar—cutting and bruising himself and loosening a few teeth. He confessed that he grew to like the job, as I suppose any nineteen-year-old would like finding that he could do a grown-up's job well.

In December (not long after his twentieth birthday) Roosevelt was appointed commanding officer of the headquarters detachment—six hundred cadets and forty officers of his own rank, who apparently had nothing to do. A week later he was moved to another new job, commanding a squadron that was in quarantine for mumps. He set to work at once, "sweating the fat off 'em and the beef on." For two days he made them clean out their barracks, then he took them out and drilled and hiked them until they were "good and tired" (and so was he). It worked like a charm, he wrote home; after two weeks they were all in fine shape. A few weeks after that he got yet another assignment, at Field Seven, the final stage of flight training at Issoudun, where he became the officer in charge of flying. The Air Service seemed to assume that he would learn to fly on his own in his spare time—which he did, though the strain showed.

Among the officers and students at Issoudun, Quentin Roosevelt stood out; he was someone that others wrote home about. They described his odd appearance: a big man, like his father, with clothes that didn't seem to fit him and a campaign hat too small for his dome of a head; a *robust* man, they said. But more than that, he was someone they liked: "a peach," "darn fine," "a wonderful boy." They noticed him partly because he was the son of a colorful president, but it was more than that: he was somebody in his own right, a forceful man who got things done. When the cadets under his command needed help, Roosevelt went up against senior officers to get it. In the winter of 1917–18, when cadets were standing guard in three feet of mud and getting pneumonia and flu, he forced the quartermaster to issue rubber boots to them all. When Waldo Heinrichs had problems, it was Roosevelt who took him to see the lieutenant colonel and state his grievances about "non-payment, shortage of pay, failure to be assigned to active duty when once sworn in etc." "Got fine satisfaction," Heinrichs said. He didn't seem surprised that a first lieutenant could confront a lieutenant colonel that way; of course he could, if he was Quentin Roosevelt.

For all his authority and presence, Roosevelt was very much one of the gang. Livingston Irving recalled life at Issoudun's Field Eight when Roosevelt was running it: "In formation flying we were under Quentin Roosevelt. He was a helluva nice boy, but the higher ups didn't like him. When they couldn't find him they would have to go searching through the hangars and usually find him shooting craps with the enlisted men. They didn't like that."

Though the men Roosevelt lived and worked with admired and praised him, they didn't know all there was to know about him. They didn't know the state of his health. He might look robust, but he wasn't; quite the contrary. He had, for example, a bad back; he had injured it years before while on a hunting trip out West with his father; his horse had slipped on a mountain track and Quentin had fallen, wrenching and twisting his back. He never fully recovered from the injury; it caused him acute pain if he exercised strenuously. (I try to imagine what it was like flying loops and spins with a back like that.)

Roosevelt was also susceptible to respiratory illnesses. Much of the time he was at Issoudun, he was more or less ill. In December 1917 he had a cough for a month, which developed into a bout of pneumonia that put him in the hospital. His life, he said, was a continual fight with the doctors; they prescribed bed rest, but he flew anyway. Later, at the gunnery school at Cazaux, he wrote that he was "not feeling awfully well" and got into a "streak of bad flying," but he went on flying. He was marked unfit for anything but light duty, but he went on with the training program; he passed the altitude test, though the high air got to his lungs and he had trouble breathing, and the next day he finished acrobatics, doing it all in one day. He was doing so much flying, he wrote, that he was tired most of the time.

This account doesn't sound like your average eager flight student. Roosevelt was certainly eager for action at the front; he continually pressed his senior officers to send him to a combat squadron, and sometimes it seemed certain that he was about to go. In September 1917 he actually had orders to report to the First Aero Squadron, but he couldn't go, because there was no one to replace him as supply officer; Colonel Bolling, the commanding officer of the training program, promised that he'd send him up with the next draft of pilots. In December he got the same promise. At the end of the year he hoped he'd be in a French escadrille within three weeks. But the weeks ran out, and he remained at Issoudun, too good an administrator to be a combat pilot.

Plenty of young men at Issoudun waited as long as Quentin Roosevelt did and tried as hard to get into combat. But Roosevelt was different in his motives: it wasn't the romance, or the danger, or the possible heroism that moved him. It was the other Roosevelt men. "I feel I owe it to the family," he wrote in January 1918, "—to father, and especially to

Arch and Ted who are out there already and facing the dangers of it, to get out myself."

Arch was his brother Archibald, a captain in the Sixteenth Infantry, already at the front (he'd be wounded two months later). Ted was his brother Theodore, a major in the Twenty-Sixth Infantry (he'd be wounded twice and gassed that spring). There was also Kermit, his third brother: he was serving as a captain with the British Expeditionary Force in Mesopotamia; later he'd transfer to the AEF in France. And there was the Old Man, Colonel Theodore Roosevelt, who had charged up San Juan Hill at the head of his Rough Riders in the Spanish-American War and who willed his sons to emulate him in their way—to go where the danger was and to do him credit. For the colonel, war was what men did, if they were men.

And there was Quentin, with his bad back and his weak eyes and his vulnerable lungs, at war because he had to be, eager to get to the fighting and get it over with before his body failed him, pleading with senior officers to send him to the front, determined not to be the *embusqué* that his brothers taunted him with being.

If the waiting pilots were lucky, they'd scrounge a plane or a couple of planes and go flying—not practicing or training (that was all behind them), but just playing—fooling around in planes for the pure, free pleasure of being up there. Sometimes they went touring: Conover and three of his buddies flew in formation to have a look at the château of Chanson, over near Tours, and then to the airfield at Pontlevoy, where they performed all the acrobatic tricks they knew while the students and instructors on the field stopped what they were doing and just watched them, and on to Chambord, near Blois, where they buzzed the château until the people inside rushed out to see them, and so back to Issoudun, "after having thoroughly enjoyed ourselves."

Sometimes they simply flew very low and as fast as the plane would move, just for the thrill of the speed (which you feel more intensely when you're close to the ground), and the danger (what if your engine fails?), and for the sense it gives you of leaving the boring old stationary world behind you. Here's Kenneth MacLeish, low and fast over the

English coast at Gosport: "The fun was quite intense today. I went bush-bouncing, better known as contour-chasing, only I went in a Camel. It's great sport to get going about 120 mph right around five feet above the ground and head straight for a hangar or a tree and stay at five feet until you get the 'wind up' and then jump the object."

Stunting, buzzing, and flat-hatting are swell fun. They're also, as MacLeish says, sport. Like other demanding physical sports—mountain climbing, deep-sea diving, auto racing—they require skill, quick responses, a certain strength, and the will to try something difficult, just to see if you can do it, to "get away with it." In some sports that something difficult is also something dangerous: the element of fear is there to be confronted and overcome, just to prove to yourself that you weren't really scared. It's something twenty-one-year-old males do—at least the ones who become pilots.

Sometimes they play at war in the air—two friends up in the sunlight, dogfighting with each other. It's what children do—aimless and free, with no goal, no score, no real winner or loser: adults play games or sports and try to defeat one another; children simply *play*. But it's also a rehearsal for the serious game that's ahead of them, when there will be real winners and real losers.

So, in the spring of 1918, as they restlessly wait for orders to the front, Quentin Roosevelt and Ham Coolidge, close friends since their Harvard days, meet in the air over Issoudun and fight. Coolidge writes a careful account of the combat in a letter to his mother. He's been given a new monoplane fighter to fly (a Morane, I assume); thinking to make a big impression, because a new plane always commands attention, he heads for an outlying field, and there spots his friend Quentin, in his gaudily painted Nieuport, circling around a target balloon over the field. Quentin sees him, flips over on his back, and dives in an attack. Ham hasn't been thinking of a fight, he says, "but one must never refuse a combat, so I hastened to manoeuvre for position." He should have the advantage—his monoplane is faster, climbs faster, and is more maneuverable—Quentin should be a dead duck. But it's only Ham's second flight in the new plane, and it's a sensitive machine that demands skillful handling; he doesn't dare "whisk it around in the slap-dash manner that would have saved the situation." And so he loses the fight.

Ham's account of the contest is wry and modest; he was cautious,

Quentin was daring, and in aerial combat daring wins. Quentin's version is even more modest: "The other day he [Ham] came over in a new type of plane, that they are just putting in on the front, and we had a bully time with it. I went up in mine, which is of course specially taken care of by the mechanics and we chased each other around for about a half an hour." He doesn't say who won; friends don't beat each other when they're playing.

It's fun up there, pretending to fight, but it's not the real thing, and the two friends aren't content with it. In a letter in early May, Quentin writes: "Ham and I both decided, independent of each other, that we were stale." "Stale" is a recurrent word among the young fliers: to be stale is to have done one thing too long. For Quentin and Ham, hanging around playing at combat has taken the edge off their keenness. They're tired of being *embusqués*; they want to be at the front, where the play is real and the winner takes all.

EIGHT

HOW TO FIGHT

January 1, 1918: the first day of the war's last year. American military units have not yet reached the Western Front—not on the ground, not in the air. Only a few determined American pilots have flown in combat, all in the forces of other nations. Most famously, there are the members of the Lafayette Escadrille (now called Escadrille N. 124). On that New Year's Day the escadrille is out of action, up in the Champagne country at a place called La Noblette Farm, waiting to be transferred from the French to the U.S. Air Service. Of the original seven pilots of the escadrille, William Thaw is acting commanding officer at La Noblette; Elliot Cowdin has been sent back to the States to be a flight instructor; Bert Hall has simply disappeared (it's rumored he's back home, making his living as a returned hero). The other four—Chapman, Prince, McConnell, and Rockwell—are dead.

A few other Americans have made their way via the ambulance service, or the Foreign Legion, or by direct enlistment, to escadrilles scattered along the French part of the front. Alan Nichols and Houston Woodward are at fields north of Paris—Nichols near Compiègne with Escadrille N. 98, Woodward in N. 94 near Montdidier. Alan Winslow and George Moseley are over on the eastern end of the line—Winslow with N. 152 at Corcieux in the Vosges, Moseley with SPA 150 near Belfort. Carroll Winslow is in SPA 112 at Beauzée-sur-Aire west of Yёrdun. The great Raoul Lufbery is with Thaw and N. 124 at La Noblette.

Some are stalled in Paris. Sidney Drew is there, vacillating over whether to stay with the Service Aéronautique or transfer to the U.S. Air Service. Charles Biddle is there, too, waiting for his American commission. Others, half trained by the RFC in Canada, are strung out along the route to the war. On New Year's Day, Edgar Taylor is aboard a troopship in the mid-Atlantic; Briggs Adams has just arrived at Glasgow and is on the train for London; George Vaughn is at the RFC training depot at Stamford, waiting to move to a British squadron in France.

As for the American squadrons—combat-ready squadrons—they don't yet exist. Wherever they are on that New Year's Day of 1918, they aren't real, complete combat squadrons; they're only the shells of squadrons, waiting to be filled with the men and machines that will do the fighting.

Even when a full complement of new pilots reports for duty, these squadrons won't be combat ready. The pilots will be jubilant and eager for action, like substitutes on a football team who have finally got off the bench and onto the field where the big game is being played. The trouble is, in spite of their flight training, their wings, and their new gold bars, despite the flying hours they've logged in their kiwi jobs, or just hanging around waiting at Issoudun, they don't really know how to play the game—don't know their way around the playing field, don't know the rules, don't even know how to find the other team. They'll have to learn new at-the-front skills before they'll be ready to meet their enemies.

There were handbooks available by 1918 to teach them those skills, though not many. War in the air had no tradition, no historic battles a pilot could study, and until 1917 no textbooks to consult, only a few personal memoirs by first-wave pilots like Carroll Winslow and James McConnell. The first book of air-war instructions by an Allied writer that I know of is *Fighting in the Air*, a thirty-page pamphlet by a British pilot, Major L.W.B. Rees, published in May 1917. Rees was a regular army officer who had spent the ten years before the war in the Royal Artillery, where he was known for his marksmanship. When war was declared, he transferred to the Royal Flying Corps and served in squadrons at the front during 1915 and early 1916, flying Vickers FB-5s and de Havilland DH-2s, the slow pusher planes that were then in use. His record was distinguished: he was credited with eight victories and was awarded both the Military Cross and the Victoria Cross, the latter for single-handedly attacking a flight of ten German planes and shooting down two. In the summer of 1916, Rees was ordered back to England and was appointed commanding officer of the RFC gunnery school at Ayr. He wrote his little book during his first year there.

An artilleryman, a marksman, and an ace: surely the perfect qualifications for writing the first handbook on how to fight in the air. He could draw on both his services: the artillery for diagrams with lines marked "line of flight" and "real path of bullet" and angles marked A, B, and C; the RFC for tactics and definitions. But any new pilot in 1918 would know from the book's first sentence that it could be of no use to him. It begins, "These notes are based on experiences of last year . . ." "Last year": that's 1916. At the rate war in the air was changing, both in the design and armament of planes and in tactics, 1916 was history. Rees recognized the problem; the sentence continues, "so that it is impossible to lay down any hard and fast rules, as the conditions alter so fast." But he didn't see that by the time it appeared, his book would be an out-of-date curiosity. As tactical advice, it's all as obsolete as cavalry charges.

Most obsolete of all are Major Rees's ideas of British pilots and of their opponents. Here's a passage from the first page:

COMPARISON OF PILOTS.

The British Pilot always likes the idea of fighting, and is self-reliant. He is a quick thinker compared with the Enemy, so that he has the advantage in manoeuvre. He fights for the sport of the affair, if for no other reason . . . Very wisely, he is not hampered by strict rules, and as a rule is allowed to conduct his own affairs.

The Enemy Pilot, on the other hand, is of a gregarious nature from long national training, and often seems to be bound by strict rules, which cramp his style to a great extent. The Enemy Pilots are often uneducated men, being looked on simply as drivers of the machine, while the Gunner or Observer is considered a grade higher than the Pilot.

This last gives a great advantage to us, as, whereas our Pilots act from a sense of "noblesse oblige," the Enemy, when in a tight corner, often fail to seize and press an advantage.

It's the old chivalric dream, air war as a gentleman's sport: the way to get killed.

The first French handbook is a very different document. Its author was Captain Albert Deullin, a French ace who had been one of the original members of Escadrille N. 3, the famous "Cigogne" (Stork) squadron, where he'd flown with great French pilots like Guynemer. In June 1917, when he wrote the first part of his handbook, Deullin was commanding officer of Escadrille SPA 73, at the front at Bergues, near Dunkerque. He'd flown both Nieuports and Spads against the Germans; he knew what there was to know about fighting in the air at the time he wrote.

Deullin called the first part of his book "La chasse en monoplane," which you might translate as "How to Hunt the Enemy in a Single-Seat Plane." And that's what it's about: one man in his plane, hunting his Boche. Deullin offers the beginner pilot basic advice for combat, which can be summarized in a few rules:

- Maneuver your plane to get into the best firing position before you fire: stay in the enemy's "dead angle" where his guns can't reach you. (Certain pilots, he says, neglect this principle and try to cut corners; such a *coup d'audace* may work sometimes, but more often those who try it are riddled with bullets and crash.)
- Stay out of your enemy's slipstream.
- Watch out for what's behind you.

And what *not* to do:

- Don't shoot until you are in point-blank range.
- Don't attack from the front, or from three-quarters rear if the enemy plane is a two-seater.

And two last rules that are pure survival:

- Be your own armorer: that is, know your machine gun—how to load it and, most important, how to unblock a jam quickly in the air (many have tried to neglect this essential principle, Deullin says, and they have always regretted it).

- There is no shame in abandoning an attack that isn't suc-
  ceeding; the greatest *chasseurs* count on one Boche shot
  down for every ten missed chances.

The second part of Deullin's treatise is dated November 1917 on
the manuscript. That's only five months after the first was written, but
in those months a change had taken place in tactics of air fighting that
the new part expresses. "La chasse en monoplane" starred the solitary
chasseur hunting his enemy; "Les patrouilles de chasse" is about planes
in formation—*la chasse* as a collective pursuit.

Deullin begins this part on a historical note, looking back a year to
the time of the Somme offensive in the summer and autumn of 1916.
(Those were the months when Major Rees was at the front learning to
fight in the air.) To Deullin, that period is the distant past. Back then,
he writes, the German aviators were completely demoralized; their artillery spotters and reconnaissance planes tried to cross the front lines
as little as possible, and their defensive patrols of two or four two-seaters
turned and scattered if even one lone Nieuport attacked them. In their
single-seat fighters they flew either alone or in twos; in either case they
maneuvered badly and refused to engage in combat, and if they did
turn and fight, they were easy prey. The result, for the French pilots on
patrol, was a sky empty of targets; enemy planes disappeared before
them, and they were almost never able to shoot down a Boche.

You might think this was a desirable situation—the Germans on
their own side of the lines, and not much fighting. But to Deullin those
were the bad old days; what was the point of flying a *chasse* plane if there
was no one to chase? And what good was an empty sky? It's an odd-
sounding complaint, but one that occurs in many letters and diaries: the
Germans were no fun; they wouldn't fight; they weren't sportsmen. Flying was still a gentleman's sport, and the Boche didn't play by the rules.

Little by little, that all changed. What happened, in Deullin's version, is that the Germans invented formation flying—not simply a lot of
planes flying in the same direction, but coordinated, disciplined group
flying. Planes working closely together could resist those one-man attacks and go on the attack themselves, easily shooting down any Frenchman who risked crossing over to the German side of the lines. "Our
hunters," Deullin writes, "were forced to admit that the time of the

solitary single-seater had passed and that we had to look for something else." There would have to be new tactics, new maneuvers, a new kind of responsibility.

The French began to experiment, first with patrols of complete squadrons, which were a flop (as one might have predicted): they took forever to assemble in the air, and once the formation was assembled, one abrupt maneuver by the flight leader could turn it into "magnificent disorder." Smaller formations, then. Try three planes, one leading, the others behind and above on either side, at an angle of forty-five degrees and a distance of about two hundred meters. Or perhaps four would work better; Deullin draws a picture of such a formation in the margin of his manuscript. It's not what pilots of my generation would have called tight formation, but apparently it worked.

The rest of "Les patrouilles" spells out the tactics and the logic of flying combat patrols in this pattern or variations of it. And there are illustrations to help—not decorations of the manuscripts, but instructional drawings like this one, showing why attacking from the front is

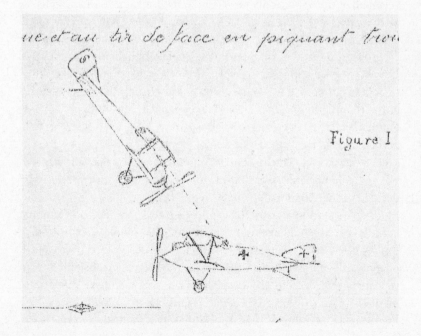

Figure I

difficult, and only for the experienced and skillful pilot. (The diving plane is a Spad, the victim an Albatros.)

"Les patrouilles de chasse" ends on a confident note. The results of the new formation tactics have been conclusive: with a good leader—experienced, clearheaded, prudent, and decisive—and well-trained pilots, "seconded by the very real superiority of our chasse machine, a fight should nearly always end successfully." In November 1917, the French have their newest and best fighter, the 180-horsepower Spad, which is more than a match for the current German fighter, the Albatros. That will change; in the new year the Germans will introduce the Fokker D.VII, probably the best plane of the war. But for now, as 1917 ends, Deullin is cheerful.

Charles Biddle was a member of Deullin's Escadrille 73 from July 1917 until the end of the year—just about long enough, he thought, to begin to learn how to fight in the air. He greatly admired his commanding officer. He wrote home in November: "I went out in the morning with the chief of the Escadrille, Captain Deullin. It was the first time I had been out alone with him on a Hun hunting expedition and I was very glad of the opportunity to watch him fighting, for he is an old hand at the game and there is probably no one in the French Army more skillful than he." (On that patrol Deullin scored his nineteenth victory.)

Toward the end of the year Biddle applied for a commission in the U.S. Air Service and spent six weeks or so hanging around Paris waiting to be transferred. He was restless and angry: after three or four months at the front he had learned how to fly in combat, but he'd only got one German plane. Now he was ready to use those skills to "bag at least two or three Huns." He wanted a squadron—French or American, he doesn't seem to have cared which—and he wanted it *now*. But instead, there he was, in a comfortable room in the Hôtel Continental, just waiting. He decided to translate Deullin's book into English.

Biddle's version is more than simply a translation: he had Deullin's permission to include material of his own. What Biddle added was testimony based on his own experience and on his observation of seasoned pilots like Deullin at work, written with the eyewitness exactness that you might expect from a Philadelphia lawyer. Some of the tactics are methods of attack that are prudent expansions of a Deullin principle. For example, Deullin writes, "Attack ahead while looking to the rear," to which Biddle adds, "It can be said, without fear of contradiction, that the overwhelming majority of pilots brought down by other single-seaters, are surprised from the rear, and this usually when their sole attention is concentrated upon a Hun whom they themselves are trying to attack."

And he extends his point, a little further on: "The oldest and wisest pilots consider it foolish for a man to go on the lines by himself, no matter how great his skill and experience. 'To attack ahead while watching to the rear' is a fundamental principle, but if sufficient attention is to be paid to the attack ahead to make it successful, it is impossible at the same time to see anything in the rear."

About gunnery: Deullin suggests a sprinkling of shots to get your correction right. Biddle adds, "Remember, however, that although in the case of a large two-seater, it may look at fifty yards as big as a battleship, the vital spots are in reality very small . . . Even where the shot is straight away with no correction to make, there is a tendency to do too much sprinkling and in one's anxiety and haste, to use the machine gun as a sort of hose with which to spray the sky." His rule is simple: "Get very close before shooting at all."

There's a strong element of cautious self-preservation in Biddle's approach to *chasse* work; some bits of advice are entirely that. For example, Deullin's advice on how to get out of a fight you're losing is to go into a spin. Biddle disagrees: "Most experienced pilots seem to agree that to break off a combat with a single-seater, the execution of *renversements*, short turns, spirals, etc. is preferable to the nose spin." And he explains why: "The former make a machine just as difficult a mark and at the same time allow the pilot to at all times keep track of his adversary and of the points of the compass." One Biddle sentence sums up his attitude toward all combat: "It would always seem better to try to watch your adversary and maneuver with the reasoned purpose of counteracting his maneuvers, rather than to do something in which one consigns oneself to blind luck and the Almighty."

Better to be reasonable than to trust to luck. You'll live longer that way.

Three manuals for war in the air, then, of which Rees is the grandfather figure, wise but useless to later generations, and Deullin is the still-active father, living by more modern rules. And Biddle? Older than the young men he addresses, but not all that much (he was twenty-nine when he made his translation), he's a kind of uncle advising his nephews on the complications of real adult life—in this case, the best, most prudent ways to kill Huns.

Major Rees's *Fighting in the Air* was published in the United States and must have circulated. Biddle's monograph was also published— according to Hall and Nordhoff's *Lafayette Flying Corps*, it was "adopted for use in the instruction of pilots in the U.S. Air Service"— but I've found no evidence in any pilots' letters that any of them read it. For some kinds of lessons, books just aren't an attractive way of learning: only direct experience will do. Sex, for instance, and ballroom dancing. Combat flying is in that category; you learn it by doing it.

Because that was true, new pilots who finally made their way to operational squadrons at the front found that though they were there, they wouldn't plunge straight into the fighting. First they'd have to have still more training. For the impatient ones it was just one more exasperating delay. Houston Woodward, new to the front in January, wrote home that before he could be put on the "available" list, "I had to undergo five hours of 'patrouilles d'entrainement' just behind the lines. Although I saw several Boches, we had strict orders to avoid unnecessary conflicts on account of my lack of experience. That was rather uninteresting work, but I became very familiar with the secteur, and, of course, with my machine."

That was the point: there were at-the-front lessons that new pilots would have to learn—important, life-and-death lessons. Experienced pilots in working squadrons knew that the first weeks at the front were a vulnerable time for new men. Until they learned the things you only learn by flying there, the odds against them would be high. And so flight leaders led their new charges on practice patrols, around behind the lines or just up to the front, not to hunt Boches, but simply to learn what it's like to fly in this dangerous new world.

Eddie Rickenbacker's memoir of his war, *Fighting the Flying Circus*, begins with an anecdote about such a learning flight. It's the sixth of March 1918 (or maybe the nineteenth—accounts vary), and Rickenbacker's squadron, the Ninety-Fourth Pursuit, has just arrived at the front. Major Raoul Lufbery, the group's commanding officer and its most celebrated pilot, announces that he's going to lead a patrol of three planes over the lines and that two of his brand-new pilots, Rickenbacker and Douglas Campbell, will fly with him. It won't be a Boche-hunting flight—the Ninety-Fourth's planes have no guns yet—only "a look at the war," but for Rickenbacker and Campbell it's an exciting occasion, their first venture into enemy airspace.

The patrol, as Rickenbacker tells it, is exciting but uneventful; he struggles to stay in formation and to follow his leader; he feels the cold at fifteen thousand feet; he sees his first antiaircraft bursts, and his stomach turns over. When they land back at their field, the two beginners assume an air of bored indifference: there wasn't much to it, they say; we crossed the lines, but we didn't see a single plane in the air—no friendlies, and no Germans. The Germans didn't dare to venture up.

Lufbery breaks in to ask them particularly what they had seen. They reply that they hadn't seen any other planes in the sky.

"Just what I expected," Lufbery says. "They are all the same!"

The two new pilots are indignant; what does he mean, addressing two expert war pilots in such terms?

"Well," Lufbery replies,

one formation of five Spads crossed under us before we passed the lines and another flight of five Spads went by about fifteen minutes later and you didn't see them, although neither one of them was more than 500 yards away. It was just as well they were not Boches!

Then there were four German Albatros two miles ahead of us when we turned back and there was another enemy two-seater nearer us than that, at about 5,000 feet above the lines. You ought to look about a bit when you get in enemy lines.

Rickenbacker draws the moral of the story: "No matter how good a flyer the scout may be and no matter how perfect his eyesight is, he must learn to see before he can distinguish objects either on the ground or in air. What is called 'vision of the air' can come only from experience and no pilot ever has it upon his first arrival at the front."

The first lesson, then, was How to See.

The second lesson was How to Read the Earth. You might think the new pilots would have looked down enough, back in their flight training, to recognize the surface of the earth below. But the front didn't look like the bucolic landscape they'd seen on their navigational flights back at Issoudun. It looked, one new man wrote, "as if somebody had taken the landscape and smudged it like a smear on a map. All the sharp outlines of field and wood seemed to fade into a dull brown and the roads and villages appeared blurred and indistinct as if they were a photograph taken out of focus." If you were a new pilot and got into a fight that separated you from your leader, or if your engine failed over that ruined landscape, you'd have trouble knowing which side of the lines you were on or which way was home. If you had to make a forced landing, you'd wonder whether you were about to be a guest of the French army or a prisoner of the Germans.

Or you might fly into bad weather. A new pilot on the Western Front would soon learn how easy it was to get lost in the weather of northern France. The prevailing westerly winds would blow you east into German airspace before you knew it, and resist you when you tried to fly back—if you knew which way back was. The snow that winter would have made it worse, erasing the ordinary world below and leaving a strange blankness in its place—a map without lines or landmarks.

Alan Nichols wrote to his family back in California about his first winter flight: "It was the first time I had ever flown when there was snow on the ground, and was surprised to see that it looks like a different world. I might have been flying over the surface of the moon, for apparently all life had vanished." You couldn't count on much out there over the front, but you could count on getting lost. You'd never entirely learn how not to, but you could learn to read what was still visible—the rivers, the straight white French roads, the wide forests, the airfields. That was another lesson that training patrols with a wise leader might teach you.

To these cautious at-the-front lessons, the old pilots added one further admonition (both Deullin and Biddle put it in their manuals): if you see that the odds are against you, *scram!* In such circumstances— and they would occur a lot—running away is not cowardice; it's just common sense. It was good advice, but common sense didn't appeal to young men who were about to become players in the big game they'd been waiting for. Their letters are full of that athletic metaphor: the war just ahead of them is "the flying game," "a glorious sport," "the best game over here," "the sporty side of war." They're right, in a way: the combat flying they expect *is* something like a sport; it's the only kind of fighting in this war in which one man competes directly against an opponent, and one of them wins and one of them loses, the only kind in which a score can be kept and individuals can become stars. Only in the air will small groups of players acting together oppose other small groups—like two football teams.

But to make the big game analogy really work, you'd have to imagine a Harvard-Yale game in which both teams are armed with lethal weapons. In that game the players would not simply be athletes; they'd be gamblers, taking risks with their own lives. General Billy Mitchell saw the flying game that way: "Pursuit squadrons are essentially an offensive element, and to enact their role successfully, they must take and maintain the offensive. They should seek the enemy and wherever found, attack and destroy him . . . One must have young men, with a good sporting instinct, willing to take big chances."

Deullin and Biddle would have disagreed, but many young pilots understood the game the way Mitchell did. Dick Blodgett, on his way to the front in January 1918, wrote to a girl back home, "I'm a very poor gambler. I just don't care for it at any time, unless I hate the people I'm playing against. Yet here I am forced to make a gambler's choice. I can play the big game safe, or double or nothing. I'm playing it double or nothing."

It's a game he will lose.

NINE

THIS KILLING BUSINESS

At the end of 1917, Alan Nichols was in Paris. It was his first Christmastime away from his family, and he was on his way to join a French escadrille at the front. In a letter to his mother back in Palo Alto he put these two discordant realities together: "It's rather queer that I should be beginning my first active work just at this time—a time especially dedicated to Peace, Goodwill towards one's fellows, and Forgiveness. Well, it certainly is not to my taste, this killing business. It is just a little job to get off our hands now."

Killing, when you're in a war, is your business—a job to do, part of a pilot's work. "We certainly can do it," he assures his mother, "without any uncertainty about whether it is necessary or not." But by denying uncertainty, he seems to admit its presence in his mind; perhaps he's thinking of the Sixth Commandment. That business lies straight ahead now, not distant any longer, not a romantic dream, but up close. He'll learn very soon what it is really like, how it's done, how you feel in the presence of violent death.

Nichols has his first lesson a few days later. He has just arrived at his new escadrille, Nieuport 98. He hasn't flown a patrol yet; he hasn't even flown a practice flight. He's just hanging around the flight line waiting when he sees a German two-seater fly over the field, taking pictures. As he watches, a Spad appears, and then another, then two more. They attack the Boche—like small birds pestering a hawk, he thinks.

The flight is so close above him that he can see the smoke of the tracers and hear the tat-tat-tat of the guns. Four fast planes against one slow one; Nichols knows how the fight will end.

> After perhaps five or ten minutes he slowly arched over until he was diving straight down and a faint streak of blue smoke trailed out. Everyone shouted, "Ça y est! Ça y est!"
>
> Then the poor devil started to vrille and while he was whirling, his gas tank blew up. Pieces of the machine flew out and fluttered like an exploding sky-rocket. Then the red-orange flame appeared and he fell straight as a stone and went out of sight behind a wood.

The Spads followed him down, and everyone was cheering. Nichols finds himself cheering, too, and feels guilty because he does: "I couldn't help thinking of the two men there, even if they were Boches, falling to their doom. They got their pictures, but no one ever saw them!" There at the very beginning of his fighting war, before he's fired a shot at a Boche, Nichols has discovered something that other men at war have learned, or will learn by witnessing it—that the enemy he must try to kill is a man like himself.

In a couple of weeks Nichols has flown his practice flights and is ready for the real thing. Now, surely, he will get his Boche—or at least have a shot at one. It isn't that simple: on his first patrol he doesn't see a single German plane. He flies another, and the weather turns the flight back. He flies another, and this time he sees planes approaching, "flying in a line stepped up like a staircase as the Boches fly." But they're Nieuports. Another flight, and the patrol passes a formation of planes that really are German, but the French flight leader refuses to engage them. Nichols and the other pilots on the patrol aren't ready; they're not yet old hands.

Two months pass, and Nichols has moved to a Spad escadrille. It's what he wanted—Spads are bigger, faster, and stronger than Nieuports and don't have the Nieuport's tendency to lose its wing fabric in a dive—but he still hasn't had a shot at a Boche. Then, on a patrol, he and his formation spot a Rumpler, all alone. They give chase. Nichols draws ahead of the others and begins shooting. His gun jams. He clears it, fires, and it jams again. He pounds on the levers with his knuckles and fires again and again, spraying bullets from side to side and up and down, looking to hit a vital spot. "I saw my luminous bullets flying all over," he writes in a letter home that night, "and by the curious effect of their curvings it looked as if they were bouncing off his machine! I was easily as close as 150 yards, all alone and under his tail."

The gun quits again, this time for good; he's fired all five hundred of his bullets. The German flies off home. Nichols is bitterly disappointed by his failure; he should have gotten his Boche. But not that way, Biddle would have told him: a machine gun isn't a fire hose, and the right distance is 50 yards, not 150.

Chasse patrols will be full of such disappointments. Mostly, they won't even engage the enemy; they'll simply fly around—maybe as protective cover for observation planes that aren't attacked, maybe as "contact patrols" looking for Boches who don't show up. Even if they do get into a fight, it probably won't end in a clear victory (Deullin reckoned the odds were ten to one against). The heroic personal combats ending in streaming smoke trails and flames and a spinning, disintegrating loser will be the stuff for the newspapers and magazines back home, but they won't be the daily life of pilots at the front. Still, most of them will get into a fight sooner or later, and some of them will shoot their opponent down. And when they do, being young and suddenly triumphant, they'll tell their stories, in their letters and in talk with their fellow pilots, who will listen admiringly and enviously.

The old hands, pilots like Deullin and Biddle and Rickenbacker and Lufbery, all taught one lesson: that to survive over the lines, you must fly as a patrol and fight as a patrol. That meant looking out for your friends and protecting them if they needed help. Air war isn't about glory; it's about mutual support—about comradeship, you might say. Letters and diaries of the new pilots show that they were taught that lesson—that's what all the practice flying was about. And some of them learned it. But not all of them. Some were so eager for the fighting to begin that when, in the middle of an ordinary working patrol, they spotted an enemy plane below, they couldn't wait for their leader's signal, couldn't just sit there in formation, but must plunge alone into an attack, moved by some force more urgent than the rules of flight discipline—the combative instinct that's in most men, or the first chance to perform the extreme act they've been trained for, or maybe the muddled notions of personal heroism that are in their heads. Here is their first fight, the first real test—of their courage, their skills, maybe also their luck.

At the beginning of 1918, Houston Woodward has been at the front with Escadrille 94 for a couple of weeks—just long enough to fly his practice flights (impatiently) and an uneventful patrol or two, and to attempt one unsuccessful attack on an enemy plane (in which his machine guns jam). One cold morning he takes off on a patrol led by an experienced French pilot, Lieutenant Parizet. (The third plane in the formation is grounded with engine trouble.) At first nothing happens; there's not a Boche in sight on their side of the lines. They cross over into enemy territory and soon see three Albatroses sailing along slightly below them.

Woodward told his story in an excited letter to his father:

> I didn't wait for Parizet, who was leading, to start for them, but piqued on one of them immediately. Parizet made a slight detour, then dove on one from the side, leaving the third, the leader, free. My Boche made a quick turn, so I redressed and began manoeuvring to get behind and above him. Finally I got him where I wanted him and piqued steep, shooting all the time. Parizet was then just ahead of and above me, and I saw him shooting at a Boche who was manoeuvring to attack me. He over piqued eventually, and the Boche fired about twenty shots at me from the side and a trifle below. He got so close I could see his face, and for a second I hesitated whether to turn on him or continue with the original one. He fell over on his side, though, so I let him go.

Woodward has attacked one Boche and been shot at by another, but there's still no score. He looks around for the German he attacked first and spots him far below, heading for home. He dives and overtakes him. When he's within a hundred meters of his target, he begins firing, a steady stream of bullets that continues until he's so close that he has to pull up to avoid a collision. This time he has better luck: "I saw him slowly slip over on the wing, then go into a slow vrille, and after a few manoeuvres to keep him always under fire, I saw that he had been hit, and made a vertical spiral to watch him vrille down to the ground."

Woodward has got his Boche, but he wants more. He's now at twenty-five hundred meters, and the other two Boches are about a thousand meters below. He sees that Parizet is still prudently hovering at three thousand meters, but prudence isn't for Woodward:

> I decided to take my chances with the other two, so threw my machine over on her side, and dropped seven hundred metres like a plummet in a couple of seconds. Both Albatros immediately continued their piquing. I followed one as low as 1,000 metres, but dared go no further after him. Then the fireworks began. One thousand metres is extremely low for five kilometers inside the German lines, and the air became black around me with their anti-aircrafts. I couldn't go in a straight line, and, as there was a heavy head wind, it took me ages to get inside our lines again.

That's the end of Woodward's story of his first fight: he has met the enemy and appears to have shot one down.

Any reader will have flinched at the mistakes Woodward made in the process: he left his leader to hunt on his own; he sprayed bullets from too great a distance; he decided to take his chances when the odds were against him; he let his plane get too low over German territory and German antiaircraft guns. But he got away with it, so he's elated. "It was very thrilling," he tells his father,

> and the most wonderful sport I have ever participated in. I was in danger only the time when the Boche fired at me, and then somehow it seemed so funny I burst out laughing. I had always rather dreaded my first combat, but there's nothing nervous or rattling about it. It was more like practice target shooting than anything else, as the aim has to be very carefully timed and corrected. There is a tremendously exhilarating thrill about it, however, and the passion of the hunt.

Woodward has had his sport and has got his Boche. But Deullin would shake his head at the story and call Woodward's victory *un coup d'audace*: This time you were lucky, but next time . . . ?

It was because of gamblers like Woodward that commanders discouraged new pilots from going Boche hunting on their own. It was all right if a group of three or four experienced pilots set out on what the French called *chasse libre*—just "poking around the sky looking for trouble," as Drew described it—but Drew's French captain would only allow beginners to go out on big patrols, which they were not to leave from the beginning of the flight till the end, unless they were having trouble with their engines. When Eddie Rickenbacker was second-in-command of the Ninety-Fourth in the spring of 1918, he made it a practice, he said, always to accompany new pilots on their first trip over the enemy lines and by advice and by actual protection from aloft to assist them through "that delicate period between the theory of the school and the hard practice of battle." In the meantime, they were *never* to take off on their own on what were called "voluntary patrols."

Experienced pilots flew voluntary patrols all the time—sometimes alone, sometimes with a pal. Rickenbacker and his friend Reed Chambers flew off together after their day's work was done whenever they felt, as Rickenbacker put it, still "mad at the Boche." He also flew voluntary patrols on his own; on the morning of his first day as commanding officer of the Ninety-Fourth (in September 1918) he took off over the lines alone and returned half an hour later with two more victories scored.

You could hardly expect new pilots not to try the same stunt: the planes were there, the front was there, maybe a German was flying around somewhere. Why not try to find him? Nobody, it appeared, would stop you. Or, why not leave your formation in the middle of a patrol and go Boche hunting alone? It all seems hopelessly undisciplined and unmilitary, just flying off when you felt like it. But they did it. That's what they imagined their role in the war to be: they were in the killing business. Death was always in their minds, the implied intention of every patrol, as it is in all war; wars are won by killing more of *them* than they kill of *you*.

———

War movies and old pilots' yarns sometimes give the impression that every contact with the enemy meant a plane shot down. Houston Woodward's calendar of the weeks after his first victory tells a different story:

January 7, 1918 (the afternoon of his victorious fight): Woodward leaves his patrol, again spots what he takes to be another Nieuport, overtakes it "and then pulled what is probably one of the dumbest biggest bonehead stunts in the war's aviation history"; he flies alongside the other plane for a while, until he realizes that he has joined up on a German Albatros. Then he attempts to engage it, but the German is "too yellow to fight" and drives away. Woodward's C.O. scolds him for leaving formation and forbids him to cross the lines alone ever again.

January 21: Woodward dives on a German observation plane and gets separated from his companion (he was always doing that); another Nieuport joins him and fires warning shots—three "Boches chasseurs" are approaching; Woodward and his new friend "beat it then."

January 21 or 22: Woodward flies a strafing attack.

January 24: He's on patrol with two others when his engine breaks down; he cuts power and glides to the nearest airfield (it's the Lafayette Escadrille's home base), where he makes a classy dead-stick landing and pulls up right in front of the hangars.

February 18: He goes on *permission de détente* (what my generation called R&R—rest and relaxation) to Paris, where he hangs out with some aristocratic Russians he's met and has his portrait painted by a Russian princess.

March 25: He's back with his squadron, now flying Spads; his engine stops in a climb; he crash-lands in a muddy plowed field, wrecking the plane.

In three months he has attacked enemy planes twice, and probably shot one down, escaped from one bad-odds fight, strafed ground troops once, and made two emergency landings. (Or at least those are the flights he has reported to his family—and Woodward was a talkative correspondent.) All of them must have provided a certain amount of excitement—the "wonderful sport" that he described in his letter about his first fight—but not a lot of heroics. Most of a pursuit pilot's work was like that.

Nevertheless, the killing business goes on; whatever a patrol sets out to do—protect an observation plane, or strafe a trench, or just prowl on a *chasse libre*—there's always a chance that a German plane will appear, and the flight will turn into Boche hunting. It's the hunting that stirs the young pilots' imaginations, not the other, ordinary pilots' work. Woodward, back from his leave in Paris, writes home about a picture he's seen in an English newspaper:

WAR IN THE AIR: A BRITISH MACHINE "PICKS" A GERMAN "OFF THE TAIL" OF A COMRADE.

"I SHOT THE ALBATROSS": A BRITISH NIEUPORT SAVES AN OBSERVING MACHINE FROM ITS GERMAN ASSAILANT IN THE NICK OF TIME.

Have you seen the *Illustrated London News* of February 9th? There is a magnificent picture of a Nieuport bringing down an Albatross in flames. It has been greatly admired by aviators . . . The details are excellent, and the artist knew flying and the two machines. Somehow the picture seems to breathe a bit of the thrill of the hunt, and you can almost see the Boche breaking up before crashing, with the Nieuport following in a vertical plunge, and spitting till the last minute. The whole thing is most realistic.

He and his fellow pilots are stirred by the diving, flaming violence of the picture; they cut it out and hang it on their wall.

Woodward writes home about the excitements of his war, and his father sends his letters to the Philadelphia newspapers, where they're published. People read them, are thrilled by his deeds, and write to him; clearly he's a hero, at least in Philadelphia. He asks his father to "please send all newspaper clippings concerning my work here." And yet he's uncomfortable with his hero's status. "I hate publicity," he writes, "and am horrified at some of the letters I have received from people I don't know. I shall have to try awful stunts now to try to live up to the reputation you somehow seem to have given me." Earlier in the letter he has described the latest "stunt" of his roommate, Pierre Marinovitch, who has shot down a German Rumpler biplane that very morning: "He already has five Boches officially, but several more unofficially . . . By the time you get this letter he will probably have several more Boches and I hope I shall, too."

The letter ends, "Will try desperately to write soon." But there will be no more letters, only this message from the commandant of his escadrille: "The first of April, in the afternoon Woodward was sent on patrol in the lines of the enemy; he was seen several times during that patrol by myself. The French patrol having attacked a certain number of enemy aeroplanes, there was a fight after which Corporal Woodward disappeared."

The commandant offers two possible hypotheses as to what happened: either Woodward "was brought down during the fight wounded or killed, or else an accident occurred to his apparatus obliging him to land in the lines of the enemy. The thick fog and the clouds which existed on that day prevented us from learning more of him."

That thick fog would persist for a long time. A month after Woodward's disappearance the commanding general of his group will issue a general order praising him as a "pilote de chasse audacieux jusqu'à la témérité et recherchant opiniâtrement l'ennemi" (a pursuit pilot daring even to foolhardiness and obstinately searching for the enemy), but adding no further information. In June a YMCA worker will write to the family to report a conversation he's had with Woodward's friend Marinovitch: "He told me . . . that he was a most daring aviator, thoroughly skillful in his mastery of the plane and absolutely courageous to the point of recklessness. For instance he said that Houston would frequently go out on solitary trips which of course means that he was without help in the event of an attack. His desire to get some Boche planes was very great."

"Daring," "foolhardiness," "recklessness": those are terms of praise from a general and a civilian, but they're not survival values.

In those messages there is no word of Woodward's fate. In August another letter from the YMCA worker reports that a wreck has been found bearing the number of Woodward's plane; he has asked the authorities to investigate. In December, a correspondent for *The Saturday Evening Post* reports to her editor back in Philadelphia: she has read through the Red Cross dossier on Woodward—several hundred pages, and they all led to "just nothing at all; the fact that he was lost in the mist and nobody could tell whether he was alive or dead." According to the Spanish report, the Germans have no record of his having been taken prisoner.

Finally, in a cable dated February 12, 1919, the YMCA man reports, "Located Houston's grave at Montdidier." He and the faithful Marinovitch have traveled to the site of the wreck and have identified the plane as Woodward's. Nearby is a rough grave dug in a shell pit and marked by a small cross made of two pieces of charred wood from the plane. There is no name, no dog tag. (Marinovitch says Woodward never carried one.) So it's him. Probably.

Woodward's story illustrates the uncertainty of death in combat. A fight takes place—but somewhere else, beyond the lines. Nobody sees it happen. A plane disappears; it must have crashed. A wreck is located (sometimes), a body is found (sooner or later, or maybe never) and identified (with more or less certainty). You can piece together a story, if you're persistent, but some of it will be guesswork; you won't *know*. Nobody will. *You* might die that way: the odds are real, and as the new men grow from beginners into seasoned working pilots, they'll learn to accept that. And learning about actual deaths will change them.

———

As more pilots came to the front, more pilots would be killed; that was just plain arithmetic. Many of the dead would be new boys, killed one way or another before they learned how to stay alive, or simply the victims of bad luck—a jammed gun, a faulty engine, a missed rendezvous, too many Germans.

Dick Blodgett has been at the front with the Ninety-Fifth Pursuit Squadron for weeks in the spring of 1918, waiting for action that can't begin until the squadron's machine guns turn up. Blodgett is very young—only twenty when he joins the squadron—and is self-conscious about his youth. "Talk about being an officer," he writes to his father, "why, unless you insist on being treated right and just refuse to let them get away with their brazen stuff, you are bossed around like a kid." It's not clear who his persecutors are—other officers? Or maybe senior enlisted men? But he *is* still a kid.

Early in May, Blodgett writes home jubilantly: at last they have guns for their planes! And he plunges at once into the story of his first trip over the lines with guns: how he was on a four-man patrol that got into a fight with two German planes, how the patrol split up, two attacking each Boche, and how his companion's guns jammed, leaving the second Boche to Blodgett alone:

> So I went in h—— bent for election. I maneuvered as much as possible so his machine gunner couldn't shoot at me, and let him have it. I shot two hundred and sixty rounds into him. I followed him all the way to his own aerodrome, killing his observer and, I think, starting a fire, as he was letting out clouds of smoke. My comrades were all split up and the last time they saw me I was following this German right home. They thought surely the anti-aircraft would get me, as I was very low, but they didn't even shoot at me. I ran out of gas just after recrossing the

lines into France; and they thought surely I had been brought down, until I telephoned in. It was a pretty exciting game.

That's the war story, but the excitement burbles on: "I love the game, and I wouldn't be in anything else for the world. It's individual work after the fight begins, and it's man to man fighting. We fought all the way from 20,000 feet altitude to about 5,000 feet. All the time we were going north into Germany. We covered about five miles."

Deullin would say: You flew too low; you followed your target too far into enemy territory (five miles is a long way back if the wind is against you); you let your plane run out of gas. Deullin would also reject Blodgett's definition of "the game" as individual work, man-to-man; hadn't this boy been listening? Why did he take such chances? Perhaps it was because on his way to the front he had made his "gambler's choice"— double or nothing. And so he went in, hell-bent and alone.

Four days later Blodgett writes again to his father. He's still keen on the work he's doing, but there's a dark side to it, too; the Ninety-Fifth has lost two captains. "It's a great game," he writes.

> But, Dad, we're giving them hell, we're winning . . . The cost is awful but it's worse for them. This sector is going to see some terrible casualties, but we've got to do it.
>
> If I go out, you can know that I went game, that before I went I brought one down.

It's his last letter.

A week later the family received a letter from an aide to the commanding general of the Army Corps. Their son is dead. The aide reports such details as he has: On May 17, Blodgett and another Ninety-Fifth pilot flew protection patrol for an observation plane, a German plane appeared, and Blodgett engaged it and drove it down behind enemy lines. The mission ended, and the two Americans turned back toward their home base, the other man low, Blodgett very high. They lost contact. The aide infers that Blodgett flew off on his own to look for another Boche. French infantry heard machine-gun fire high above them but because of the altitude and poor visibility could not see the planes. He can find no witnesses to the combat.

When Blodgett reappeared over his own lines, the aide continues, his flying was erratic. He seemed to be attempting to land, though he was still far from his own field. Suddenly his plane went into a slip (or into a vertical dive—accounts differ) and crashed. Help arrived quickly, and he was carried to a nearby hospital, but in less than an hour he was dead. There were two bullet holes in the underside of his plane, and a colonel to whom the aide spoke concluded that Blodgett had been in a fight, had been wounded—probably in the head—and had flown toward home until he lost consciousness. His death was classified as Killed in Action.

The diary of Waldo Heinrichs, also of the Ninety-Fifth, adds a few terse pilot's details: "Dick Blodgett returning from patrol got in fight with Boche, got two bullets and glided home, fainted in air & crashed. Neck broken, skull fractured."

———

Dick Blodgett was a beginner, killed on his second combat flight. But it wasn't only the new boys who fought and died in the air; old, experienced pilots fell in combat, too. Two days after Blodgett's death Raoul Lufbery—the man Rickenbacker called "the American Ace of Aces, the most revered American aviator in France"—was shot down within a few miles of the field at Toul where both the Ninety-Fourth and the Ninety-Fifth Squadrons were based.

The basic frame of the story is in the squadron combat report: "Alert 8h 55 to 9h 34, 3 planes, Major Lufbery, Major Huffer and Lt. Gude. Answered to St. Mihiel, altitude 1500 meters. Major Lufbery killed in action. 2 combats. See Pilots' Report."

If you flesh out that terse report, you'll get something like this: On the morning of May 19 at 8:55, three planes take off in response to a report from an observer at St. Mihiel that an enemy plane is in the air. The three pilots are two experienced majors—Lufbery and John Huffer— and one first lieutenant, Oscar J. Gude (who has never been in combat before). They climb to fifteen hundred meters, find the German plane (it's a biplace Albatros, and somebody engages it—apparently twice). Major Lufbery is killed.

There is one individual combat report filed for that day and time— Lieutenant Gude's:

Date—May 19, 1918.   Altitude, 1500 meters.   Squadron No. 94.
Hour of leaving, 8.55   Hours of arrival, 9.18.
Name of pilot, Lt. Gude.   Mission—Alert—Toul.

Combat with one Boche—350 to 400 rounds, at 9h 00 to 9h 10.
Attacked six times. Saw him go into a vrille near river southeast
of Camp, near Foret de Haye. Conf'n Asked. (sgd) O. J. Gude,
1st Lt. ASSRC.

On details of Lufbery's death personal accounts differ, but they
agree on some crucial points: that Lufbery engaged the enemy Albatros, that his plane fell, and that Lufbery jumped or fell from it and
struck the ground near a French village.

Eddie Rickenbacker was flying a patrol when the fight occurred.
When he landed, he heard the news from Major Huffer, the Ninety-
Fourth's commanding officer (who in this version had not been in the
air), and drove at once to the village where Lufbery's body had struck
the earth. He describes the scene: the body had fallen on a white picket
fence surrounding a peasant's garden, but already the villagers had rev-
erently removed it to the village town hall, where it lay in state, covered
with flowers. There was only one wound on the body, Rickenbacker
said: a bullet had cut away the thumb of Lufbery's right hand, the hand
that clasped the joystick.

Billy Mitchell was in his office in Toul when he heard of the fight;
he also drove to the village and got his version from the village shoe-
maker. Lufbery had flown so close to the enemy plane that they seemed
to touch and had fired four or five shots. The German did not reply.
Again he approached and fired, and this time the German replied with
a few rounds. The American plane pulled away and rolled over, and
what looked like a sack full of something fell out. The plane caught fire,
crashed, and burned up. There was no mark on Lufbery's body except
one bullet wound through the left hand.

Colonel Frank Lahm was umpiring a baseball game when he heard.
He wrote in his diary,

Word came in about 1 P.M. that Lufbery had been brought
down. It seems a two seater Boche came down over Toul, then on
to Ochey. Our people got the alerte [sic] and went up—Lufbery

had been up, came down & heard the report, jumped into an-other machine, found the Boche near Pont-St. Vincent and attacked, but was set on fire and jumped out of his machine to keep from being burned up. Too bad.

Three versions of the death of a great flier, none quite an eyewit-ness account. They tell essentially the same story, with a few variations—right hand or left hand—and a few more details (Lahm has apparently done his from a map). But on one crucial question they differ, and it's a question to which pilots wanted to know the answer: Did Lufbery jump?

To the young pilots Lufbery flew with, he was more than simply a more experienced flier; he was an older and wiser friend (he was thirty-three when he died) with whom they could talk about the techniques and problems and fears of combat flying. One question in particular came up a lot: If your plane catches fire in the air, what do you do? A latter-day pilot would say, "Bail out!" But in 1918, Allied pilots did not carry parachutes; you jumped or you burned. It was a terrible choice to contemplate, and so they *did* contemplate it. Even Billy Mitchell, that great cheerleader for war in the air, thought about it. In his memoir, in the middle of an enthusiastic account of the arrival of American avia-tion at the front, he pauses to think for a moment about death. "We had our losses, too," he writes, "which I shall not mention in this chronicle." So this will be a war story without the dying part; that's like him. But he goes on: "The burning of a pilot in the air as his ship catches fire from the hostile flaming bullets is a terrible thing. He is there alone, suspended in space, with no companion to share his misery, no man at his elbow to support him, as in the infantry on the ground. When he is wounded and falls, it is for thousands of feet, instead of two or three, as a man on the ground does."

Then Mitchell recovers his spirit: "We were inflicting a loss of at least three to one on the enemy, though, which was remarkable for a new outfit. Our men were full of dash and exceptionally cool in combat."

But for those few lines he has let the military mask slip and re-vealed the sympathetic man behind it, who can imagine what it must be like to burn to death in the air.

Lufbery had that kind of imagination, too; he thought about death by burning a lot. Alan Winslow remembered him remarking, a night or two before he fought his last fight, that if his plane should ever burst into flame, he would do his best to bring it down without jumping. Winslow thought that the circumstances of Lufbery's death proved, however, that to leap under such conditions is instinctive, and that Lufbery had jumped.

Rickenbacker also recalled a conversation with Lufbery on the subject of catching fire in the air (perhaps it was the same conversation that Winslow recalled; they were all in the same squadron):

> I had asked Luf what he would do in a case of this kind—jump or stay with the machine? All of us had a vast respect for Major Lufbery's experience and we all leaned forward to hear his response to this question.
>
> "I should always stay with the machine," Luf responded. "If you jump you certainly haven't got a chance. On the other hand there is always a good chance of side-slipping your aeroplane down in such a way that you fan the flames away from yourself and the wings. Perhaps you can even put the fire out before you reach the ground. It has been done. Me for staying with the old 'bus, every time!"

Yet, Rickenbacker concluded, Lufbery "had preferred to leap to certain death rather than endure the slow torture of burning to a crisp." There was a small stream below him; perhaps he was trying to jump into the water—as though that would make the leap rational.

Mitchell, too, tried to find an alternative to that suicidal jump. "I doubt very much," he wrote, "if an old pilot like Lufbery would have jumped on account of fire. All the eyewitnesses I have talked to said Lufbery fell out before the plane caught fire. I think it quite probable that Lufbery, in his hurry to get after the German plane, failed to tie himself in the plane with his belt; that the German shots cut his controls, his airplane turned over and he fell out." And he drew a planner's conclusion: "Just think—if he had had a parachute he could easily have been saved!"

Pilots' recollections of the events of that engagement differ in details, but they agree in including one other pilot in the story—the untried

Lieutenant Gude, the only pilot on the field prepared for flight when the invading Albatros first appeared, who took off to engage the enemy and returned with his ammunition entirely used up to claim a victory.

But there had been no victory; the German plane was still up there, so Lufbery took off to finish the job and died. His death wasn't exactly Gude's fault; Gude was on his way home when Lufbery attacked. But there was fault to be found in his performance. Rickenbacker describes it in two dismissive sentences: "His encounter was plainly seen by all the spectators who gathered about our hangars . . . Gude began firing at an impossible range and continued firing until all his ammunition was exhausted, without inflicting any appreciable injury upon the two-seater Albatros."

So did Mitchell: "As I left my automobile [at the airfield], I could see one of our airplanes engage the German ship but in an utterly futile way. The pilot did not close up but expended all his ammunition uselessly in the air." And he adds, "For this performance I sent the pilot to the rear."

The rest of Gude's story can be briefly told. He stayed with the Ninety-Fourth for nearly two months (he was still flying patrols with the squadron in early July). Then he was moved to the Ninety-Third and flew with them until mid-October. On October 22 he took off alone in a plane that belonged to his C.O., Major Huffer; he flew directly to a German-held airfield (at Metz, or Mars-la-Tour, or Tichémont—stories differ), landed, and surrendered, saying (in some versions), "Fini la Guerre." German pilots gathered round the captured Spad and had their pictures taken. Gude was put in a German POW camp, where other captured pilots knew him, and added their own recollections to the growing story. Alan Winslow put him in one of his *Liberty* articles in 1933, though he gave the character a pseudonym because Gude was still alive. "A good pilot," Winslow wrote, "but in combat a complete washout . . . he not only knew he was yellow in combat but would admit it."

Three pilots of the First Pursuit Group: two dead, one disgraced. The two dead men are very different in their combat experience: Dick Blodgett is new to the game, on his second combat patrol; Raoul Lufbery is the Ace of Aces, nobody knows more about the killing business. Their deaths occur two days apart, and so do their funerals.

Waldo Heinrichs attended both funerals and describes them in his diary. First Blodgett: On Saturday, May 18, the Ninety-Fifth forms for the funeral and rides in trucks to the cemetery on the grounds of the evacuation hospital nearby. All of the squadron's flying officers are there (Heinrichs notes that they march very well in the funeral procession), as well as some from the Ninety-Fourth, and a small group of nurses. Members of Blodgett's flight are pallbearers. An honor guard fires volleys in salute, and taps is sounded over the grave. Most impressive, Heinrichs says—a formal, military, reverent ceremony, as a soldier's funeral should be.

Two days later it's Lufbery's turn. His funeral is at the same hospital burial ground. This time there are two generals present—one American, the other French (they both make speeches)—and many French and American aviators, and Red Cross nurses galore. Five planes fly low over the grave and drop flowers. Taps sounds and echoes from the woods; very beautiful, Heinrichs says. It's a more elaborate funeral than Blodgett's, but it's the same solemn ceremony; in death they are the same and merit the same honors. They are buried side by side.

TEN

ABROAD II:
GETTING ACQUAINTED

Apilot's work is never a full-time job, not even when there's a war going on. Wherever you are in the system—whether you're in flight training, or stuck in some *embusqué* post, or in a combat squadron at the front—you'll spend most of your time on the ground. On your busiest day there will be time between flights, and mealtimes, and just sitting-around-waiting time. Evenings will be free, and for most pilots the night, and (at least at the training fields) Sundays. Some days will be no-fly days: the weather will be bad, or there won't be enough operational planes, or no missions will be scheduled. It won't be like life in the trenches, where the war is always present and there is no chance to escape the mud and the shells.

The life of a pilot left plenty of opportunities to get away from planes and airfields and become acquainted with the country beyond. You might commandeer a squadron car (there seemed to be a lot of them available) and drive to the nearest town and just look around. Weekends were sometimes free; you might take a train to Paris or London. *Permissions* for a few days of rest and relaxation were possible: you could travel farther, to some seaside resort—Deauville, or Cannes, or Nice, or Biarritz, or, if you were based in England, Bournemouth. Wherever you went, you'd have opportunities to taste the life in this strange new country—life as it was lived away from war—and to learn your way around in it.

Issoudun is in a pretty part of France, and the students seemed to have plenty of free time to explore it. They could walk out into the countryside, away from the roar and bustle of the airfield, and enjoy the old France that war hadn't changed: there'd be a château, or an old church, or a peasant plowing with oxen, or a little inn where the inn-keeper in his big blue apron would invite you to stop and have some beer, "car vous devez avoir soif sur la grande route." If you were one of the flying officers there, doing an *embusqué* job, you might have a motor-cycle at your command (as Quentin Roosevelt and Ham Coolidge both had) and ride it off to towns like Bourges and Nantes, and even Char-tres (Roosevelt stopped at the cathedral there to light a candle). Or a couple of you might borrow planes and just tour the neighborhood, buzzing châteaus and doing stunts for the folks on the ground. In warm weather they swam in local streams; in cold weather they found an inn and drank with the peasants and practiced their French on the patron's daughters.

In England the members of what had been the Italian detachment, and became the Oxford detachment, learned to take the pleasures that Oxford offered. John Grider and his friend Larry Callahan rode bicy-cles out into the Oxfordshire countryside and took tea at "Lady Some-body's house." Archie Taber rode a hunter from the local livery stable across the fields, "jumping hedges and fences and water-hazards," and hoped to ride in a meet with the Heythrop hounds; he also rowed on the Thames with the Queen's and Exeter crews. George Vaughn and Callahan played ragtime piano at college parties, and Callahan taught the English students how to mix cocktails. Forty years later Callahan remembered that "we never had more fun in our lives than we did at Oxford." That fun had nothing to do with the war; it had everything to do with being young and back in college.

Wherever they trained, in England or in Scotland or in France, the young Americans found the local gentry hospitable and eager to invite them to their country houses for dinner or for weekends. The pilots were impressed by the style of the lives these people lived; they wrote home about the country-house life or stored the details in their memo-ries, to be recounted many years later. George Vaughn was training at the School of Aerial Fighting at Ayr, in Scotland, when he was invited, along with three other Americans and a dozen British officers from the school, to a private dance at a large estate nearby. "There were just about enough girls to go around," he recalled, "and we certainly had an enjoyable evening. The house was an immense one, with a history dating way back somewhere, but still so remodeled inside that it is very modern." (That mixture of a vague sense of the presence of history and approval of modern improvements is a very American reaction.)

The party sounds very proper and sedate; no doubt it is well chaperoned. A few days later Vaughn goes to a dance at another country house and has a good time. He's invited back for an afternoon of tennis and tea. He concludes that he has "quite broken into the high society of Ayr and the vicinity."

The country houses of France were just as hospitable. Doug Campbell wrote home from Issoudun in the late autumn of 1917 to tell the folks about Sunday dinner at a château belonging to a French general— about the château itself ("late 1400's, fitted up and improved in splendid taste") and the perfectly wonderful meal, all kinds of hors d'oeuvres and three meat courses. And about the four kinds of wine, including champagne and burgundy. Campbell's host is the grandson of one of Napoleon's marshals; he shows his American guests an epaulet worn by Napoleon at Waterloo. The whole party is a new experience for them: formal splendor, surrounded by time and history.

Roland Richardson recalled another invitation at Issoudun during the time when he and a lot of other student pilots were building the base. One day, on a road that ran beside the camp, a car pulled up and a Frenchman got out. Were there any Americans present who spoke French? he asked. Richardson replied that he did, whereupon the Frenchman invited him to his house for dinner, along with any other French-speaking pilots he knew. Richardson could only think of Quentin Roosevelt. That evening the Frenchman (his name was M. Normant) sent his car for the two of them, and, Richardson recalled, they had a very pleasant evening with the Normant family. Roosevelt would pay many more visits to the Normants' house, often with his friend Hamilton Coolidge. Coolidge described one such visit in a letter to his mother in the spring of 1918: "Yesterday Q. and I sailed up to the Normants! Side by side we flew in our little buses, making faces at each other occasionally just for amusement. Golly, it's fun, mammy! They always meet us at the field [not an airfield, a pasture] in their auto and take us to the house not much over a mile away." They spend a "glorious, peaceful day there." Quentin would come to regard the Normants as his "family in France." Not many Americans would penetrate that far into the heart of their host society.

The Americans training in the Oxford ground school also received invitations. John Grider described some of them in letters to his friends back in Arkansas: he has lunch with "Lord and Lady Ostler, the famous doctor"; he dines with an official of the American Embassy in London and with a woman violinist—"the perfect example of the more intellectual type of society woman"—who is also busy with war work, two days a week plowing and the rest driving an Army car. A Miss Cannon invites him to tea, and he accepts and discovers that his hostess wears a monocle and that he can hardly understand anything she says and she can't understand him. That doesn't prevent her from extending another invitation, this time to ten of the Americans at the ground school, to come to a little dance. They all come. "I picked out a very select company," Grider writes, "all of them showed up sober except two."

One of the two drunks performs an Indian war dance in the middle of the floor; Grider says he never laughed so much in his life. It isn't quite the sort of dancing Miss Cannon had in mind, but the incident doesn't seem to have soured the relationship; in a letter a few days later Grider reports, "I have an awfully sweet girl in Oxford, a Miss Cannon."

Parties in London are bigger and classier. Grider writes to his hometown friend Emma (who is also his banker), explaining why he has just drawn six hundred dollars from his empty account: "I had a wonderful party at the Savoy last week and drew for six hundred. If you don't take care of me, I'll be put in jail. This London is *some* place, you would love it! I had dinner there several nights and all the women wear evening gowns, all the men in uniform, having fourteen days' leave from the front. It is some wild place."

In Grider's mind, wildness is a desirable quality—not only at parties, but everywhere in a flier's life. When he and his friends Larry Callahan and Elliott Springs (Grider thinks of the three of them as the Three Musketeers) are selected by the RAF ace Billy Bishop to join his 85 Squadron, Grider is delighted. It's one of the finest squadrons in existence, he tells Emma, "made up of the best there is, a hard fighting, hard flying, hard drinking lot of perfect princes!"—which is another way of saying they're wild all the time, like Grider. So getting drunk at the Savoy isn't a pointless, dissolute thing to do; it's simply one more expression of a basic pilot's value, another kind of risk taking.

There are plenty of agreeable young women in London to take risks with. Grider describes his London doings in a letter to Emma in February: "Emma, I have had more wild parties at the Savoy. That is the greatest hotel in the world. Three of us go down and get a suite, have dinner served in the rooms for six and the party is on."

But in May, the tone changes. "Emma," he writes,

at last I am having real romance. I wish you could see the girl. The only trouble with her is her salary. She gets five thousand pounds a year and has a very nice private income besides. She is one of the most sought after women in London and almost every evening I strut into the Carlton or the Ritz with this wonderful vision on my arm. All the women hate her and copy her clothes.

The vision's name is Billie Carleton; she is a popular actress on the London stage, and the country boy from Arkansas is dazzled by the company she keeps: "We are going with the fastest, keenest crowd in London," he writes to Emma, "and I have gotten away with the handsomest, most charming and sought after girl in the drove. Some class!"

Two weeks later, when 85 Squadron was ordered to the front, Grider took with him a good-luck charm from Billie: "I wish you could see the mascot I have, a beautiful doll with hair from the donor's head and dressed exactly in a duplicate of my favorite costume. Billie Carleton gave her to me and she rides in a mica case in the back of my fuselage."

He flew with his mascot until a patrol on June 18, when he left it behind in the hangar. He didn't return and was reported Missing in Action; later, a German message drop confirmed that Grider—the risk taker, the wild man—was dead.

Billie Carleton died some six months later in her London flat, of a cocaine overdose. An inquest into her death began in early December and was reported in the London *Times* in headlines that were, for the staid *Times*, sensational:

MISS BILLIE CARLETON'S
DEATH.
MYSTERY OF A GOLD BOX.
STORY OF GIFT OF DRUGS.

The cast of characters at the inquest might have come from a West End melodrama: a cinema actor, an English woman married to a Russian, an Army officer, Mrs. Vernon Castle (the popular ballroom dancer), a woman named Lo Ping You. Their testimony was just as theatrical: they told of furtive drug dealing, of cocaine sniffing at the London Victory Ball, and of opium-smoking orgies in Mayfair.

Grider doesn't seem to have known that his wonderful vision was an addict.

Across the Channel, the pilots at Issoudun and Tours—both the flight students and the *embusqués*—spend as much of their on-the-ground time in Paris as the Three Musketeers spend in London, but less wildly, with less attention to hard drinking and more attention to girls, or more often to one girl. That difference may simply reflect a different city life. In Paris the parties happen not in hotel suites but in the cafés and bars where pilots congregate. The pilots name those places in their journals and memoirs: the Grande Bretagne bar, the Astra bar across the street, Ciro's, Henri's, the Crillon, Tourelle's, the Brasserie Universelle, the Café de la Paix, the Café des Sports, the Artistes. In such public, convivial places, with a girl you like, getting falling-down drunk isn't an option. The language problem must also be a factor: if your girl speaks only French, and your command of that language is uncertain, you'd better stay sober or you won't get anywhere.

At first the girls have no names—they're simply "a girl I met," or "our French girl," or "ma femme." But gradually they become persons: they're called Madi, or Maria, or Jeanne, or Georgette. They're all pretty, and some of them have further, or more individual, qualities: one has a good head on her shoulders; another has a sense of humor. All of them are different from the girls back home.

As in London, most of the pilots' meetings with these girls are brief encounters, but others have such permanence as wartime allows. Walter Avery meets his Jeanne in May 1918, while he's at Le Bourget flying with a Defense of Paris squadron, and for the next two months they are often together—in the Bois de Boulogne, on the boulevard Montparnasse, in the Luxembourg Gardens and the Tuileries. She seems to be showing him her town. Then, in July, Avery gets his orders to the front. He and Jeanne have a farewell party à deux, and the romance seems to be over.

But it isn't. In late August, Avery returns to Paris (he's taking his friend Waldo Heinrichs to a hospital there) and spends the afternoon in the Jardin du Luxembourg, "loafing, reading and looking for Jeanne *chez-elle*." He seems to have found her, for his next day's journal reads, "Goodbye Jeanne 1 P.M." He misses his ride back to the airfield and stays another night.

The women the young pilots meet in Paris are not all French. As the war goes on and the American role in it expands, more and more young American women come on the scene. They're Red Cross girls, who serve coffee and cookies and hand out letter paper in the Red Cross huts that are in every camp, or they're nurses or nurses' aides in the American military hospitals. They have the comfortable attractiveness that familiar people and things have: a group of you—young men and women—can go out together to a party, or supper in the country, or dance to a phonograph in some girl's room, and feel easy because you're behaving by the social rules you learned back home. "It has been great fun," George Moseley wrote in his journal of evenings with his friend Stuff Spencer and some American girls, "as it is a treat to be able to talk without any effort to someone who understands you." The nurses give dances at their hospital residences and invite the young pilots. The pilots come, and though the ratios are not ideal—there tend to be five males for every female—there's a certain comfort in that, too. These are nice girls: there'll be no wildness here.

For some of the young pilots that's a relief. Percival Gates goes on meeting Bernadine, the nurse he danced with on the troopship coming over. Later he visits her at her hospital in Limoges; they take another town walk. "I had a wonderful time," Gates writes in his journal, "talking over our trip across and everything we had done together at Brest and what we had each done in the meantime. Anyone outside the Army and outside of France cannot possibly appreciate what it means to have lady friends over here. Especially when they are just like sisters. That is the way most of the American girls are who come over here."

He visits her again three weeks later. They have dinner in a hotel and go out in the country on bicycles for a couple of hours. "Bernadine is only a friend and a pal," he insists, "nothing more . . . She is a peach and like an older sister to me."

One must remember, among all the stories of parties and drinking binges and wild women on street corners, that there were also straitlaced young men like Gates, who abstained from both the drinking and the girls and viewed the goings-on of their fellow pilots with a severe distaste. Many of them were the sons of clergymen—Gates's father was a Baptist minister, and so was Waldo Heinrichs's—and their letters home sometimes read like sermons on the wickedness of the world, full of reprehensions of the drinking and gambling and smutty language and of "orgies" with harlots.

Some of these censorious lads mellow in the pilots' atmosphere of hard living and hard flying. Once Heinrichs joins the notoriously wild Ninety-Fifth, his journal entries change, and he begins to confess attraction for the girls he meets. There's a very pretty French mademoiselle "who could not keep her pretty eyes at home"; he'd like "walking, talking, dining with her," but decides to think it over. And an American nurse named Janette, whom he actually takes out walking and afterwards laments "this wretched war that takes men from the company of fine girls." And he actually goes into a bar in Bar-le-Duc and buys some liquor. You might call Heinrichs's change a kind of conversion experience, the consequence of his exposure to France and to the war.

But they're still young Americans just past the years of their boyhood, and they retain the tastes and habits of those years and revert to them in their on-the-ground leisure. They play baseball: at Dunkerque in the spring of 1918, Kenneth MacLeish and the other Americans in RAF Squadron 213 play a team that's mostly Canadian and beat them 16–1; they have a game down on the beach nearly every evening, he says, and the whole town turns out to watch them. And in Paris, Harvey Conover takes time out from the partying to watch a ball game out in St. Cloud, in the western suburbs. At their field near Toul, the Ninety-Fifth plays a close one with the Ninety-Fourth and wins 14–13. Some of the boys play horseshoes; it's a farmers' game, back home.

Conover spends an evening at the Casino in Paris, where Gaby Deslys and a chorus of English girls are performing, and is moved by "the Jazz Band imported from New York, which makes you shed tears of homesickness." Food makes them homesick, too. Gates goes to a Red Cross dance at Issoudun. "It was too crowded to dance much," he writes in his journal, "but there were a lot of American girls there from various Canteens and they had some ice cream and cake which reminded me more of America than most anything else." In a letter written the same day, he is still thinking about the food: "We actually had ice cream and cake and lemonade! That is one thing I think I missed more than anything else in the food line—ice cream."

At their fields at the front, when the weather is fine, they go swimming in the local river. Lance Holden is at Saints with the Ninety-Fifth:

This afternoon a bunch of us went to Melun for a swim in the Seine. Wow! But it felt good to get in the water again. They had a spring board 10 ft off the water that gave good diving. Somehow swimming and diving around with a bunch of boys in trunks—was a pleasant relief from the constant reminder of war that a uniform gives. I almost thought I was leading the old carefree vacation life when I noticed the scar on Gill's leg where a bullet had gone in. It seemed scarcely possible that next day we would be trying to kill men.

For an afternoon they're boys again, back home. But the river isn't the Wabash or the Tombigbee; it's the Seine. Beyond the horizon the guns roar, shells burst, planes dive and climb. The war goes on, and they are part of it.

ELEVEN

IN PURSUIT

I n the early weeks of 1918 more American pilots moved up to the front—not many, but a few. Some arrived with newly formed squadrons: the Ninety-Fifth reached the French airfield at Villeneuve-les-Vertus, south of Reims, in February; the Ninety-Fourth came up a month later to the same field. Back at Issoudun, Quentin Roosevelt heard about the Ninety-Fifth's move and rushed to his commanding officer to demand a place in the squadron. The colonel said no and explained why: the move was only a political gesture so the U.S. Air Service could say it had a squadron at the front. "They haven't even got machines for them yet," he said, "or any sort of an organization to allow for breakage and spare parts. What will happen to them is that they will move out into a camp that is not yet finished, up in the zone of advance,—and then sit there for a month." He promised Roosevelt a place in a *real* squadron as soon as one turned up.

A scattering of other new pilots moved up individually from where they waited—at Issoudun or Tours, or at training fields in England, or (a few) from fields down in the foot of the Italian boot. As they moved to the front, they heard sounds and rumors of war in progress. Tom Buffum, on his way to join Escadrille SPA 77 at Fère-en-Tardenois, paused for a night in Paris and woke the next morning—he remembered that it was March 21, the first day of spring—to the sound of explosions, which continued through the day and the following night. The Parisians began to show signs of hysteria, he said; they didn't know what was happening. Neither did he. When he reached Fère the next day, he was told that pilots of his new squadron had searched the skies over Paris the night before looking for enemy bombers but had found none. Of course they didn't: the explosions weren't bombs, they were shells from Big Bertha, the huge German gun fired on Paris from seventy kilometers north of the city. The shelling was the beginning of the German spring offensive.

American pilots too far from the attack to hear the thunder of the guns heard rumors of it. George Moseley, based at a U.S. naval seaplane station near Dunkerque, was aware that something was going on somewhere and wrote home enviously a week after the offensive began: "This front has been fairly quiet since the big push farther inland. I certainly do wish that I was in it. It is the biggest battle in the history of the world. It is hard to be so close and yet so far from it."

Ham Coolidge, still back at Issoudun testing planes, heard the rumors, too. He wrote to his mother about them on Easter Sunday, March 31:

It seems absurd to discuss such insignificant things as our little private doings here when this terrific drive is going on, but I absolutely cannot say anything about it that I should like to say. Suffice it though, that the work of the French and British Flying Corps in dispersing infantry attacks sends little thrills up my spine every time I think of it, and makes me more impatient than ever before to get up there and into the *mêlée*.

Ten days later, Alan Nichols wrote to his parents, explaining how rumor works in a war. He'd been out hunting (rabbits, not Boches):

When we came back, we discovered all the pilots closely grouped around the Captain, who was giving orders right and left, handing out maps and information all at once. This is what they told us, "The Boches have attacked on the English front. They are *on the Somme* already." All sorts of wild speculations began to fly. If you will take a map and trace the Somme, you will see how little information that gave us. Were they on the part that

runs north and south, or were they farther? Perhaps even as far
as Amiens? No one knew, but everyone had an idea.

Nichols's escadrille was ordered to prepare to move the following morning. All night the men worked loading trucks. In the morning the orders
were canceled. The pilots began to speculate again. But nothing happened. "All we heard was rumor," Nichols wrote. "No newspapers, no
letters, just talk. Speculation ran riot." That's the way news travels in a
war zone; you don't know anything about what's happening, not even
what your own unit is doing, or will do tomorrow. And so you make it
all up. The young pilots knew that a battle was being fought, somewhere, and in their imaginations they made it huge, terrific, the biggest
ever. They wanted to be in it, wherever it was.

The spring offensive wasn't an American battle; there were no
American ground troops engaged, and no Air Service squadrons. But
Americans were there, in French escadrilles and in Royal Flying Corps
squadrons. The stories they told of those days at the end of March 1918
describe war at its most chaotic—and what they learned from it.

Curtis Kinney had just joined the RFC's No. 3 Squadron at a field
near Albert; he was still in what he called his "breaking-in period," flying his practice flights, when the offensive began. By March 25, No. 3's
planes were within range of the German guns. Shortly before dusk that
day the squadron was ordered to move all its planes and equipment
west to a field at Doullens. The pilots grabbed their flying gear and ran
to their planes, and Kinney ran with them. He was the last to take off.
In his haste he forgot to fasten his seat belt.

Once in the air, Kinney looked around for the other planes but
didn't see a single one. He flew on alone through the gathering night,
and as he flew, the flashes of the German guns got bigger and brighter—
not because of the increasing darkness, but because he was flying toward them. There was no point in turning back—there was no place to
go back to—and he had no idea where Doullens was, so he looked for a
flat place to put his plane down.

A full moon rose, and that helped a little; he found what looked like
an open field and settled in for a landing. As the plane rolled along the
ground, a wing struck a post he hadn't seen, and the plane flipped over.
Because he hadn't fastened his belt, he was thrown halfway out of the
cockpit—not crushed by the wreckage, but pinned to the ground and

unable to move. He heard voices approaching. *Germans?* They came nearer. "'Ere, mates," a Cockney voice called. "'E's over 'ere." He was carried to a field hospital, but when he saw that the wounded soldiers around him were all worse off than he was, he slipped away and returned to his squadron and went on flying.

You might call Kinney's adventure another breaking-in lesson, not in how to retreat—no training manual would recommend taking off at sundown in a plane you haven't entirely learned to fly, with your safety belt unfastened, to look for a field you've never flown into—but in what a retreat *feels* like, the confusion, the uninformed disorder, the muddle of it all.

American pilots with active squadrons described the chaos of that first day of the offensive. G. de Freest Larner was with the French escadrille SPA 86 near Noyon. He flew a patrol that morning into German airspace at five hundred meters altitude, in a fog so heavy that he couldn't tell where he was and almost landed on a German field. "All the French balloons were brought down," he wrote, "making it impossible to tell what was going on behind the enemy lines, and all our aviation fields had to be abandoned. No telephones, no balloons, no observation planes—we did not even know the location of our own lines." It was all too vast, he wrote, for him to describe. And then he described it: "the burning towns; exploding ammunition dumps, abandoned by the French; dead horses and men, scattered along the roads; the hammer-blows of machine guns, shooting up fountains of fiery bullets as you sweep low overhead."

The fog that Larner flew in seems an apt metaphor for what the retreat was like—war without information about either side. At the beginning, troop positions changed hour by hour, and lines of communication broke down; nobody knew where the enemy forces were or what planes and pilots were at hand to oppose them. Missions to be flown were not assigned to squadrons trained and equipped for that particular job; you simply did what had to be done. On one French-held stretch of the lines, two escadrilles of Breguets and one group of Spads were all the planes there were; they flew every kind of flight—reconnaissance, infantry liaison, ground attacks—and they flew all the time. One American flying with a French escadrille looked back from the end of the offensive at the work his squadron had done: "We flew six hours a day; mostly reconnaissance, flying very low over the enemy, shooting the troops in the trenches, the cavalry on the roads, and detachments of cannon and *ravitaillement* [supplies]."

And he added, as though in an afterthought, "Three men were brought down, including myself." A bullet from the ground had cut a magneto wire and stopped his engine. He managed to land between the lines and ran toward the French trenches while German troops took potshots at him with machine guns. He escaped uninjured.

New pilots who came to fighting squadrons during the spring offensive learned a complex, useful lesson: how to retreat and fight an attacking enemy at the same time. They also learned that even if they were pursuit pilots, they wouldn't always be up at ten thousand feet, each a solitary knight hunting his Boche. They might spend most of their time down below in the smoke and tumult of the common soldiers' war, roaring along at ground level, many planes together making one offensive weapon, or low over enemy territory looking for troops, or supplies, or anything else that moved—doing what was ordered, what was needed.

Pilots called that kind of flying "low work"—attacking at ground level whatever lay in front of your own troops, clearing their way to advance, or giving them time to retreat. There was nothing glorious about it, but there was exhilaration. Flying close to the ground always stirs the blood: the lower you are, the greater your sense of speed. Things on the earth below rush toward you, seem to rear up suddenly into sight and just as quickly stream beneath and are gone behind you, into the past, the place where you have just been. Landscape is different down there, hills you pass are higher than you are, trees are horizons, towns are sudden rooftops, water towers are monuments. Even the weather is different: earth weather, below the cloud cover, in a space full of smoke and haze that you fly *through*, not over or under.

If you're a combat pilot attacking a ground target, what you see is different: your vision is narrowed, confined to what you see through your gun sight. Your sensations are different, too: you feel a tension that is close to fear and a rush of adrenaline as your guns chatter and the tracers spout up at you from below. It's flying outside ordinary time, a headlong moment; one pass and you're gone, before the debris has had time to settle back to earth. You've gotten away with it again. There'd be little room in that anonymous storm of attack for personal heroism, but there'd be excitement enough. "This offensive," Larner wrote, "is proving the most instructive, the most exhausting, and the most thrilling experience I ever expect to have." To an adventurous young man at war, all those adjectives are positive—war *ought* to be like that.

Frederick Ordway, who joined the Twenty-Seventh Pursuit Squadron later that spring, cataloged the low work his squadron did in a letter home: "I have been flying over the lines every day, sometimes two or three times a day. Have been patrolling, protecting bombing, artillery spotting, and photography machines, fighting, scouting, strafing, and running barrages of anti-aircraft guns." "Strafing," from the German *strafen*: to punish; it meant low-flying planes machine-gunning ground targets, especially trenches.

Other pursuit squadrons had other low-work jobs to do. Sometimes they carried bombs—small bombs, twenty-pounders that they dropped on low-work targets. Sometimes they dropped other things: supplies to their own troops, and cigarettes, and newspapers; and propaganda leaflets on the Germans (who dropped propaganda back on them). Sometimes they flew "contact patrols," low flights over the front to establish exactly where the lines were that day. That was dangerous work—flying so low that you were in the same air that artillery shells from both sides passed through, and close enough to the ground to be sniped at by every rifle and machine gun below you, including your own troops, who didn't always distinguish between their planes and the enemy's. Pilots back at their airfields after such flights counted the bullet holes in their planes. It was a point of pride, a kind of small-boy boasting, like coming home from a football game with your jersey torn—evidence that you had been in the thick of it.

Other patrols—offensive patrols, they called them—were explicitly for Boche hunting. They'd be flown a bit higher. Such patrols might amount to just a lot of flying around over the lines looking for your enemies, who might not show up or might appear in distant formation but decline to fight, turning back to their own safe territory, leaving the sky empty again. Or they might stay in sight, hovering just out of reach, and your flight leader might choose—for reasons you wouldn't understand—not to engage them. Whatever he did, your job was to follow his lead. Looking for a fight was a collective action that you did in formation; that was the safest way, especially for beginners.

Up there in formation, new pursuit pilots learn further combat lessons. About antiaircraft fire (which the British call Archie), and what to do about it. First you see puffs of smoke—black if they're German, white if they're from Allied guns. If the burst is close, you'll feel the concussion and hear it—like a loud cough; if it's *very* near, you can even smell it—like burned rags—and you'll jerk your controls about, bank sharply, or dive, to throw the gunners down below off their aim.

Alan Nichols, new to the front that winter, wasn't used to being shot at when he described his complex feelings about antiaircraft fire. Like all artillery fire, it came without warning:

> We were peacefully plowing along when they opened up. The way they got the altitude was uncanny, but they missed on distance and position.
>
> I was on the Boche side of the patrol. The first black puff opened up in front of me and to my right, but on my level. It had an angry red flame in it. Then came the "ker-blam!" just like the sound on the ground, only muffled by the roar of my motor.
>
> The second puff popped to my left, just opposite the other. [He's being bracketed; the next shell should burst midway between the other two—just where his plane is flying.] Now the puffs looked wicked, no longer beautiful, because I thought how full they were of flying lead.
>
> I looked at each wing, half expecting to see great holes, and I waited a long moment for the third shot. It went off behind and under to the right, but by then I had her wide open, climbing and "S"ing. It excited me with an exalted thrill. I didn't have time to be afraid. Afterwards, I was disappointed not to find any holes.

It's a convincing account of the event itself: where the shells burst, and what Nichols did to evade the next one. But what's most interesting is how the language of emotions enters the story. Nichols's first response to the bursting shells is aesthetic: the puffs of smoke that linger in the air are beautiful. Only after he thinks of the flying shrapnel around him do they become wicked. Still, he's exhilarated. By what, exactly? By the danger that he has just passed through? Or by his vigorous response to it? Or simply by the fact that at last he's been in the war—all the way in—and hasn't faltered. His realization, after the event, that he wasn't afraid is a reaction that many combat pilots will recognize: in the middle of an action you're too busy doing your job to have time for fear.

On those first patrols they learn more about tactics. They learn that patrols don't usually go over the lines in a single formation but in layers, one group leading, the other behind and higher to protect the first. If the lower formation is attacked, the higher one dives and attacks the attackers. The Germans may also be flying in layers, and their upper flight will plunge in, until there are more planes in the fight than you can count, all milling, twisting, turning, diving, and the air is full of the smoke trails of tracer bullets. It won't be much like the friendly dogfight games they played back in Issoudun.

They'll learn to look up, and behind, and toward the sun (where an enemy patrol may be hovering). And when to refuse a fight. You might spot a German two-seater alone below you; it's tempting—it looks like an easy kill. But look up: there are ten Boches above you, waiting to pounce, and maybe still more off to the west, between you and home. A trap! Both sides set them and admire each other's skill (Lance Holden describes escaping from one and adds, "It had been a beautiful trap"—as though outsmarting your enemy were an art form).

And so they flew their first patrols and saw what the earth at war was like: the treeless, shell-torn ground, the blown-in trenches, the ruined towns, and beyond the front the French roads, white and straight and bordered by poplars, that are the only dependable guides to where you are. And they felt the strange beauty of it all: how the flashes of the artillery show up most brilliantly in the hours before first light, and how sunrise is more splendid seen from the air high above the mud and desolation, how the dawn repays the discomfort and the danger. And saw—or didn't see—their first German plane. And learned—or didn't learn—the lessons of flying disciplines.

———

Not all the pursuit squadron flights that winter and spring were flown close to the ground; there was plenty of high work to do, too. High might mean Boche-hunting patrols at 5,000 or 10,000 feet, or it might mean altitudes up to 20,000 feet, or even higher, depending on the plane you were flying. By pilots' accounts a Spad might reach 20,000 feet (Dick Blodgett got that high); Rickenbacker got a Nieuport to 22,000; Bogart Rogers made it to 20,000 in a Camel (it took him an hour to get there); Fred Libby took a fully loaded DH-4 to 22,500 (higher, he noted proudly, than a Camel or an SE-5 could go); Minor Markham managed 17,000 in a Salmson.

These high flights were flown without oxygen: the technology for putting oxygen in pursuit planes simply didn't exist in 1918, and aviation medicine doctors were still working to understand what altitude sickness was and how it affected pilots. But the pilots knew; they mention the physical effects they feel of breathing the thin air at high altitudes: the violent headaches, feelings of faintness and weakness, breathlessness, and pressure on their eardrums coming down. Rickenbacker tells the story of a fellow pilot who had fainting spells at altitude and spun in. But they don't complain; they just climb. When Fred Libby lands after his high-altitude adventure, his adjutant simply gives him a shot of oxygen and a couple of scotch and sodas, and that, Libby says, clears up the old head.

You might be ordered to attack—or try to attack—a German photographic plane, which would have oxygen tanks aboard and would cross the lines at twenty-two thousand feet. If you were in a Spad, you'd get to nineteen thousand or twenty thousand feet, where you'd just have to hang on your prop and squirt your guns up at the intruding Boche above you. Your bullets would fall short of their target, gravity would seize them, and they'd fall to earth like rain. And so would you, stalled in the thin air.

Imagine what it was like, sitting up there at twenty thousand feet on a patrol, in an open cockpit the size of a barrel, with only a meager windshield to protect you from the slipstream that strikes your face at a hundred miles an hour, with no heating system except what blows back from the engine. Remember where they're flying. The Western Front lay across northern France between the forty-eighth and fiftieth north latitudes. If you run that line on eastward, it will cross Ukraine and Kazakhstan and northern Mongolia, reach the Pacific at Russia's Sakhalin Island, and cross the Pacific just south of the Aleutians. Run it west and it will touch the top of Newfoundland and continue across Canada past Winnipeg, missing the United States entirely. It's cold along that line in the winter. And in the spring, too.

It's not surprising that the young pilots, new to this refrigerated flying, describe in detail the clothes they wore: on their feet heavy woolen socks and fur-lined boots, on their legs woolen long underwear (maybe two pairs), heavy breeches, and woolen leggings. On their bodies an undershirt or two, a jersey, a shirt, a heavy sweater knit by Mom, and a leather coat, and on top of it all the heavy fur coverall that they called a "teddy bear." On their heads fur helmets, on their hands fur gloves on top of lighter gloves. How, one wonders, did a pilot dressed in all those clothes ever get himself into the cramped cockpit of a Nieuport?

In spite of all that wool and fur, they froze. I don't simply mean they were chilly; they *froze*. In a March letter Waldo Heinrichs writes an apologetic letter to his mother, explaining why he isn't keeping up with his piano playing: "I have been unable to continue my practicing because I froze the fingers on my left hand. I was up about 20,000 feet, and it was cold. I also froze my cheeks and nose, and I'm a great looking sight now. My face is peeling and I look as though I've been in an awful fight."

Dick Blodgett, who brought his violin to the front with him, complains (also in March, also to his mother) that he can't play it because he's frozen the fingertips of his right hand. A month later, Kenneth MacLeish, flying with the Royal Navy at Dunkerque, goes to twenty thousand feet and freezes three fingers and the thumb of his right hand. "These high patrols are torture," he tells his aunt Mary, "torture of the worst kind."

And yet, for all the discomfort, what they feel most is the exhilaration of being there. MacLeish, having told Aunt Mary how cold he is, goes on: "Oh, it's a wonderful, wonderful game, in spite of all the uncomfortable high patrols. A man can use his skill and his brain, and once in a while his nerve, if he has any. It's glorious. I wouldn't trade my experience for any other in the world."

————

In Fred Ordway's list of the pursuit pilot's work, fighting is only one job among many, but it's there; they *did* fight, plane against plane. Sometimes a fight occurred on a protection patrol; you're flying cover for an observation plane when Fokkers dive down on the slower, clumsier two-seater, and you dive, too, to protect it, or you're on a combat offensive patrol, sent out over the lines to attack any German plane you can find, and one turns up. Or you're sent up in a hasty takeoff from your airfield to intercept Germans who have appeared where they shouldn't be— right over your head.

One of the most told stories of the American air war concerns events in the sky above Toul on April 14, 1918—the first day on which an American squadron (it was the Ninety-Fourth) began regular patrols over the front. For the basic facts of the action, the squadron's daily operations report, written the same day, is the place to go:

> Two planes sent out on alert at 8:44, brought down two German Albatrosses D.A.5, one about 100 meters away from the Gengoult flying field by Lieutenant A. F. Winslow, the other

was brought down in flames about 200 meters from the same field by Lieutenant Douglas Campbell at 8:50. The German pilots were made prisoners. One of them being wounded, and the other one uninjured.

These took place at 500 meters altitude.

All the details of the action are there—the time, the place, the altitudes, the pilots, the planes, the prisoners. But it isn't a story, really; it's only the bare bones of one, as plain as a recipe; it leaves out the answers to the questions that any curious reader would impatiently ask: What happened up there? How did they do it? And, most important, what was it like? For answers to those normal human questions you'll have to go to the stories the men themselves told.

A letter Campbell wrote the following day begins, "It was a great war yesterday." He and Winslow are scheduled to stand by "on alert" that morning. At 8:45 the phone rings: two Boche planes have been sighted fifteen miles away. Five minutes later they're in the air. Visibility is poor; the air is misty; Winslow is flying at two hundred meters when Campbell joins him. Suddenly Winslow turns and chases a plane that's just above him, not over three hundred meters high. It has black crosses on its wings! Campbell hears Winslow shoot. He banks at ninety degrees to get a view below him, so as to help Winslow if necessary, and it's lucky he does, for just as he turns, he hears the pop-pop-pop of a machine gun behind him; another Boche is shooting at him. And another fight begins:

> For some reason or other I thought his tail was turned toward me as he shot, and the thought "Biplace, keep under him" flashed into my brain. He turned out afterwards to be an Albatross monoplane, but I had guessed wrong, and instead of getting above him, which would have been easier, I kept below him, maneuvering so as to try to get under his tail without letting him point toward me or get a shot at me from a broadside. In a biplace, you see, the gunner-passenger can shoot through a 180 degree arc behind the wings above the tail, and through large arcs down at the sides; while the pilot can shoot to the front by aiming his plane just as we do. It took over a minute to maneuver

into a position behind and under his tail without exposing myself to his fire (I thought), but I finally found myself right under
him. Then I pulled my nose straight up into the air and let him
have the bullets, and I think he got some in his motor, for I saw
some tracers hitting his nose. The next thing I knew, he was
diving at about 45 degrees, and I was behind and above him but
behind his tail. Then I got a good aim, pulled the trigger, and
held on to it. Two or three tracers hit him, and after about 50
rounds had been fired a streak of flame came shooting out of
his fuselage near the motor. I ceased firing, and watched him
land and crash in a ploughed field, his plane a mass of flame
and wreckage. The pilot had had sense enough to unfasten his
belt, and was thrown clear of the machine, escaping with some
bad burns and broken bones.

The story of a first victory couldn't be more immediate than that; the
emotions are still pulsing, the sights and sounds are still in Campbell's
head—the black crosses, the popping machine guns, the streak of flame,
the wreck. And the beginner's blunders that might have made the ending different—how *could* he have mistaken a monoplace for a biplace?

It's more than a beginner's excited story, though; it's also a kind of
instruction manual—Campbell's own "Chasse en monoplane," putting
down the lessons he's learned in his first fight, for his own benefit
and for the folks back home, to help them imagine an unimaginable
experience.

Winslow had got his Boche a minute or two earlier; Campbell saw
it fall, make a rough landing in a plowed field, and turn over. The entire
double victory had happened within five or six minutes. Both fights had
been fought directly above the Ninety-Fourth's airfield, so close and so
low—under a thousand feet—that witnesses on the ground—the pilots
and mechanics on the field, and even the citizens of Toul—could watch
the whole performance as from a grandstand, so near that Campbell
could land his plane and run to the wreck of his opponent's plane in
time to grab a few pieces as souvenirs. And so could everybody else:
gawkers streamed to the crash sites from the airfield and the town, on
foot, on bicycles, on motorcycles, and in automobiles, to stare and pick
at the wreckage.

Other pilots who were at Toul that day came, too, and later told their versions of the story. Colonel Frank Lahm, at that time an Air Service staff officer, in town on balloon company business, drives out to the airfield, past the hurrying crowds, in time to meet the two German pilots. The first, he wrote in his diary, is "a nice looking fellow under 20." Lahm asks him, "Offizier?" And the German replies, in perfect French, "Je suis adjutant." The pilot of the other plane is "a big husky typical German, 24 years old." He's lying on a stretcher; his face is badly burned, his legs, too, and one ankle has an ugly break.

Lahm moves on to examine the wrecks. One turned over in landing—the top wing surface is damaged, and the top of the tail is broken; souvenir hunters are already at it. The other wrecked plane is a smoldering ruin. Lahm thinks the pilot was lucky to be fighting so low; if he'd been higher, he'd have been completely burned before he got to the ground. The whole scene is observed with a pilot's eyes: What were the enemy pilots like? What shape were they in? What was left of their planes? The Boches, he learns, were from a newly formed squadron that had been assigned to that relatively quiet sector to get some experience.

Eddie Rickenbacker was there, too, flying a patrol up in the fog and mist while the fighting took place below him. When he landed, the two German planes were still burning. The pilots had been pulled from the wreckage, and Rickenbacker interviewed one (the other was beyond talking—he died shortly after). How did they happen to be above an American field in such weather? The survivor replied that they were lost and were trying to find their way home; they thought they were over Metz and that the field below them might be their own. So beginners had stumbled on beginners and had scored the first victories by American pilots in an American squadron.

The two victors are instantly famous in Toul. At a ceremony in the town square a French major pins the Croix de Guerre on both, and in any Toul café the drinks are free. Famous back home, too; Lance Holden's mother reads about the exploit in her local newspaper and sends a clipping to her son, who replies in June, with evident pride, that he has had dinner with Campbell—in Paris, at Madame Adrian's. Campbell, he says, is in Paris on a three-week leave, recovering from a bullet wound in the back:

Of course we talked flying and he described his fights. He has seven Boches now—each one means a thrilling story—He is to be ordered home, but expects to be able to get that changed—says he has just begun and why stop now. I hope they make him go, so you can see the type of man that is really doing the work of our air service—But don't you see, the real sports will insist on sticking right here without the cheers and welcomes they would get at home—Be careful who gets your applause. I used to think I wanted to get a couple of Boches and get home but examples like Doug's make things seem different. Such men make the world worth living in . . . But he is going with a smile into a game that has but one ending—what an end though! How I long to get a good machine and get out fighting with my friends who have done so well.

Holden reports his conversation with Campbell in the language of the young pilots: the "work" (by which he clearly means single combat between *chasse* planes); the "real sports" (the pilots who stay at the front to finish the job); the "game" (the whole fighting life, right up to the one dark ending). Add to those terms Campbell's wound, which Campbell, being the game pilot he is, ignores. It all makes one heroic myth in the mind of the admiring Holden, for whom it is all still ahead.

Campbell told his story of that first victory immediately, in letters and in conversation. Winslow waited fifteen years and then wrote his version in a series of articles that he published in *Liberty* magazine. His account is essentially the same as Campbell's as far as the facts go, but less individual, less excited, more a conventional war story, written in a style you might expect in the pages of a popular weekly: planes roar, guns bark, bullets scream. Any good journalist could have written it.

Only once does he seem to speak in his own voice. This is when, back at the field after the fight, he meets his opponent face-to-face:

He was badly shaken, but was perhaps not less nervous than I. It was a curious sensation to be face to face with the man with whom I had been having a machine-gun duel in the air but a few minutes before.

The crowd became silent; I felt awkward. I asked in German if he were wounded. Replying in perfect French he said that he had only been bruised in the crash, that the rudder controls of his plane—an Albatross D5—had been shot away and his engine put out of commission, but that fortunately my bullets had spared him . . .

I noticed that he was a non-commissioned officer; I had understood that all pilots of German pursuit planes held at least the rank of second lieutenant. Generally this was true, he said. He had been a pursuit pilot for over two years, but had not yet received his commission.

"*Pourquoi?*"

Bitterly he replied:

"Because I am a Pole."

He was then led away. As he left he raised his hand in a gesture indicating his relief at being alive, and remarked:

"That's all, then. This war is over, as far as I'm concerned!"

It's not the fight that moves Winslow; it's the man he fought—nervous and bitter and relieved to be done with war—a man Winslow can understand and feel sympathy for, a man like himself.

Doug Campbell's combat history ended two months later when he took that bullet in his back. After a stretch in a hospital he was ordered back to the States to inspect the training of *chasse* pilots; he never returned to the war. Winslow remained at the front with the Ninety-Fourth. He scored one more official victory and one unofficial one for which there were no witnesses. Then, on the last day of July 1918, on a patrol somewhere between Soissons and Reims, he was caught in a melee of German and American planes and hit by a blast of bullets that stopped his engine and shattered bones in his left arm. He managed to make a one-armed landing behind the German lines and spent the rest of the war in a prisoner of war camp, where a German surgeon cut off his damaged arm.

Two very different young men fought in that first victory: Campbell—confident of his skills and certain of his cause—who would almost immediately shoot down another Boche, and then another, and in less than two months would win his fifth confirmed victory and become an ace; and Winslow—*not* confident, *not* certain, inclined to get a plane in his gun sight and then hold his fire for fear it might be French, always conscious of the dark possibilities of war—the same young man who lay on the window ledge of the Biltmore to test his courage. Different, but for a few minutes in April over Toul they shared a spectacular action and shot down the Ninety-Fourth's first two Boches, while all the squadron watched.

Two truths about pursuit tactics and pilot behavior in combat emerge from the stories that Campbell and Winslow told. One is the wisdom of mutual responsibility—how you must fly as a patrol and fight as a patrol, looking out always for each other. In their accounts of the double victory that they share, both men mention how in the swirl of their separate flights each looked round for the other, to help him if he needed help. The other truth is that at the moment of actual engagement they fought as individuals.

That headlong excitement is in many of the letters that new pilots wrote that spring, as they began to reach the front in substantial numbers and found that flying in a pursuit squadron was indeed the great adventure they'd hoped it would be. John Grider, the good ol' boy from Arkansas, put it this way after his first fight:

> He didn't crash so I don't suppose I got him, but I won the fight and it was just him and me and Jesus there and he had all the advantage.
>
> It is the only sport there is. I swear I never felt anything like it!

One mustn't forget, though, that among all those exulting new pilots there were always the others—the ones who felt the exultation but realized with a pang of regret that the planes they shot down had men in them. An anonymous Lafayette Flying Corps pilot shoots down his second Boche in the dark days of the German spring offensive and thinks, "Oh, it was a wonderful sight! I watched him fall all the way to his last resting place, in the middle of a railroad track, amidst a cloud and explosion of smoke and flame, just as if a shell had hit the ground, instead of an airplane." But he adds that it was "a machine which two minutes before contained two human beings." A sense of the humanity of your enemy is probably an inconvenience in wartime, but sometimes it's there.

TWELVE

LOOKING AT THE WAR

Back at the training fields in the spring of 1918—at Issoudun and Tours and Ayr and Hendon—most flight students dreamed of being *chasse* pilots and assumed that if they did well in training, they'd get what they wanted and be ordered up to a *chasse* squadron; any other assignment would be unjust, if their records were good. But assignments didn't always depend on how well a man could fly and shoot; sometimes they were simply what was available.

Pilots who flew observation planes don't figure in the myth of the war much; not many collections of their letters exist, and no memoirs that I've come across (though there are a couple by observers). Yet at the end of the spring of 1918 there were more American observation squadrons at the front than there were pursuit squadrons, and they did their work and took their losses.

On an ordinary day at the front an observation pilot might be assigned to any of a number of missions: reconnaissance, or a contact patrol, or a photography run; or he might fly protection for a squadron mate, or *réglage* for an artillery battery, or even a propaganda drop. Their stories of such missions, when they bother to tell them, make it clear that observation flying could be challenging, difficult, and dangerous.

George Hughes was a prudent, sensible, unemotional man, to judge from his letters, who never felt the joy that flying gives most pilots or any great impatience to get to the front. Hughes wrote to two people: his mother and his younger brother, Jerry, who was also a pilot, but further back in the program (for the first half of 1918 he was a flight instructor in Texas). To his mother, George wrote about everyday matters—the weather, French crops, family business, his daily routine. To Jerry, he was the older, more experienced brother, advising the kid on the path his career in the Air Service should take, as though Jerry were a young man on the verge of a business career, trying to choose between banking and real estate. "Business" is a word George used a lot; he was older than most of the new pilots (he was twenty-five when he moved to the front in May with the Twelfth Observation Squadron), and he had had some experience of the business world before he enlisted. Observation flying, to his mind, wasn't a game or a sport; it was simply another kind of business, though a dangerous one.

Hughes didn't keep a journal, and there are sometimes long breaks between letters home. During his time with the Twelfth he was twice shot down and had to make difficult forced landings. One of these incidents he never mentioned in his letters; the other he described in a letter to his brother. He's been on an early morning *réglage* flight, working with the American infantry. For *réglage*, that is, artillery adjustment, or ranging, or registration (pilots used all those terms), a single observation plane would be sent across the lines to find an enemy target—an observation post, an artillery installation, a command post—and signal the location back to its own artillery, which would open fire. The observer would note where the first shells fell and send back corrections until the gunners got a hit.

The weather was bad that morning, and the German antiaircraft fire was heavy; the planes on Hughes's patrol that started at seven thousand feet ended up at less than six hundred feet above the German trenches, where they stayed for two hours or more, going back of the lines at an altitude of less than a thousand feet: "How those devils did shoot at us—rifles, machine guns and every now and then the Archies would open up and plaster the skies. But I was always lucky enough to be elsewhere when they broke. One shell did break just under me so close that I expected to find myself minus a landing chassis . . . I couldn't see a living soul even when we got down to where our wheels were dragging on the ground."

Finally, he sees five Germans (he calls them Dutchmen, as American pilots often did) standing on a hill that commands the heights and the swamps below, where the American infantry is attacking. Hughes comes along just at the Dutchmen's level; they look like a firing squad getting ready to fire at him. Another man might swerve toward them and begin firing. Not George; he turns around and beats it out of there, "hell bent for election."

> Well [he goes on], they simply perforated that ship of mine, but only one shot came close to me. It entered my lower left wing at a slight angle and came into the fuselage under my arm, passing somewhere along about the tip of my nose and piercing the center section of the wing some three inches back of the leading edge, just above my head. I'll bet those German officers sure cussed their gunners out, because they'll never get a chance like that again. At least not with me for some time to come.

A prudent man jokes about getting shot up. And that's all: he doesn't describe what he was doing out there over the lines; he doesn't even mention the crash landing that ended the flight. But his exploit must have impressed someone higher up in the Air Service and eventually reached the desk of the Chief of Air Service. After the war ended, Hughes and his observer, Captain William Saunders, received commendations "for gallantry in action."

What they did certainly took courage: flying around low over enemy territory (Hughes later recalled that at the end they were down to about 150 feet), while every gun on the ground below took potshots at you, would strain any pilot's nerves, and a dead-stick landing among the shell holes of No-Man's-Land, that would be stressful, too. But what they got was not a medal; it was only a commendation. They'd been brave, but they weren't attacking; they were only observing. Jerry Hughes remembered that his brother was recommended by the French for the Croix de Guerre, but it never went through.

Photography missions were also part of the work of observation squadrons. Observing the enemy with a camera was sometimes simply a matter of one plane flying along the lines while the observer photographed enemy depots and facilities, gun emplacements, any target that might have been moved, or enemy defenses at a point in the line where American troops were preparing to attack; sometimes the objective was broader—recording a stretch of the front or mapping a wide area, perhaps six or eight miles into German territory. For these larger tasks a plane equipped with a camera built into the bottom of the fuselage was used (pilots called such planes camera kites), capable of taking a continuous series of images. To do the job successfully, the pilot had to fly at a constant altitude and in a straight line. That made him vulnerable to attack, so he was customarily accompanied either by *chasse* planes or, if they weren't available, by planes from his own observation squadron.

We have the recollections of both the pilot and the observer of a strenuous photography mission flown in the summer of 1918. Lieutenant Donald Cole (pilot) and Lieutenant Percival Hart (observer), of the 135th Squadron, were assigned to take a consecutive sequence of pictures along the course of a small river southeast of Verdun. The trip began well enough; the weather was good as they crossed the lines at fourteen thousand feet. Cole headed the plane up the middle of the stream, while Hart, on his hands and knees in the rear cockpit, concentrated on the camera in the cockpit floor. But the plane had drifted off course, and after much hand waving (which was the only means of communication between pilot and observer) they turned back to begin again.

Here's Hart's version of what happened next:

I heard a lot of shooting and the pilot was jumping and wiggling the plane back and forth, trying to get my attention.

An Albatros was coming down on us! I grabbed my guns but couldn't get a shot at him because the top wing was in the way. Cole then turned to the left and I started shooting at the Albatros. Cole had kicked our plane into a spin at the same instant that he was hit by the German. The first that I realized that there was anything wrong was when I smelled gasoline and noticed that the engine was off. Cole turned around, gesticulating to me, to tell me that he had been wounded and that our engine had been knocked out.

We had enough altitude so we kept gliding and gliding, skimming over the front trenches and we landed behind our own lines. Just before we landed a group of German soldiers came

pouring out of their lines and began shooting at us with their
pistols and rifles. I leaned over the side and I popped back at
them with my machine gun. Cole had been wounded twice; in
the leg and in the thigh. Neither bullet had hit the bone and they
were just flesh wounds. He was taken to the hospital at Toul.

And here's Cole's version, beginning at the point at which they discover they're off course:

I motioned to go ahead and take the rest [of the pictures] and
that at the finish point I would turn around and get the right line
on the way back. This all took a minute or so and when I turned
front again there were two German fighters coming at us. As I
started a left bank to get my two Marlin machine guns on them,
I felt a hammer blow on my left knee and the plane fell away in
a spin. I knew I had been hit.

There's gas everywhere; the bullet that hit his knee has also pierced the
gas filter. He stops the spin and cuts off the gas flow. They're at fourteen thousand feet, six miles behind the German lines, with no power.
Cole sets the plane in a glide for his own side of the lines: "I had to pick
a field to reach and land in, knowing that with a dead engine I had only
one try. We crossed the lines at 500 feet and Perc Hart emptied his
guns on the German trenches. I made a good landing just behind our
trenches, was helped out of the plane and taken to the Evacuation Hospital #1 near Toul."

Forty years after it happened, two elderly men remember a mission
they shared. The story returns to them slightly differently, of course: they
experienced the flight from different places in the plane and played different roles in what happened. The pilot remembers what it was like to
be wounded and how he got his damaged plane out of a spin; the observer remembers his gunnery. But it's essentially the same narrative:
the assignment, the attacking German planes, the spin and recovery, the
emergency landing. And the excitement of it all—that's still there, too:
two young airmen doing their job, fighting the enemy, getting the plane
back to their own side of the lines.

Was it a successful flight? No, not in terms of what they accomplished; they didn't get the photographs, the pilot was wounded, and

though Cole got the plane on the ground safely, it was wrecked by the crew that came to salvage it. But to the two crew members it was a success, in a way; when crises came, they had acted, and they had survived.

Photo planes needed protection, either from a pursuit squadron or from one of their own observation planes. Cole and Hart were accompanied by one protection plane, but it doesn't appear in their story until the fighting is over and the wounded plane is gliding for home.

For how protection should be done, there is the example of Fletcher McCordic of the Eighty-Eighth Observation Squadron. McCordic was something of an odd man out among the pilots he flew with. Though he came from a professional family—his father was a lawyer back in Winnetka, Illinois—Fletcher did not go to college, but chose a technical school instead. His interests were entirely mechanical: from an early age he loved machines—first the family automobile and then, increasingly, airplanes. He built plane models and then his own full-sized plane. In the fall of 1916 he entered the Wright Flying School on Long Island, and when he enlisted in the Air Service the following year, he had an Aero Club pilot's license. He was twenty-five, older than most enlistees and far better trained. And more serious about his war. The other guys called him the General, or simply the Gen.

McCordic had an engineer's mind, practical and exact; he saw his flying duties as technical procedures, to be performed thoroughly and correctly, and as often as possible. He would spend hours waiting around the squadron headquarters, or nearby, within calling distance, so that he'd be the first pilot on hand when a special mission was to be dispatched. By the end of the war he had flown more than 125 hours over the lines, had fought many fights, and was credited with two enemy planes.

McCordic's letters mention flying many protection patrols, but he was a man of few words, and he never said much about exactly what he did in the air or how he felt about it. For that we must depend on the testimonies of his admiring fellow officers, as in this account by an observer in his squadron:

One time he [McCordic] was sent up to protect another plane which was taking the photographs. Four Boches came in to attack and McCordic, who should have held his place in rear of

the photo plane, swung over to the Boche side, making it certain that he would have to be shot down before the photo ship could be touched. He had his guns working and before any other [Allied] planes came the Boches had decided that they didn't care to fight any one so aggressive and turned off. Then the "Gen." swung his plane back in rear of the photo ship. I was taking the photographs and my heart certainly went out to him when I saw that he meant to make them get him first, as they certainly would have if they had continued to fight. When we got home I rushed over and bragged on him for it. "Well, I was protection, wasn't I?" he said and let it go at that.

A contact patrol was as close to the infantry war as a pilot—any pilot—could get. The job was to fly low over an attack in progress, right down in the rough air near the ground, through the ground fire from the trenches and the trajectory of shells from the big guns, and locate the troops that were fighting there.

On the eve of a contact patrol, the observation pilot Harvey Conover wrote, "This is by far the most dangerous work in all aviation so everyone is wondering who of us will be bumped off. However, everyone is also very anxious to get into it and see the most wonderful spectacle in the world—that of charging troops & tanks immediately below you."

After the battle, he described what he'd actually seen and how it had felt to be there: "The sight is most magnificent: watching our men fighting their way from shell hole to shell hole, shells bursting all around you, and machine guns tack-tacking below you. It makes you want to yell to the men to give them hell, and it is more exciting than anything I have ever participated in."

Conover thought the contact patrols that observation pilots flew were the most dangerous of aviation duties (Billy Mitchell had called such work "the most hazardous, but most important of all missions"). Either might have added that in spite of that, observation flying was generally considered the least adventurous thing you could do in the air. The pilot on such flights wasn't even regarded as the most important person in the plane, at least by many observers; it was the guy in the backseat who was in command, who made the decisions and guided the team on its mission; the pilots were simply deliverymen, truck drivers. In both the German and the French air services, the pilots of two-seaters were often of lower rank than the observers/bombardiers; often an enlisted man in the front seat would be flying an officer in the back.

To make this relationship absolutely clear, some observers attached strings (which they called reins) to the pilot's arms and ran them back to the rear cockpit, where the observer tugged them this way or that to steer the pilot in the right direction—like a farmer driving his mule.

If being an observation pilot wasn't considered adventurous, being an observer was even less so. The women they met made that abundantly clear. Elmer Haslett, an observer with the Twelfth Aero Squadron, recalls an incident at the airfield at Amanty. He's been asked to drive to a nearby town to pick up three YMCA girls who are coming to Amanty to entertain the troops. The girls greet him warmly: they can see by the leather coat he's wearing that he's an aviator—"Hero Number One of Heroes All," as Haslett puts it. They demand to be taken up in his airplane. Then he opens his coat, and one of the girls sees that the flying insignia on his chest has only one wing on it, not the two wings that a pilot would wear. "Wild eyed and with marked disdain, she exclaimed sneeringly to the others, 'Oh, he's only an observer! A half aviator!'" Half an aviator, half a man.

It must have been that perception of observation fliers—both observers and pilots—that moved many pilot-observer teams to seek occasions to fly a different war, not simply observing, but attacking, and to record the flights on which they did so. In some accounts, a flight of observation planes goes out on a patrol in a fiercely belligerent mood, like some urban street gang strutting out into disputed territory to pick a fight with a rival gang. They may be observers, but what they're looking for is not some activity on the ground but trouble in the air—enemy planes to engage in a dogfight that will make their observation squadron for one intense moment a *chasse* squadron.

As you might expect, Harvey Conover, always eager for action, felt the need for a *chasse*-pilot adventure more than most observation pilots—so much so that he tried one on his own. He explains in his journal how it happened. The Boches have just shot down three American balloons; Conover and his observer decide to try their luck on German balloons in retaliation. Their flight hasn't been ordered—the squadron report doesn't even mention it—they just fly it. They know that what they're doing is foolhardy. "This is practically an impossible task in a two-seater," Conover writes, "but we thought we would try it anyway."

They load their guns with incendiary bullets and take off into solid cloud cover, climb up through it, and head off toward Germany. The clouds are so thick that they can't find an opening in them, and they have to navigate by guesswork and by compass. After a while Conover reckons they must be about five kilometers into German airspace; he dives down through the clouds and comes out not among Boche balloons but over a German hospital, and they have to go down to twelve hundred meters to see even that.

Conover's reaction is what you'd expect of him:

> There I received the thrill of my life, for nowhere were there
> signs of trenches, the sun was invisible, and my compass was
> whirling hopelessly. I therefore had to guess our direction &
> opened the throttle wide. Visions of landing in Germany, of
> being brought down, for at that height our position was hopeless,

and a thousand similar thoughts flashed through my brain. However, luck was with us, and we had apparently done such a foolhardy thing that no one had suspected us.

They pass over trucks and camions and can almost distinguish the Hun troops below them. Finally, after what seems an age, they sight the Boche trenches ahead. "Never have I seen a more welcome sight," Conover writes. "Over we went with a black boche barrage popping around us and returned to report no German balloons up, to thank our stars that we were not in bocheland, and to wonder how we got back. After consulting a map, we learned that we had been some 15 to 20 kilometers deep in Hunland."

The whole flight has been a wild and irresponsible game. They've put themselves in danger without authority, and they've accomplished nothing. Except the thrill, which must have been the greater because it was free and unauthorized. Now they can go back to their observing.

———

Occasionally, some general in the field might praise an observation squadron's work, as Major General Robert Lee Bullard did in September 1918, when he wrote a general order about McCordic's Eighty-Eighth: "This Squadron has repeatedly performed missions involving great hazard, has repeatedly, in the accomplishments of its mission, fought largely superior enemy forces and has, under great difficulties, achieved excellent results."

What the general said was true enough—the Eighty-Eighth had done its work well—and those adjectives—"great" hazard, "great" difficulties, "excellent" results—are what one expects on such occasions. But there's a note of special pleading in it, as though he were addressing some arrogant *chasse* pilot, who didn't think of observation as serious work for a real flier.

Observation squadron histories have something of the same tone: let me tell you, they say, what our squadron *really* did, and how tough it was, and most of all how important it was in the large story of the war. When Captain Daniel Morse, a pilot and C.O. of the Fiftieth, wrote his squadron's history, he inserted this paragraph:

It might be explained here that the 50th Squadron was a Corps Observation Squadron, assigned to do divisional aviation duties. This sort of work, in fact, is the real reason for having aviation in modern warfare, as these squadrons work directly with the infantry and artillery on the ground. They are the ones who get all the information of enemy movements, etc., and do the extremely important work of infantry contact patrol, which is to find out and tell the divisional headquarters where their front line troops are when communications are cut. They are the only means of communication in many cases during a battle. It is also a fact that the general public knows little about this end of aviation, even though this is the most important branch of aviation. Its proper or non-functioning can save or destroy thousands of lives of our own troops, and it also can be the means of the success or failure of an offensive. This is not known by the general public because of the notoriety given the "chasse" planes when they bring a Hun plane down. No mention has ever been made when the observation planes *saved* hundreds or even thousands of our own troops. It is the most constructive work in the combatant arm of the army.

It's a plaintive appeal for respect for what observation squadrons did. And it had justice on its side: observation missions *were* important.

Justice, but not romance, not personal exploits to be remembered and retold. The myth would remain what it had been from the early days of the war—stories of rattling guns and burning, spinning planes that would provide plots for novels and movies and pulp magazines for years to come. A generation later, small boys like me, who wore helmets and goggles to school in the winter, would run around the school yard at recess, their arms stuck out like wings, uttering what they hoped was the sound of machine guns and shouting, "Look at me! I'm Eddie Rickenbacker!" or "I'm the Red Baron!" And when our war came along, we'd know that we *had* to be pilots—not just any pilots, *fighter* pilots, because they were the heroes, they were the solitary knights of the air who fought their war personally, one plane against another.

THIRTEEN

A SHORT HISTORY
OF BOMBING

Bombing is another story. Ever since men first began devising ways of lifting themselves above the surface of the earth, other men have worked at ways of dropping things—grenades, artillery shells, bombs, whatever would explode—on their enemies below. At first they tried unmanned balloons (imagine a balloon with a bomb dangling from it, floating on the wind over some battlefield!). Then, as powered flight became possible, they turned to dirigibles and airplanes. It was all experimental, as the technology of war always is. By 1907, nations were alarmed enough to meet in conference at The Hague and agree that aerial bombardment should be prohibited. But as usual, war, when it came, trumped that peaceable resolution.

When the First World War began seven years later, air raids were flown almost at once. In the first months of the war two German zeppelins raided Antwerp and Namur (*The Times* of London reported the attack on August 26). By the end of the year they had reached England (*The New York Times* reported that attack on Christmas Day). British and French aircraft retaliated, and the bombing war was on.

By the time American pilots began to arrive at the front to serve with the Service Aéronautique, the French had organized and equipped squadrons specifically intended for bombing. Some Americans flew with them. Norman Prince, one of the founding members of what became the Lafayette Escadrille, began his combat career in May 1915 with a French bombing escadrille. His account is the best record I know of what it was like to fly a bombing mission in those first years of the war.

Prince told the first part of his bombing story in a talk he gave back in Boston on Christmas night 1915, while he was on a short furlough. The scene was the Tavern Club, and the audience would have known him—a local boy born in Prides Crossing who had learned to fly at Marblehead, just up the coast—though he must have seemed different now, a veteran pilot who had fought in a foreign war, speaking to civilians.

In that talk, he told about his first "bombarding expedition," back in May, in the Pas-de-Calais. He was sent with two or three other members of his squadron to attack a railway station not far within the enemy's lines, where ammunition was being unloaded. They took off and spent the next forty minutes just climbing, to reach a sufficient altitude to cross the lines. Then they headed for the target. But separately— Prince could see the other planes far ahead of him and could see that they were being heavily shelled by German antiaircraft batteries. He decided to climb still higher before he crossed the lines, and it was only when he saw that his gas supply was getting low that he started over and ran into his own baptism of fire: "The impression made upon me by the terrible racket and the spectacle of shells aimed at me and exploding near by made me shiver for a moment. Though I was confident and unafraid, my limbs began to tremble."

Any old combat pilot will recognize that feeling—the first surprised awareness that war is personal and that the gunners down there are shooting at *you*. Still, Prince goes on, "I kept straight on my course. I would not have changed it for the world. My legs were so wobbly from nervous excitement that I tried to hide them from my observer, who was an old hand at the game. I confess to a feeling of relief when I reached the point where our bombs were to be thrown over."

It's a primitive sort of raid, as Prince describes it: three or four planes, widely separated from one another and at different altitudes, heading for a target that's never named. What he tells his Boston audience about is his feelings on the way to the target and on the way home. He says nothing about the actual attack. Who threw the bombs over (nobody seems to have aimed them)? Did they hit anything? He doesn't say how big the bombs were (surely an important detail), though he does say that the

Voisin he was flying could carry a payload of up to seven hundred pounds (which would be a lot of work for the thrower).

In the next thirty days pilots of Prince's squadron flew seventeen more raids and, as he says, "got to be old hands at this kind of warfare." As their experience grew, so did the size of the raids and the distances they flew. On a raid on the railway station at Douai, twenty planes flew twenty-five kilometers into enemy territory. On the way in they were attacked four or five times by German fighters, and four of them were hit. Only four of the twenty bombers reached their target. One was Prince. For his service he was awarded the Croix de Guerre.

In August, the squadron moved east to Lorraine, near Nancy, and the raids got bigger, and flew farther. On one occasion the president of France and the king of the Belgians came to witness the takeoff of four bombing squadrons, ninety planes in all, flying four abreast and headed for a target a hundred kilometers beyond the enemy lines. Prince notes that the president and the king "were highly complimentary in their salutations to us Americans." On another raid that month, this time of thirty planes, Prince's plane is attacked by six Germans, the engine stops, and he glides to the French lines, powers off, and makes an emergency landing in a field covered with white crosses (they mark the graves of French and German soldiers killed in a battle there the year before).

These raids were flown in the spring and summer of 1915. The war is still in its first year, but already you can see the direction that aerial warfare is taking: three or four planes, then twenty, then ninety, and then even more. As the flotillas of bombers grow larger, they begin to be celebrated in the press back home. In August 1915 the French War Office reports an attack by French planes on a German arms factory, and *Flying* magazine picks up the story for its American readers: four air groups totaling sixty-two planes, *Flying* reports in its October issue, "threw down with precision over 150 bombs, thirty of which were of large caliber." A "stupendous raid," *Flying* calls it. In the months and years ahead there will be more such stupendous raids: British and French squadrons will join forces to send more bombing planes farther, and raids will be measured by the number of planes involved, and by the distance flown, and by the total weight of the bombs dropped, which will be measured in tons. And sometimes by the cost, in crews lost and in planes shot down.

Prince flew on a raid like that in the autumn of 1916. It wasn't one of the giant operations, only fifty or sixty planes, but it attacked an important target, the Mauser munitions works at Oberndorf, fifty miles beyond the Rhine from the French lines in Alsace. As usual, the raid was made up of both French and British bombers. To protect the bombers, there were *chasse* planes, including French Nieuports, four of them flown by Americans of the Lafayette Escadrille, including Prince, who had transferred from his bombing squadron to N. 124.

The story of the raid was told not by Prince but by another Lafayette pilot, James McConnell. He wasn't on the mission, but he saw it take off and return; the rest of the story he must have heard from pilots who flew it. English Sopwiths took off first, climbed to altitude, and joined up in a V formation; it resembled a flight of geese. Breguets and Farmans followed. Above the bombers the *chasse* planes darted and circled, watching for enemy planes. But Nieuports have a limited range, and when they'd escorted the bombers across the Rhine, they had to turn back to refuel. The bombers, unprotected now, continued to the target and dropped their bombs and turned for home—what was left of them: six had been shot down, some in flames.

By then the Nieuports were back, to cover the bombers on their return flight and to clear the air of German planes: there were fights, Lufbery shot down three planes, and Prince got one. The sun had set by then, but the *chasse* pilots stayed in the air, doing their job. The earth below them was in darkness before they looked for a landing field and found one at Corcieux. Lufbery went in and landed. Ten minutes later Prince followed, spiraling down through the gloom (there were no landing lights on the field), skimming over the trees at the edge of the field. In the dark he didn't see the high-tension line that was strung just above the treetops. His landing gear caught the line, and his plane dove forward, hitting the ground nose down and somersaulting. Prince was thrown from the plane. Both his legs were broken, and he suffered internal injuries. He died three days later.

An ordinary bombing raid of the mid-war period, but it tells a lot about the bombing story: how scrambled together the flights were out of whatever squadrons were available; how unprotected they were on the longer runs; how anonymous the dying was, when it was bomber pilots who died. Only the *chasse* pilots have personal stories, and names, and, it seems, friends to grieve for them. And what was accomplished? Fires burned; air raids always leave fires behind them. But did Mauser stop making its rifles? Nobody will know until the war is over.

In the spring of 1917 an American pilot arrived in France who would affect the bombing story more than any other American, although he was not a bomber pilot and would never fly on a bombing raid. The United States had been at war for four days when Major William Mitchell appeared at the American Embassy in Paris and began at once to arrange an office for, as he put it, "handling aviation." Mitchell had been in Spain on a mission as a military observer when his country declared war. He caught the next train north.

Mitchell must have been an impressive man to meet: tall, lean, handsome in a stern-faced way, a man who in photographs always seems to stand straighter, more at attention, than the men around him. What photographs can't show are the conviction that was growing in him—that he knew how to win the war and could accomplish that goal if only the decision makers in Paris and Washington would listen to him—and the driven determination to *make* them listen.

He began his "handling" job at once, covering the Zone of Advance like a traveling salesman covering his territory. He hadn't been in France two weeks before he was visiting frontline squadrons to talk to pilots and their commanders and to see how the air war was being fought and training fields to see how new French pilots were being prepared for combat. Sometimes he flew there in his own plane, a Nieuport or a Spad; sometimes he traveled by car to ground units at the front, to see what their problems were and how airplanes could help.

As he went, Mitchell kept a careful diary of what he had seen and his conclusions, but he waited ten years to publish that record. By then the war was long over, and Mitchell was out of the Air Service. The book that appeared then is a mixture, part his daily notes and part retrospective judgments, and often the line between the two parts is blurred. The diary is exact and factual; the judgments are often bitter and angry. Together they record the process by which Mitchell evolved from an ambitious regular pilot, new to the front and eager to play a role there, to an airpower strategist. More than that, his book is the testament of a visionary—a true believer and increasingly vocal witness to the dream that was in his mind of a new, absolute kind of war, a war that would fall from the sky and that would be invincible.

Mitchell was quick to come to judgments. Two weeks after he arrived, he observed that he in his plane could cross the lines in a few minutes, whereas the armies below him "had been locked in the struggle, immovable, powerless to advance, for three years," and concluded, "It looked as though the war would keep up indefinitely until either the airplanes brought an end to the war or the contending nations dropped from sheer exhaustion."

Already it was either-or: stalemated war of attrition or airpower.

After many conversations with French officers, Mitchell drew some conclusions about the state of French aviation. The pilots he'd met had been in this work too long, he thought; in many cases they had lost their nerve and were flying cautiously and defensively. Defensive flying—by which Mitchell meant only opposing enemy planes that entered French airspace—might be necessary, given the depressed state of the French air service, but it wouldn't win the war. If the war was to end in victory for the Allies, there must be more planes, they must be used offensively, and more of them must be flown by American pilots.

The following month, May 1917, Mitchell traveled from Paris to Abbeville, on the English stretch of the front, to the field headquarters of the RFC, and there he met Major General Sir Hugh Trenchard, General Officer Commanding the Royal Flying Corps in the field. Trenchard was impressive: he was six years older than Mitchell and outranked him by several grades; Mitchell must have seen in him what he himself aspired to be. He was also physically impressive; Mitchell described him as "about six feet in height, erect of carriage, decided in manner and very direct in speech"—which sounds a lot like a description of Mitchell.

In this meeting between two decided, direct men, Mitchell explained why he was there: he wanted to learn everything there was to know about British air operations. Trenchard responded by reading aloud a paper he'd written on the role of aviation in war.

What Trenchard said was that the airplane is not a defense against another airplane (the sky was too wide, a plane was too small); rather, it was—or should be—an offensive weapon. And not singly, but in large numbers, attacking at many places. Air attacks should be carried as far as possible into enemy country; he thought it perfectly practical for planes to attack the rear of the German army and to destroy all its means of supply, subsistence, and replacement. *All* its means, note that: what Trenchard was imagining was a war of perfect destruction. And not simply for a few miles behind the lines, something vaster and more Wagnerian than that. He visualized planes with the capacity for ten-hour flights that would so increase the radius of attack that even Berlin could be reached, which would mean that the whole of Germany would become the target—not only military installations, but *everything*. And not only by daylight: night bombings such as the German Gothas flew could inflict thousands of casualties in a single night. It could all happen, he thought, but only if his nation's flying forces were unified under a single commander. That would be him, of course.

Trenchard had one other strategic point to make. He observed that when a hostile airplane appeared over the front, whistles blew and men hid in their trenches, even if the plane was flying far too high to be a threat to them. He thought this "moral effect" should be exploited: "Not only was the material effect of bombardment to be reckoned with, and it was constantly increasing, but the moral effect on the people was even greater. Women and children were paralyzed with fear. It was a menace from an entirely new quarter." That assumption—that air raids could have psychological as well as physical effects—would become part of the long-range destructive strategy in the months to come. Fear would become a weapon.

Mitchell was impressed by what he heard—so much so that he quoted the whole of Trenchard's paper in his *Memoirs*. He also attached the paper as an appendix to a memorandum that he sent that spring to the Chief of Staff, American Expeditionary Forces. In that memorandum he argued that the U.S. Air Service should adopt what was essentially Trenchard's offensive air strategy of heavy bombing.

Consider the impertinent irregularity of that memorandum: a *major* telling a *general* how to conduct his war! For the moment Mitchell's assertiveness seemed to work; he was promoted to lieutenant colonel and for a short time was put in command of the entire Air Service of the AEF. (That's not as grand an appointment as it sounds; in July 1917 the Air Service in France apparently consisted of one Nieuport, which

Mitchell used in his travels.) Sooner or later such a thrusting young officer would surely get into trouble.

Spring became summer, and Mitchell went on covering his territory and waiting impatiently for his own air service to turn up. He visited British and French bombing squadrons at their fields, admiring the planes they had and carefully recording their performance figures. In June he saw the first heavy bombardment squadrons of the RFC and noted that each Handley Page could carry more than a ton of bombs, that they had a range of about two hundred miles, and that their cruising speed was only sixty-five miles an hour. That made them vulnerable to German pursuit planes in daylight, and they were mostly used at night. *Every* night, in fact, in raids on Bruges, where they demolished railroad yards, barracks, ammunition dumps, and depots of supplies.

In August he was near Verdun, observing operations of the French First Bombardment Group. On one day the French bombers dropped more than twelve thousand pounds of bombs on troop concentrations at St. Juvin, Grandpré, and Fléville, while Mitchell watched from a Sopwith above the lines and saw the smoke and fire rising from the targets. That night they dropped twenty tons of bombs on railroad stations at Longuyon, and a great fire was reported. (Notice that *pounds* have become *tons*.)

You can see what Mitchell was doing: he was studying the bombing operations of other air services in preparation for the day when American bombing squadrons would be operating at the front and he could put Trenchard's principles into practice. He not only studied Allied bombers; he listened and watched when German Gothas flew over in the darkness, and hurried to inspect the damage they'd done, and he recorded reports of German raids that he didn't himself witness—a daylight raid on London, for example: how many planes, at what altitude, and with what losses.

The American day would be a long time coming, though. By mid-1917, American troops had landed in France, and General Pershing was established in Paris, but the Air Service wasn't visible. Young men classified as "aviators" were beginning to arrive, but they were only partially trained at best, and some had had no flight training at all; it would be months before any of them were combat ready. For the rest of the year Mitchell worked to establish flight schools and to equip them with planes and instructors. The combat squadrons would have to wait.

Looking back, Mitchell wrote that the spring of 1917 "had seen the real beginning of grand tactics in air warfare, that is, large numbers of airplanes acting together under a common leader." That beginning had taken place in his mind and in Trenchard's, but it had yet to happen on the scale they imagined. Nineteen eighteen would be different: the grand tactics, and the grand strategy, could begin.

———

In late March 1918, Kenneth MacLeish had been training at the RFC's School of Aerial Fighting at Ayr, in Scotland, when orders came for him to join a Royal Navy squadron at Dunkerque. He arrived at the air station to find other Yale men already there, some in his new squadron, others in squadrons nearby: Bob Lovett, Di Gates, Shorty Smith, George Moseley—he names them in euphoric letters home. "This is the most wonderful thing that ever happened to me," he wrote on March 28, "as the people I came to fly with are the best in the world, and the machines are absolutely A-1."

It wasn't only the company of familiar faces that raised his spirits; it was what they would be doing together. At the end of March the German spring offensive was already being fought along the lines south and east of Dunkerque; air station rumor said it would begin along the British stretch of the front any day. And MacLeish's squadron would be in it: "I will be way down the line where things are happening these days, right in the middle of the greatest battle the world has ever known. Won't that be worth—doubly worth—all the weary months I spent waiting for my chance . . ." When he wrote that letter, MacLeish had not yet flown a single combat flight. His excitement is the excitement of innocence.

A couple of weeks passed, and MacLeish flew high patrols and froze—fingers, nose, lips, cheeks—but saw no action. Then, early in April, he flew his first bombing raid. The Camels were rigged with bomb racks, each loaded with one fifty-pound bomb. The idea, he explained in a letter, was to make a surprise low-level attack in broad daylight on German installations at Zeebrugge. It would be a short run—less than fifty miles.

The ceiling was low that morning—only a thousand feet. The seven planes would have to fly below it until they approached their target, then pull up into the overcast and when they thought they were directly over Zeebrugge dive down to three or four hundred feet and drop their bombs and get out. It would be a daring, dangerous stunt to try, but it sounds possible, in theory.

The actual attack was something else. MacLeish described it in a letter the same day. The first man to dive had an easy time; the German gunners didn't even shoot at him. The second man got a little ground fire, the third more, the fourth had a hell of a time. The fifth had to turn back and try it again; the sixth wasn't much more successful. And then it was MacLeish's tail-end-Charlie turn.

> In my wildest dreams of all hell turned loose, I never pictured anything like that. There must have been a thousand machine guns working on a twenty-four-hour day schedule. The tracer bullets were doing loops and split turns around my neck. I got dizzy watching them. I put my fingers on both triggers and had my two guns going full blast while I dove. It was no use. I saw in a second that I never in the world could get there. The rapid fire pom-poms were putting up a barrage in front of me, and it was getting closer and closer as I dove. There were so many bursts of smoke that I lost sight of the target. I thought of home and Mother and zoomed back into the clouds.

When he emerged from the cloud cover, he was completely lost: he couldn't even see land. And he still had his bomb aboard. He flew by compass until he saw the coastline and followed it west, toward home, while enemy antiaircraft batteries blazed away at him. Eventually, he came to a town he recognized; it was twenty miles from Zeebrugge, but he didn't like the idea of going back, so he found a target below, dove, and dropped his bomb (his "pill," he called it), zoomed back up into the clouds, and headed for the air station. From the experience he drew one moral: "Today I learned never to be the last machine in a daylight, low bombing stunt."

MacLeish's story of his initiation into actual war is a frank and honest account. The tone of the telling is the tone of a twenty-three-year-old ex–college boy—at once tense and jaunty, as though his flight had been both a terrifying experience and a joke on him. Now he knows what a low-level bombing raid is like when you're in it: the smoke, the antiaircraft bursts, the presence of other diving planes, and most of all the *feeling* of attacking—that heightened state between fear and exhilaration that comes as the target slides under your plane's nose and the tracers begin to float up. It hasn't been the epic kind of raid that Trenchard and Mitchell imagined, only a small-scale, ordinary piece of a bomber pilot's work, and his part in it, though brave enough in the prudent way that Biddle and Deullin would approve, has not been heroic (a hero would have stayed in his dive into the furious ground fire and would probably be dead). He has not lost his confidence, nor his enthusiasm for flying, nor his sense of the thrill of an attack, but now he knows what it is like.

A month after that first raid, MacLeish heard of "a great big project," the newly conceived Northern Bombing Group. This was to be the Navy's way of claiming a piece of the strategic bombing action. It would be composed of both day-bombing and night-bombing squadrons that would fly raids deep into Germany around the clock, and it would be all Navy. Billy Mitchell must have been furious when he heard of the plan (and he would have heard; he was alert for such schemes). In his opinion, the place for the Navy was on the water; or if it insisted on flying (and he didn't see why it should), it ought to be in planes that were as seagoing as its ships were—floatplanes, or flying boats. The land belonged to the Air Service, and so should every plane that landed on wheels on solid ground.

The idea of a Navy bombing group sounded good to MacLeish, as it did to many of his Yale friends at Dunkerque. He volunteered to join it and at the end of May moved to the bombardment school at Clermont-Ferrand to become a Navy bomber pilot in a Navy squadron. That didn't happen; the Northern Bombing Group had trouble getting organized and equipped, and by July he was back at Dunkerque, attached to an RAF squadron. Before his war ended, he would have many other jobs, most of them connected with the Navy's efforts to make the NBG operational: in Paris, testing and inspecting equipment, then *almost* commanding a day-bombing squadron in the group, then testing and inspecting again, this time at Eastleigh on the English coast, before he wound up once more at Dunkerque with his old RAF squadron.

The last year of the war was the year of the big bombing raids. By then, all the combatant air services had planes that were capable of flying long distances carrying heavy bomb loads. They were huge planes, by First World War standards; British Handley Pages had a wingspan of a hundred feet, nearly as wide as the Flying Fortresses of the next war. Other Allied air services had comparable planes. The Italians had the Caproni, an odd-looking biplane with a wingspan of more than seventy feet and three engines—two facing forward and one aft—and three tails. It was the Allies' most effective bomber; two French bombing squadrons also flew them.

The Germans had their big bombers, too—Gothas, twin-engined biplanes the size of the Caproni. Colonel Mitchell heard of a Gotha raid that summer and carefully recorded the details: how an armada of thirty-five Gothas had flown across the Channel in broad daylight at an altitude of only thirty-five hundred feet, undetected by any Allied aircraft, and had dropped their bombs on London and returned to their base without losing a plane. He was appalled and blamed everybody: the Navy, which was responsible for defending the air over the Channel; the Army, which had no planes along the coast to fight the Germans off; the antiaircraft batteries, which were ineffectual. But still, wherever the blame lay, the Germans had done it; daylight raids were possible.

Most German raids weren't daylight operations, though. They came by night and were largely unopposed; the art and technology of night *chasse* flying had not yet been worked out. Allied pilots didn't meet the big planes in the air, but they sometimes saw them and heard them from the ground—rumbling ghosts in the darkness over Paris, or London, or Dunkerque, dropping destruction on the night streets below. Lance Holden, stationed at Le Bourget in a Defense of Paris squadron in the spring of 1918, described a raid:

> Last night we had our first raid. The lights went out. A moment later the barrage started. We stood out on the field—watching the bursting shrapnel and the flash of the guns. Search lights were playing on the sky and finally centered just over us. The firing increased and soon we heard the "thrum" of the Boche

motors. Then the whistle of a bomb before she hit. The whole thing was beautiful and thrilling. It reminded me of a show at the Hippodrome one year long ago. Some battle in the air scene. How theatrical it seemed at the time.

It's a spectacle, a *son et lumière*.

All that spring there were no American bombing squadrons at the front. Pursuit squadrons moved up—by April both the Ninety-Fourth and the Ninety-Fifth were flying combat patrols—and so did observation squadrons: the First in April, the Twelfth and the Eighty-Eighth in May. But no bombers. American pilots did fly on bombing raids with British and French squadrons, and some of those raids were on a scale that Mitchell would have approved; in May, for example, Alan Nichols and his French colleagues in SPA 85 flew cover for a raid at fifteen thousand feet on airfields at Cappy, where Richthofen's fliers were supposed to be. On the raid were thirty Spads—in front, "to clear the way," Nichols explained—followed by twenty-seven Breguet bombers, followed by another twenty-five Spads: eighty-two planes in all. The expedition was a great success, Nichols said; the fields were "well bombed" (though for him the high point was not the bombing but the dogfighting, in which he got his first Boche). Nichols's French commander called the raid "a Grande Promenade Militaire."

———

To be quite accurate, there was one American squadron—or sort of squadron—in existence in France at the turn of the year. The Ninety-Sixth had been at the bombing school at Clermont-Ferrand since November 1917, training in clapped-out Breguets that were rejects from French bombing squadrons at the front and waiting for better, newer planes and a few experienced pilots. The squadron didn't get new planes, but on April 11 it got a new commanding officer.

Major Harry Brown was something rare among flying commanders—an army regular, a West Point graduate who had served in the infantry back in Texas. Brown had no more flight time at the front than any junior pilot in his squadron, but he had professional ambition: he was eager that his squadron should be the first American bombing squadron to fly combat missions at the front, even if they had to fly them in tired old Breguets. And they did; in May the squadron flew what planes it had up to the airfield at Amanty, and on June 12 it launched its first raid.

That launching was an event: Trenchard came to watch it with members of his staff and officials representing British, French, and American aviation; pictures were taken. It turned out to be an ordinary sort of bombing raid (which is surprising when you consider that only two of the pilots and observers who flew on it had crossed the lines before). The ancient Breguets took a while to reach twelve thousand feet, and two planes had to drop out with engine trouble, but the rest reached their target (it was Dommary-Baroncourt) without opposition. They ran into antiaircraft fire there but dropped their bombs on a railway yard and a warehouse. On the way back the formation was attacked by enemy fighters, but there were no casualties, and all landed safely. That evening the squadron celebrated the success of the first American bombing raid. Brown had what he wanted.

Still, it wasn't quite what Billy Mitchell had in mind: ten old Breguets don't make an armada. He got his chance in July. By then he was Chief of Air Service, First Army, in the Château-Thierry sector. He proposed to the French a joint attack on German supply points at Fère-en-Tardenois that would mass their bombardment and pursuit squadrons and destroy German ammunition dumps and supplies. The French expressed regret; they had no squadrons to spare. They asked the British if they had any bombing squadrons available, and the British—meaning Trenchard, one assumes—replied by sending a brigade of the RAF: three squadrons of DH-9 bombers and four squadrons of pursuit planes.

The raid—250 planes in all—was flown the following day. Mitchell was delighted with the results and praised in particular the "tremendous valor" of the British bomber pilots:

> They came down in broad daylight to within a few hundred feet of the ground, blowing up several ammunition dumps which could be plainly seen by our ground troops. The Germans were taken completely by surprise and now had to stand on the defensive in the air, as this was their key point. If we blew up all their ammunition there and wrecked their supplies, their movement into the Château-Thierry area would be brought to a standstill.

Unfortunately, he adds, the British lost twelve bombardment airplanes in the attack, but the raid had been a success that confirmed his strategic theories: "It was the first case on record where we, with an inferior air force, were able to put the superior air force on the defensive and attack whenever we pleased, without the danger of the Germans sending great masses of pursuit aviation over to our side of the line." You'd think he'd have been content. But his account of the raid continues for one more sentence: "What we could have done if we had had one thousand good airplanes instead of a measly two hundred and fifty!"

Major Brown and the Ninety-Sixth spoiled the good bombing news. After their first raid, pilots of the squadron flew a couple of uneventful missions, but then both the weather and their old planes turned against them. On June 22 a formation set out for Conflans but was forced by clouds and high winds to turn back. On the twenty-fifth a formation of four planes got to Conflans and dropped, but poor visibility obscured the results. On June 26, 27, and 28, Brown attempted to lead attacks on Longuyon but had to return: the cloud ceiling was impenetrable. All this action wore the already worn planes out, and more and more had to turn back before they crossed the lines.

Early July was much the same: either the weather was foul, or there weren't enough planes; no missions were flown. Major Brown must have felt desperate; how could he and his squadron make their reputations with such weather and such planes? July 10 looked no better: cloudy and rainy, with poor visibility and only six planes available. But in the late afternoon the clouds seemed to lift, and Brown decided to take a chance and fly a raid. By the time he and the five other pilots took off, it was almost evening. As they climbed, they were immediately swallowed up in the overcast and disappeared. That was the last that was seen of them.

The squadron log for that day records what squadron members back at Amanty knew about the raid:

July 10—6 planes left our airdrome tonight at 6.05 p.m. to bomb the railroad station and yards at Conflans. Up to 11.30 p.m. no word had been received as to the whereabouts of them. Weather cloudy and rainy. Visibility poor. The formation was in command of Major Brown.

The next day's entry is from the Germans:

> *July 11*—Today at 4.00 p.m. the following extract from an inter-
> cepted German Communique was received by G-2, GHQ&EF
> (via 'phone): "Out of a squadron of six American aeroplanes
> which intended to attack Coblenz we captured five together
> with their crews." It is believed that the 6th plane landed within
> the German lines farther south than the others.

If that was true, the Ninety-Sixth had lost its commanding officer, most
of its flight crews, and nearly all its working aircraft in a single operation and without dropping a single bomb.

A story like that was bound to enter the Air Service rumor net, and
so it did. Harvey Conover drew a pilot's moral from the story:

> This may take some of the damn foolishness out of the Ameri-
> cans. They have been forced to fly planes entirely unfit for this
> work and discarded by the French. Not a word of this has been
> allowed to get into the paper. If it were put in we might benefit
> by the experience and our countrymen might lose some of their
> conceit and cockiness. A grand and glorious ending for the first
> American bombing squadron together with their commander.

The following day *The New York Times* had the story, from the German source. It went like this: The flight had climbed out of Amanty
into a solid overcast and had flown above it until, by the major's reckon-
ing, they were over Conflans. But the major hadn't allowed for the fact
that the winds above the clouds were stronger than the winds at ground
level—were in fact gale-force winds out of the southwest, blowing toward their target at something like seventy miles an hour. When Brown
led his formation down through the overcast to where he thought Conflans was, he found a strange city—Coblenz, a hundred miles farther
east. He indicated to the others that he was lost, and they all turned,
apparently each man on his own, and headed in what they hoped was
the direction of their home field. Flying against that fierce headwind
and still carrying their bombs, they all ran out of gas and made emergency landings in Germany. The sixth plane that the Germans couldn't

account for was Major Brown's. He, too, was down; it just took longer to find him.

Billy Mitchell heard the story, too, and drew his own angry moral from it:

> Our bombardment group was not in good condition. It was poorly commanded, the morale was weak and it would take some time to get it on its feet. This was largely due to the fact that when I was away in Château-Thierry, the 96th Squadron was left behind in the Toul area. The Major who was then in command of the 96th flew over into Germany with what ships he had available for duty. He lost his way in the fog and landed in Germany with every ship intact. Not one single ship was burned or destroyed and the Germans captured the whole outfit complete. This was the most glaring exhibition of worthlessness we had had on the front.

To Mitchell, the worst part of the history was the enemies' impudent response to the incident: "The Germans sent back a humorous message which was dropped on one of our airdromes. It said, 'We thank you for the fine airplanes and equipment which you have sent us, but what shall we do with the Major?'"

Mitchell did not respond, and the six crews spent the rest of the war as prisoners of the Germans. As for Major Brown, Mitchell wrote bitterly, "he was better off in Germany at that time than he would have been with us." As Mitchell saw the case, Brown's incompetence had humiliated his commander and effectively grounded the Air Service's first bombing squadron. With only two pilots and two planes left, the Ninety-Sixth would fly no more missions until replacements arrived. And Mitchell would have to start over building the strategic bombing force that he wanted so much.

FOURTEEN

SUMMER: 1918

O n the first day of spring 1918 only one American squadron was at the front and operating. That was the old Lafayette Escadrille, which had been transferred from the Service Aéronautique to the U.S. Air Service in February and was now the 103rd Pursuit, flying patrols from a field near Reims. Two other pursuit squadrons—the Ninety-Fourth and the Ninety-Fifth—had made it to the front, but neither got there equipped to fight: the Ninety-Fifth had no guns, and its pilots had not been trained in gunnery (they were promptly sent back to Cazaux to learn how to shoot); the Ninety-Fourth first had no planes and then had no guns to go in them. There were no other American squadrons on the lines—no observation, no bombing squadrons. The Air Service war in the air simply hadn't begun.

On the first day of summer, twelve squadrons were present and operating: five pursuit, six observation, and one bombing (the unfortunate Ninety-Sixth). Not a large number, when you consider how many French and British squadrons were strung along the front and fighting, and certainly not the tidal wave of pilots and planes that Congress had so optimistically promised a year before. Still, the flow had begun.

All that spring Americans moved up. In June two very restless *embusqués* finally escaped their jobs at Issoudun and joined the First Pursuit Group at Toul: Ham Coolidge went to the Ninety-Fourth Squadron, and his friend Quentin Roosevelt to the Ninety-Fifth.

Two other flying friends went up together in July. Walter Avery and Lance Holden had been in the same Defense of Paris squadron at Le Bourget field since April. In their months of waiting around, they'd heard stories of what squadrons at the front were doing and knew the reputations that some of those squadrons had gained. When their defense squadron was disbanded in July, the American pilots in it were offered a choice of assignments. "I faced a big decision yesterday," Holden wrote in a letter home, "I had the opportunity to go where I liked—To stay behind the lines—to go to the front with the French—or to get into the very thick of it with my friends in the best American Squadron—Gale, Willard, Avery and I looked at each other and sort of smiled—then they left it up to me, where we should we go. You are such a good sport that you will understand my choice." He chose the First Pursuit Group (composed of the Ninety-Fourth and the Ninety-Fifth Squadrons): "It is the crowd you have read so much about—Campbell—Rickenbacker— and all my friends—Their esprit de corps is marvelous—the wildest bunch on the front . . . I never was so happy."

Esprit de corps—of course: that's a virtue in any military unit. But *wildness*? That must mean extreme behavior beyond ordinary rules, both in the air and on the ground: chance taking over the lines, hard drinking after hours, furniture-breaking parties—the legends of fighting squadrons you hear before you ever see one in action.

————

Before 1918, the war on the Western Front had been mostly a static, entrenched confrontation; attacks might be launched, and troops would advance and withdraw, but the front remained essentially stationary, a meandering scar across France shaped like an arm with the elbow bent, the shoulder at the Channel, the upper arm running south to around Amiens and the forearm reaching east from there to the German border beyond Toul and Nancy.

In the spring and summer of 1918 that changed, and the war became a war of movement that remained in motion until the Armistice. Squadrons that had been flying from the same familiar field had to move up, in order to keep within the reach of the shifting lines, and then move again—forward as the enemy withdrew, or sometimes laterally, as fighting flared up on another part of the front. Moving became so customary that Ham Coolidge complained, "I feel like a travelling salesman going from place to place with all kinds of disreputable looking baggage." Squadron members—not only pilots, but mechanics and quartermasters and clerks and cooks—became skilled at packing up everything it takes to run a squadron, hauling it off to somewhere else, and unpacking it in time for the next morning's patrols.

Pilots' letters of that time are full of names of new airfields that are hard to find on maps: Épiez, Ourches, St. Pol, Amanty, Touquin, Flin, Francheville, Saints, La Ferté, Ferme des Greves, Lisle-en-Barrois, Vaucouleurs, Delouze, Coincy, Rembercourt, Érize-la-Petite, Bicquelay. A few of these fields are in the British sector, where some Americans are still flying with the RAF, but most are in the neighborhood of Château-Thierry, where American squadrons first enter the war in significant numbers, and later farther east, in the Toul sector.

Sometimes the new field a squadron moved up to would be an established, comfortable airfield: the landing spaces would be flat and smoothed out and long and wide enough to get down on without any trouble, and there'd be permanent hangars for the planes. Toul was like that—at least in memory. Harold Buckley looked back on it as "like the promised land with its fine airdrome, splendid quarters, and hot and cold showers." That sounds ideal, but there's more: memory adds the two cities nearby (Toul and Nancy), "of sufficient size to promise occasional opportunities to indulge the lighter sides of our natures." Hot showers and two towns to party in—what more could a pilot want?

Other fields would be new, might not even be airfields yet, but simply the biggest open space around—like the patch that the Ninety-Sixth Squadron flew into in May. Charles Codman remembered that flight:

The map was being scanned for Neufchâteau when without warning the leading plane banked to the left and slowly spiraled earthward. Motor trouble perhaps. Directly beneath, the terrain was thickly wooded. No visible landing place, unless you counted the small open space hemmed in on three sides by the woods and sloping sharply off on the fourth into a tiny village. It could be made in a pinch all right, but one would hardly choose it for an *atterissage* [landing field]. Two more planes nosed down. The formation scattered, circled, and one by one in a somewhat gingerly manner slid over the tree tops. A slight bump and we were on a stubby patch of what had been a wheat field, abandoned apparently, and liberally strewn with rocks. Across the middle of it a small white country road, originating presumably in the now invisible village, wandered off into the forest. No sign of human habitation. Where were we, and what now?

They were at Amanty. The airfield there would become an important base in the last stage of the war, but first the squadron would have to build it. That shouldn't have surprised the squadron members; Americans had been building the fields they flew from since the first student pilots arrived at Issoudun.

New airfields meant new quarters—all kinds of quarters. "This is the queerest life you ever saw," Ham Coolidge wrote to his family at home. "One week we live in a château, the next we are billeted in dingy farmhouses. Sometimes we eat like kings, again we almost starve because of all being broke." At Toul, in June, they were housed in a stone barracks with good food and hot and cold shower baths, and then, at Touquin, southwest of Château-Thierry, in a real château with flowers and vegetables in its gardens and fish in its lake. In September they lived in a tent, which Coolidge found far preferable to a billet.

Quentin Roosevelt found a room in a charming French house—"one of those white, plaster houses with tile roofs that sag in between the rafters"—with a little old lady and her dog. Initially, both regarded him with suspicion, but he won them over—first the old lady, by speaking French to her, and then the dog, who barked and growled but before the first evening was over was wagging his tail and putting his head on Roosevelt's knee. Roosevelt was an irresistibly charming young man.

———

Wherever they lodged, the pilots' work they did would be essentially what earlier pilots had done: the same patrolling, protecting bombers and artillery spotters and photo planes, the same fighting, scouting, and strafing, the same low work through the same artillery barrages. The same, but with a difference: in July the war heated up, and the Battle of

Château-Thierry was fought. The pilots were aware of the change; Lance Holden wrote, at the end of the month, "We are in a sector where there is more aerial fighting than there has been in the history of the war and undoubtedly the battle between Soisson and Rheims is one of the most terrific in history."

In that most terrific battle the fighting—on the ground and in the air—will grow more and more intense; there will be more troops below and more planes above. More planes will mean changes in tactics; pursuit planes will fly in larger formations, and dogfights will be congested and scary. Sumner Sewall, a pilot in the Ninety-Fifth, described a fight he got into that month in a letter to his mother:

> We were patrolling about over the lines in a big formation of ten planes when we sighted a formation of six Boche machines about five kilometers inside their lines. Well we dived on them and attacked. I wish you could have seen the mess that followed. Sixteen planes just rushing around upside down and on their ear some climbing and others diving. Black crosses would go swirling around. Really it was the darndest stew I have ever seen.

Fifteen years later, Alan Winslow remembers such congested battles: "These massed aerial combats are not adequately described by the expression 'dog fights,'" he wrote; "they were violent mob riots of the air."

There will be more bombers in the air, too—flotillas of them (Billy Mitchell's "measly two hundred and fifty" plane raid was flown during the Château-Thierry operations), with more pursuit planes stacked above at different altitudes to protect them. Observation squadrons will be drawn into the mass attacks; George Hughes remembered that in the drive on Hill 204 "there must have been fully 150 Allied planes in the air at one time. It was like running a taxi on 5th Avenue; it was all you could do to keep from colliding."

With all those planes in the air, and the antiaircraft fire heavier from below, there will be more casualties: more wounds, more crashes, more accidents, more planes that just disappear, more dead. As more new men come to the front, live through their first weeks there, and join in the ordinary business of combat flying, the dark events of war will become a steady presence in their minds, and they will search for a way of writing about them. Walter Avery, at Saints with the Ninety-Fifth, recorded the squadron's daily losses in his journal. Here are entries for a few days in early August:

> *Saturday.* Had my second Boche today . . . Holden, Bailey and Gill failed to return. At supper we learned by phone that Holden and Bailey had been driven down just inside our lines . . . Gill has not been heard from.
>
> *Sunday.* Gill got back, wounded in the leg . . . We found "Rabbit" Curry's machine near Azy. He had fallen about 50 ft. in a nose dive and died before they got him out of the plane . . . Russell is missing . . . Curry is buried near Azy where he fell.
>
> *Monday.* Russell was seen to go down in yesterday's fight. Buried near Bazoches Hospital.
>
> *Tuesday.* Milhau, a transfer pilot, leaving our field in a Type 28 [Nieuport] went into a *vrille* at 100M and couldn't get out of it. He was killed instantly. He and the plane were a bad mess.

The tone of the writing is flat and reportorial—ordinary words for ordinary dying, the tone they've used for death since their training days. Avery provides the details that pilots always want to know—what happened, and where and how. And nothing more.

When the plane shot down is his own, a pilot will write about it in his letters or journal—if he does—in the same cool tone. When Lance Holden is shot down that August, he mentions the incident in a single paragraph, almost parenthetically:

> *Aug. 5–19, 1918.* The 10th we were attacked by 7 while protecting a French biplace Spad. Buckley and Avery each got one. Gill was wounded. Bailey and I were shot down. He with an explosive bullet in his tank. I with a bullet through my intake manifold and cylinder—besides others. That was an entirely successful fight. The biplace returned with all its pictures.

Doug Campbell is wounded in the fight with a German biplace that ends his combat career:

I heard a loud crashing sound and felt myself hit in the back; it appears that a bullet struck a wire just behind me, and one of the fragments lodged in the flesh of my lumbar regions.

Fortunately, it didn't disable me for flying, and I made a bee-line for home, landing safely. Inside of half an hour the bullet had been located by X-ray . . . The wound is perfectly clean, and they sewed it up tight . . . I am sleeping and eating well, and am as comfortable as could be expected with a hole in my back.

Two war stories that you'd expect would be told with some sense of excitement. Holden tells his in plain descriptive terms; Campbell is off-hand and cheerful (the letter is to his mother). Nothing to get excited about; it's all part of the game.

That tough tone became the pilots' style as they settled into the customariness of everyday war. Only occasionally does one see the mask of toughness slip. In August, Holden sketches four deaths in three days as curtly and exactly as any pilot could wish: "In three days—4 men have been killed in accidents. 2 crashed on our field. Then Walt Smyth and Alec Bruce collided in the air when a Boche piqued on their formation. Walt fell 3000 metres without wings, Bruce fell with jammed ailerons." And then he adds one word, from the heart: "Horrible!" The deaths of Smyth and Bruce are horrible because he knew them.

One of the dead that summer was Quentin Roosevelt. He had come to the front—at last—early in July, flew his practice flights, and made his first patrol on the tenth. Over the lines the formation broke up, and Roosevelt found himself alone until he saw three planes together and flew to join them. He was nearly in formation with them when he saw that they were German. He attacked one and saw the enemy plane spin down. He had probably got his Boche. Four days later, on his second patrol, he again lost his formation (one thinks of those nearsighted eyes) and simply disappeared. He was declared Missing in Action. Several days later a German plane crossed the lines to drop a note: Lieutenant Roosevelt had been killed in action and buried at Chamery.

None of Roosevelt's fellow pilots saw his last fight, but they wrote home about his death and—being pilots—speculated on what happened: he forgot about the strong wind against him and was blown far into German space; he was too eager and let himself be drawn into a trap; he got lost in a bank of clouds. But after the tough speculations come the testimonies and the strong feelings for the special young man that Roosevelt was: he was a "wonderful boy"; "everyone loved him"; "one of the finest and most courageous boys I ever knew"; "a daring flier and was very popular with his companions"; and, from his dear friend Ham Coolidge, who had made a pilgrimage to Roosevelt's grave and afterwards wrote home: "Bursting shrapnel, onion rockets, machine gun bullets and Boche planes give you a start at first, but you get used to all that. What you can never get used to, though, is to have your very best friends 'go West.'"

Theodore Roosevelt wrote of his son's death to his friend Edith Wharton: "There is no use of my writing about Quentin; for I should break down if I tried. His death is heartbreaking. But it would have been far worse if he had lived at the cost of the slightest failure to perform his duty."

The score of the dead was a statistic that living pilots learned to accept. Another kind of score keeping seemed, in their minds, to make up for the losses: the score of personal victories that they all hoped to achieve. When one of them won his first fight, he wrote home to share the news— modestly or triumphantly, according to his nature. After his first fight Quentin Roosevelt wrote cautiously, "I got my first real excitement on the front for I think I got a Boche." Ham Coolidge simply announced, "I got a Boche today." And Avery wrote, "Day before yesterday while making my second patrol over the front with this squadron, the 95th, . . . I brought down my first Boche." All matter-of-fact statements of matters of fact.

But as they move into their separate stories and the details pile up, their excitement invades their narratives: they describe how the enemy's tracer bullets flew past their ears; how the Boche's tail suddenly tipped up and he went into a *vrille*; how the biplace Rumpler burst into flames; how the Pfalz threw out clouds of smoke. And how they felt afterwards: "I shall never forget the sensation of seeing a stream of flaming tracer bullets from my guns sink into its body"; "now feel quite sure that I am really in the war"; "you bet I was happy."

The folks at home are thrilled and proud; they pass the letters on to their local papers, and because the stories are dramatic and the heroes are hometown boys, the papers publish them, with the local reference in the headlines. Occasionally, a story comes straight from a correspondent at the front. When Walter Avery shoots down a Boche who turns out to be a German ace, the Cleveland *Plain Dealer* runs this story:

OHIOAN DROPS FOE ACE
WALTER AVERY OF COLUMBUS TAKES HIM PRISONER
(By Plain Dealer Special Cable)

WITH THE AMERICANS AT THE MARNE, July 26.— Walter Avery of Columbus, O., an American aviator who has scored a number of brilliant successes, today shot down and took prisoner Capt. Meinkopf, one of the Leading German "aces" who had sixteen aerial victories to his credit.

Avery's feat occurred near Chateau-Thierry.

Getting it slightly wrong, of course; Avery hadn't scored "a number of brilliant successes"; this was his first fight. He didn't copy the *Plain Dealer* piece into his journal, but he did preserve the report from the London *Daily Mail*, which identifies his victim as "the most famous living German airman." "The duel," the *Mail*'s correspondent wrote from France, "was one of the most exciting I have ever seen. The two machines went at each other like two fighting cocks at 900 feet up. Lieutenant Avery's mastery was incontestable, and he won more by manoeuvring than with his machine guns." The reporter interviews Carl Menckhoff (like the *Plain Dealer*'s man, he gets the spelling wrong), who wants to know who the pilot was who shot him down. "He is a good fighter," he says, "and it might gratify him to know my name." He's surprised to learn that his conqueror was an American flying a French Spad.

The story of Avery's victory will last longer than most; an American beginner beating a German ace is just too good to let go. Billy Mitchell will tell it in his *Memoirs*, improving it slightly; in his version, as Menckhoff was hustled back to a prison camp, "he bitterly complained of his hard luck in being downed by a *kind*."

Ham Coolidge's first victory was reported from the field by a war correspondent for the *Boston Herald*, which published the account twice, on consecutive days, in essentially the same words. In the *Herald*'s version, the fight went like this:

> Driving a big, new French biplane, mounting four guns, he was sent with Lt. James A. Meisner of Brooklyn on a photographic mission behind the German lines. There they were attacked by a squadron of seven Hun fighting planes. Instead of fleeing, Coolidge turned on his attackers, sending one to the ground in flames. The others made off. Lt. Coolidge completed his mission and returned to his hangar. He was grazed on the chin by one bullet, two bullets pierced his gasoline tank through the protected armor and more than 30 struck the plane. When he landed his plane was collapsing because Boche bullets had cut the wires.

You can imagine how thrilled and alarmed the folks at home were. They must have mailed a cutting to their son at once. Three weeks later, when the *Herald* story reached him, Coolidge wrote back:

I hasten to correct an account of my adventures which gives me considerable pain! The *Herald* obviously had my name confused with that of an observer in one of the biplace observation groups. I do not drive a *big* French biplane, but a small one. It is not equipped with four guns. I did not turn upon seven attackers and send one down in flames . . . It is true that I have official credit for downing the biplace Rumpler. It is nothing but pure luck that my bullets happened to be the ones to bring out the flames, for certainly the other two boys deserve exactly as much credit for downing it as I do. Also it is the sort of thing that happens every day and they shouldn't have stuck in my picture and written all that junk. It's a pity.

Pilots know that the newspaper version will miss the important details: the roles the other pilots on the patrol played, and what the Boche did, and the weather, and the way luck enters in, and fear, and nerves. Civilians won't get it right, because they can't: they haven't been there—not even the special correspondent who says he saw it all.

And so pilots at the front withdraw into their pilots' world, where there are other young men like themselves who understand the contingencies of combat. It isn't that they don't enjoy their moment of celebrity—it's like scoring a touchdown in the Harvard-Yale game—but they distrust the civilian storyteller. The language they trust is the plain talk of pilots: exact altitudes, and the names of targets, and the numbers and kinds of planes, and of the guns they carry, and words for the weather, and for certain maneuvers and disasters.

Dick Blodgett and the Ninety-Fifth have barely begun to fly combat missions when he writes: "The magazines in the States are full of the greatest yarns I ever heard. You might think we'd done something yet, besides make a lot of promises. They write up reams of junk just because a few darling sons left home." And he adds, for emphasis, "And just remember that I said that everything I had read in print about aviation is to say the least gross exaggeration and really nothing but newspaper lies. They get me quite stirred up."

And Holden, writing in September: "It seems to me all aviation stories are written about the fights in which the pilot gloriously brings down Boches and balloons like falling leaves." It isn't *like* that: the balloon *doesn't* burn, and he flies home wiggling and twisting to avoid streams of German bullets.

Most of all, they're embarrassed at being called heroes. It's a role they imagined, back at the beginning: meeting your enemy in the air in single combat and defeating him; that would be splendid beyond anything their college-boy minds could conceive. But now they know that a fight in the air isn't like the hero stories the newspapers tell and that onetime winners aren't heroes. The real heroes are the pilots who came to the war months or years before, made their reputations among their fellow pilots, scored their victories, and were modest about them.

Among the storytelling pilots there were also the other kind: the self-promoters, the exaggerators, the flat-out liars. Holden in a letter praises the modesty of his friend Doug Campbell and goes on, "Oh how unspeakably we hate the other kind—Bert Hall—Wright and the rest." Bert Hall and Harold Wright: those two names turn up again and again that summer in the letters of pilots in France, and always with contempt. Real combat pilots despise the two of them as a banker might despise a forger—for debasing the currency.

Bert Hall's war, so far as it went, was a creditable one. He joined the French Foreign Legion in 1914, transferred to the Service Aéronautique, flew with the Lafayette Escadrille (he's there in the photograph of the first seven Americans), shot down three—or perhaps four—Boches, and was decorated for valor (Hall and Nordhoff name the decorations: Médaille Militaire, Croix de Guerre). In 1916, Kiffin Rockwell describes one of Hall's fights: "Bertie Hall attacked a Boche this afternoon at 4,000 meters high, brought him down. He followed him to one thousand meters high and saw him hit the ground and go to pieces just in the German lines. Bertie's machine was hit in the fight." And in his next letter, he asks his brother to "give Bertie Hall some publicity."

But in the middle of the war Hall seems to have lost his taste for combat: perhaps prudence set in, or a sense of self-preservation. And from that point Hall's war story becomes the subject of speculation and rumor: Was he kicked out of the Lafayette? Did he really join a French aviation mission to Romania? Historians of the Lafayette venture many other possible Bert Hall stories: that before the war he had flown in the First Balkan War; that he conned the Chinese air force out of a large

sum of money; that he did time in a federal penitentiary. And they find
many colorful terms to describe him: con man, card shark, forger, liar,
bounder, scoundrel.

Certainly Hall was back in the United States before the war ended,
"supposedly," Hall and Nordhoff wrote, "for the purpose of entering the
United States Air Force." (There's a lot of doubt in that "supposedly.")
He didn't, in fact, join the Air Service; instead, he wrote about the adventures he'd had, in a book titled *En l'Air!* and in at least one magazine
article. You can get a sense of Hall's relaxed way with the truth from the
heading of the article he wrote for *The American Magazine* in the summer of 1918:

FAST FIGHTING AND NARROW
ESCAPES IN THE AIR
Some of My Experiences in a Battle Plane
By Lieutenant Bert Hall
An American Who Became an "Ace" in the French Flying Corps

Hall was never a lieutenant in any service, and he wasn't an ace: two
lies already, and he hasn't even begun to tell his story!

The tale he told to the folks back home is a lively one, suited to
popular taste. It's full of fights against odds, and burning planes, and
the blood of Boches, and of his own victories and decorations. But it's
also full of praise for the men he flew with and their "splendid loyalty
and devotion" to one another. You can't help liking the man who tells
the story. The only trouble is, it isn't the story of the pilots' work that we
get from other men who were there but a romantic tale with himself as
hero: not lies, exactly, but selective improvements of the truth, such as
a likable rascal might tell.

The case of "Sergeant Pilot Wright" was altogether different. Wright
was simply a liar who did essentially nothing during a short hitch with
the Lafayette Flying Corps and claimed to have done everything. Hall and
Nordhoff put the facts of Wright's war in a bare summary in their book:

Date of Enlistment: March 20, 1917.

Aviation Schools: March 25 to September 8, 1917, Avord,
Pau G.D.E.

Breveted: July 18, 1917 (Caudron).

At the Front: Escadrille Spad 155, September 11 to December 23, 1917.

Final Rank: *Sergent*.

Two and a half months in a squadron. No victories. No decorations. Just *there*.

Wright's version of his flying career is something else: a tall tale of planes and balloons shot down in thrilling fights, a man-to-man combat with Baron von Richthofen at twenty thousand feet, a one-man scrap against seven Germans, a "hair-raising" battle of forty Allied planes (one of them *him*) against fifty-five Boches—the whole story decorated with blood-splashed wings and flaming planes. He must have written it back in the States in the spring of 1918; it was published in *The Saturday Evening Post* in five weekly installments between June 8 and July 6, under the title "Aces High."

It took a while for copies of the *Post* to reach pilots at the front, but when they did, the reactions were uniformly hostile: not so much angry as contemptuous and dismissive. In July, Roland Richardson wrote, "If you want to read a funny article on Aviation read 'Aces High' by Sgt. Pilot Harold D. Wright in the S.E.P. June 15, 1918. He sure does sling the bull so to speak about himself and aviation in general, whatever you do though, don't believe all of it, for we have just read it and most of the article is ridiculous. His figures are way off and the whole thing is pretty much of a farce."

In August, *Plane News*, a paper published in France for the troops, ran an item on Wright under this heading:

"AVIATOR" FAILS
TO KID TROOPS
AND ESCADRILLE
"Soldier" Who Failed as Flyer
Putting Over Heavy Stuff

The article summarizes Wright's real career: he was briefly with the Lafayette Escadrille, but failed to qualify as a pilot, and flew only thirteen hours over the front. It ends,

It is another instance of kidding the public and seeking the limelight of fame.

The hero does not seek publicity.

You can see what is happening: pilots at the front are reading Wright's stories, or maybe only hearing about them from other pilots, and are spreading the word. As accounts circulate, details are added to them: the thirteen (or thirty) total hours of flight time, the single trip over the front, the discharge for cowardice. And so an antithetical version builds that will overwhelm Wright's inventions and replace them with the story of a cowardly liar. As Hall and Nordhoff wryly remarked, Wright had turned out to be not Baron von Richthofen but Baron von Münchhausen.

If you eliminate the liars, the journalists, and the headline writers back home from your list of possible tellers of the air-war story, what are you left with? Only the pilots' own versions, the bare truths that come from direct experience—factual, blunt, emptied of war's big words, and filled with plain particulars of men and how they behave in the air, how they depend on one another and how they act alone, and what the enemy does, of machines and the ways in which they can fail you, of weather and terrain. And luck. And the odds. It will be the story that pilots tell one another, in the language of their own pilot culture; the rest of us can listen in if we want to.

FIFTEEN

SEPTEMBER: ST. MIHIEL

By the summer's end the Battle of Château-Thierry is over, and won, and there are rumors of the next one, an even bigger offensive that will engage still more American troops and more American squadrons. Lester Egbert, the supply officer of the Twenty-Second Pursuit Squadron, remembered waiting, back at Orly, for orders to the front: "Rumor had it that the Americans were about to make their first offensive. We understood that the Americans were forming their first army, an army bigger than the one Grant led into Richmond, and would take over the lines near Toul and Nancy; and that's where we were to go." That's the way military news spreads—by rumor, not by some general's announcement.

Lance Holden hears the rumor in early September; he and the Ninety-Fifth have moved to a new sector between Verdun and St. Mihiel and are flying with the First Pursuit Group from a field near Rembercourt: "When the attack breaks for which we have come down here there is going to be some great fights. There are something like 3000 planes in this sector. It will be an all American offensive. Probably to straighten the St. Mihiel salient and possibly to capture Metz. I should like to be billeted in Metz this winter."

Other squadrons have moved up, too; by mid-September twenty-nine Air Service squadrons are at the front. There's a bustle along the lines: new billets to find, new fields to learn (the length of the landing space, the slopes, the obstacles), new planes to bring up. And muddle, too, as the changing needs of the offensive require sudden squadron changes. A squadron might train as a bombing squadron, organize for that work, and then be told there is a greater need for scout planes and go to the front as a pursuit squadron, where it will be given Spads—which the pilots have never flown and the mechanics have neither the tools nor the spare parts to service (as happened to the Twenty-Second Squadron that summer).

Or a squadron might come to the front as a biplace pursuit squadron (which sounds a little odd) and be ordered to turn itself into a bombing squadron overnight and fly a bombing mission the next morning. That happened to the Twentieth Squadron at Amanty in September. Orders came on the evening of the thirteenth to bomb Conflans the next morning. The squadron had no bombs, and ground crews worked all night hauling a supply from Colombey-les-Belles. It flew the mission as scheduled, in DH-4s with Liberty engines (which many of the pilots had never flown before), over enemy lines (none of them had ever crossed the front). One pilot crashed on takeoff and was killed, but the others apparently reached their target and completed the mission, thus becoming the first American squadron flying American-built planes to drop bombs on the enemy—another of those *firsts* that American squadrons so eagerly claimed. The organization of the American air war would never lose this state of extemporized disorder—of a military force that had come to the war too late and could never quite catch up with itself.

––––––

The flying weather on the Western Front during the last months of the war was awful—rain, mist, low-lying clouds, and high winds that blew planes deep into German airspace. Squadron historians looking back on those months sprinkle their pages with the dreariness: "rained in the night and a gusty wind at dawn"; "cold and rainy and the clouds low"; "dud weather now set in with a vengeance"; "low-hanging mists and drizzling rain" (those are all from Frederick Clapp's history of the Seventeenth, on the English front with the RAF). "It never ceased to rain and at one time the fellows wore their boots for nearly a month without putting on shoes" (that's from C. G. Barth's history of the Twentieth, in the American sector in the east).

They catalog the problems such weather caused as the front moved and men and planes tried to move with it. The 104th Squadron is ordered to move up to Souilly, south of Verdun, in early September, in time for the St. Mihiel offensive, which is to begin on the twelfth. The squadron's enlisted men drive all night on the seventh through rain and get there, but the pilots and the planes are grounded, back at Luxeuil. The C.O. hopes to lead them up on the eighth, but rain and high winds make flying impossible—that day, and the next, and the next, and the next, while the squadron commander "literally tore his hair and read an occasional telegram from the Group Commander." (That's from the squadron historian's account.) The Battle of St. Mihiel is scheduled to begin the next morning, and the 104th has ten observers but only two pilots (neither of whom has flown over the lines).

On the twelfth the squadron's second echelon tries to move up through the same weather:

> In the morning Lts. Coffin, Jacobi, Ball, Houck, Davis, Wallace and Johnston started in the rain. Coffin and Jacobi actually reached Souilly and Coffin flew over the lines that afternoon. Ball landed at Amanty in a hard rain storm and collided with two Breguets of the First Bombardment Group that were on the ground. Davis, Wallace and Houck followed Ball down and broke their propellers in the mud. 1st Lt. Donald Johnston failed to report.

(That's the historian again.)

When dawn broke on September 12, the D-day of the St. Mihiel offensive, pilots looked out from their tents and saw that the weather was what it had been for so many days: low-hanging clouds, a fine, driving rain, and heavy winds blowing out of the southwest, straight into Germany—unflyable weather. But at 5:00 a.m. the infantry left its trenches, and the ground assault began; its progress had to be observed and reported, and fighters had to support it. And so they flew. Percival Hart, of the 135th Observation Squadron, described that day as "by far the most eventful day in the Squadron's existence. Every pilot and observer, except the missing six, had flown twice, and some of them three times; at least two planes had been over the lines at all times from before dawn until dusk, flying under weather conditions which would ordinarily have been considered impossible." (The missing six were the crews of the three planes that had not returned from their first mission of the day; two of them had been shot down in flames; the third had got lost in the clouds and made a forced landing in Switzerland and was interned.)

Joe Eastman, of the Ninety-Fourth, flew two patrols that day and wrote a sensitive description of what he saw and felt. His story begins on the flight line that morning, where he and the other pilots on the early patrol stand, "smelling the turbulent weather dubiously." They'll have to fly in pairs, trying to keep track of each other in the mist and rain.

Eastman and his partner, a pilot named Thorne Taylor, take off, get to two hundred meters, and head for the lines. Taylor, in the lead plane, slips in and out of sight in the tatters of cloud that trail below the overcast, and Eastman struggles to avoid colliding with him. The air becomes more violently agitated, and gale-force winds toss the planes around. They pass a balloon; it's higher than they are. The planes "flop and skid from the air 'bumps' of forests, gale, clouds, barrages and cannon fire."

It's a rough patrol that Eastman flies that morning. And yet what impresses him most, out there in the misty grayness, is not the weather, or the sounds of battle, or the waves of attacking troops, but something nearly the opposite: "Along in the trenches could be distinguished our troops lined up ready for the word. Of German infantry nothing at all was visible. Except for the few groups of doughboys to be seen, the effect generally was of the greatest loneliness. Now and then a few trucks, otherwise the roads stretched white and blank—not a soul. Where *was* everyone?" The loneliness of a battlefield before the battle: it takes a kind of poet to see and feel that.

On another patrol later that day, Eastman has a different unexpected impression:

Strangest, from our point of view, was that instead of the battle being a distant impersonal scene of flickers along a sweep of dull colored blotches—we were in it, surrounded by it at no more than a good bellowing range. Camions were not doubtful

tiny specs. We could see the harness on the horses' backs! And
the shells that sent Buddy [his term for an American soldier] flat
on his back, would like to have done the same to us.

Words alone are not enough to make that patrol real; Eastman adds
drawings to his account.

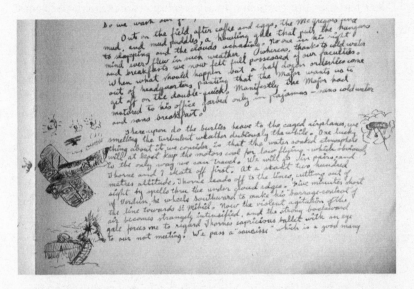

What they did, in those last months of the war, was mostly done
close to the ground. This concentration of low flying was partly a consequence of the weather: if you couldn't fly high and hunt the Boche
there, then fly low and go after the infantry and transport. But it was
also partly tactical: the front was shifting and uncertain, and the enemy
retreating along roads and rail lines was vulnerable to attack. Allied
troops were also moving; their exact location at any given time could
only be determined by flying low and looking for them.

Ham Coolidge flew a liaison patrol on the first day of the St. Mihiel
offensive and in a letter to his mother a few days later tried to explain
what it had been like. Describing the events of such a vast action, he
wrote, was "like trying to recall all that one sees from an express train
window after the journey is over, only we have the added difficulty of
having to pay considerable attention to our little express train itself. We

are the engineers as well as the passengers." Nevertheless, he tries: "Thursday morning we went out in groups of threes and fours, flying at a height of perhaps two hundred feet. Our object was to see everything possible on the ground and to try and establish the location of the lines . . . Well, you never saw such a sight or heard such sounds."

The patrol starts out along their own lines. Below them, Allied artillery batteries fire continuously; the explosions rock the little planes about and threaten to dash them into the treetops. Coolidge can see very few men moving down there: the color of American uniforms is hard to distinguish against earth colors, and the planes are tossing wildly in the turbulent air. They move into Bocheland: burning villages, dumps, and storehouses stand out sharply. Then they are over woods again, but are they Boche woods? Or Allied? Coolidge can see officers on horses rushing to and fro on the roads, and trucks, wagons, and men moving madly along, but he doesn't dare fire on them—they might be Americans. He simply can't tell.

At this point, Coolidge's story shifts from the ground below to the air he's flying in: "Then the party began for us. The Archies opened up full blast, hanging hideously close, when suddenly, sharp and distinct through the noise of our motors came the unmistakable ra ta ta ta ta of machine gun bullets."

He thinks there must be a German plane on his tail, but it's a machine-gun nest in the woods; they're not firing tracers, so he can't see them rise, but they're there. The plane on his left takes seven hits and leaves the formation. Another has a *panne de moteur*—engine failure—and barely gets back across the lines. Coolidge and the fourth plane turn back, into a heavy headwind, with antiaircraft shells bursting all around them, and the rattle of machine guns below. Just as they cross the lines, Coolidge's engine groans and dies. He glides down a little valley and worms his way into a tiny patch of good ground, past telegraph wires, barbed-wire entanglements, and shell holes, and rolls to a stop a few feet from one of the holes. "A Spad," he observes wryly, "is heavy and lands fast at best, so it's no fun to have forced landings." He walks to a French headquarters nearby and finds that the fourth pilot from the patrol has also *panned* and is there.

Four planes go out on an infantry liaison, and not one completes the flight. And what have they learned about the moving front? Nothing that Coolidge mentions; his story is about chaotic confusion and destruction below and a storm of enemy gunfire above. Their only accomplishment has been their own survival.

Pursuit pilots like Coolidge don't seem disappointed not to be high up, dogfighting; flying low-work missions is exciting. Lance Holden flew another kind of low mission the day after Coolidge's—the second day of St. Mihiel. His account of what it was like is less tense than Coolidge's and more high-spirited, with more of the fun of low flying in it (apparently nobody is shooting at him, or at least he doesn't mention anyone):

> We rolled out of bed this morning while it was still dark with orders to strafe troops on the roads as they were retreating. I was leading a patrol of 3. But the other two had dropped out with motor trouble by the time we crossed what used to be the lines before the Americans advanced. The clouds were only 300 ft. off the ground so I was hopping along over the tree tops when along came a wagon train of Germans. It was a fine, long, straight road and in 30 seconds what used to be a very orderly string of wagons became a riot! My guns were working perfectly. The drivers were diving under the wagons—the horses were rearing and plunging.

He turns from that target, strafes a camp in passing, and flies on up the road. There are no wagons for some distance, but he spots a German officer riding his horse: "Say! when my tracer bullets started bouncing off the road beneath that horse you should have seen the circus. Off went the officer's hat—away went the horse with the dutchman crouched over his neck. That fellow knew how to ride! But I don't know if he has stopped yet—He was still going—a speck in the distance as I turned for home."

It's a comic incident, a circus. He sails on home, still laughing.
The story has one more detail:

> I looked behind and there just a measured inch from my head was a bullet hole. It must have gone through my hair.

The bullet that missed is part of the joke.

Balloon hunting was another patrol a pursuit pilot could fly when the ceiling was low. The First Pursuit Group flew a lot of them that fall. To the armchair aviator a balloon might seem an easy target: it floats there at the end of its cable, a few hundred feet from the ground, it can't move, it can't fight back, and it's flammable. Just get in close, take aim at the fat bag of gas, and blast away—and then get out of there fast.

It wasn't that easy. Ham Coolidge explained in a letter written in September, "Shooting down balloons is pretty risky work—a good deal more so than combat with enemy planes. You see they send up a fierce barrage of machine gun fire, Archies, flaming 'onion' rockets, etc., in a circle around the old sausage." Balloon-hunting patrols were dangerous.

Nevertheless, in those autumn months of 1918, American pilots flew more and more attacks on balloons—sometimes on orders, sometimes voluntarily. No doubt there were more Boche balloons out there to shoot at, as movement along the lines accelerated, and both sides needed accurate information on the exact location of troops, artillery, supplies— all the necessities of war in progress. And there were more American squadrons at the front to attack the watching balloons. The planes the pursuit squadrons flew—new Spad VIIs—were better suited to such attacks, stronger and faster than the old Nieuports, and armed with two Vickers guns that could be loaded with incendiary bullets, or sometimes with an eleven-millimeter "balloon gun." Balloon busting had become a special pursuit pilot's job, with its own equipment and its own appeal: a balloon counted the same as a plane in a pilot's individual score—get five, and you'd be an ace.

A few of Lance Holden's encounters with balloons, as recorded in his journal for August and September, show the excitement with which pilots pursued this kind of low work. On August 2, Holden is returning from a patrol when he comes on a balloon at two hundred feet: "I fired at close range. Zoomed over it and looking over my shoulder saw a column of smoke and flame appear on top. Then the whole envelope burst into flame." It seems so casual: he just happens on a balloon, he fires, it burns. Years later, he drew a picture of a successful attack; Harold Buckley put it in his history of the Ninety-Fifth.

By the end of September Holden's impatience to raise his score to five is growing as the war moves toward its end. And then an opportu-

nity comes: "At last! At last—my chance came last night and I brought down another balloon in flames that is certain to be confirmed and become an official victory. It makes me all the happier because it is something I have had my heart set on and been systematically trying to accomplish." He's excited; he must make the story vivid to the folks back home. He goes on:

It was so dark by this time I figured the Huns must have gone— The gunners, I don't think saw me till I had started shooting— the balloon was only 100 metres up—I waited patiently as I could till I was very close then fired—my guns jammed! They were shooting machine guns and "flaming onions." I was so mad it didn't phase [sic] me—I just got out the hammer and started fixing the guns—I got the guns fixed and was turning to fire again when up she went. Can you picture that great sausage wrapped in flames in the dead of night? . . . I don't know if the observer escaped or not—I don't see how he could have—if he had jumped the balloon would have fallen on him—if he stayed he was burned.

It's a graphic story, another kind of air show—in which, perhaps, a man burns to death.

————

Balloons counted in the victory score, and sometimes pilots went balloon hunting on their own, hoping to score a point before the game ended. But the strategy of the war's endgame was not individual, it was large-scale—more planes in the air, flying larger and longer missions, against fiercer opposition both from the air and from the ground. By the time the St. Mihiel offensive began, there were three pursuit groups (that's twelve squadrons), six observation groups (thirteen squadrons), and, for the first time on the front, a bombing group—enough planes to fly the sorts of missions that Trenchard and Mitchell had dreamed of.

They flew those missions in the war's last months, and pilots who flew them remembered them long afterwards with a certain pride; they had been there when the *big* air battles were fought. They recalled not numbers of planes—who could have counted them?—but the dense whirl of them, like gnats in a beam of summer sunlight, each plane a dot in a swarm of dots. They're pleased with the size of the attacks: bigger is better, more destructive, more overpowering. The more planes the Allies put in the air over the German lines, the closer they come to final victory.

Billy Mitchell agreed, of course; for the initial attack at St. Mihiel, he planned to launch a force of two thousand planes to cover and support the offensive and to oppose the massed power of the German air force. Kenneth Littauer, C.O. of the Eighty-Eighth Observation Squadron, was at Souilly on September 13 to witness what he called "General Mitchell's famous 'thousand-plane raid'" (actually comprising 1,481 aircraft): "I was climbing into an airplane to start out on a mission when I heard some noise overhead. I looked up and wave after wave of airplanes came over. I'd never seen anything like it. Of course, it was delightful doing a mission after that. The air was swept clean. There was nothing out there after that mass of airplanes went through."

I can imagine how Littauer felt as he looked up from the ground at that grand sight: no one had ever before seen so many planes in the air together, moving in one coordinated action against the enemy.

A lot of planes will be lost in those final months; sometimes they'll be counted in small numbers, one here, one there, a couple somewhere else, as squadrons launch such raids as they can with the planes they have. On the first five days of the St. Mihiel offensive the Ninety-Sixth Bombing Squadron flew nine raids, in spite of the worst flying weather in many months. The first raid, on the twelfth, was a single plane attack on Buxières; the plane did not return and was later reported to have gone down in flames. The second raid, of eight planes (or maybe nine—reports vary), attacked Buxerulles; eight planes returned, one made a forced landing at Vaucouleurs. On the third mission, five planes were ordered to bomb troops at Vigneulles. The takeoff was delayed, and the flight didn't leave until 6:35 in the evening. The planes dropped their bombs blindly and headed for home in the dark. Only one landed successfully; one crashed in a forest, two piled up on the airfield, and one crashed in a plowed field, killing the pilot.

That wasn't all. During the day many planes from other squadrons made emergency landings on the Ninety-Sixth's field. One Salmson, trying to land near the squadron hangar, drifted in the fierce wind into two of the Ninety-Sixth's Breguets, destroying all three planes. Score, after one day's actions: three fliers killed and eight planes wrecked or out of commission.

On the thirteenth, the five flyable Breguets that were left were ordered to bomb roads between Chambley and Mars-la-Tour. Four got off, but one was forced to land in a nearby field. The other three continued and made low-level bombing runs on troops along the road. They were surrounded by fifteen German pursuit planes, and two of the Ninety-Sixth's planes were shot down—one out of control, the other in flames.

On the third raid of the day, eight planes took off late—it was 5:00 p.m.—to bomb Conflans once more. The squadron operations report tells the bare story of what happened: "Planes #14, 20, 4 and 1 did not return, and have no report of them to the present time. Others did not reach objective." The missing planes were never heard from.

Bruce Hopper, the squadron historian, summed up the Ninety-Sixth's rough time at St. Mihiel: "During the entire St. Mihiel offensive

the squadron was operating under the most discouraging conditions of
adverse weather, and shortage of planes, and flying personnel. The losses
in four days were 16 fliers . . . and 14 planes destroyed in combat or
forced down in hostile territory."

And he drew this strategic conclusion: "The big lesson learned from
the many combats with Germany's ace squadrons, which had been
moved to the sector, was that big, tight formations were necessary to
successful bombing operations. The heavy losses were due to small formations of three or four planes being completely wiped out. A large
formation, with a tight rear line, attains a degree of self-protection."

In theory that sounds reasonable enough: bigger will be safer. But
in practice there was no safety in either large or small operations: as the
number of planes in the air and the number of missions flown increased,
so did the casualties. Pilots said there were more and better German
squadrons facing them, and that would have been a factor; and some
missions were flown deeper into German territory, and that would increase the odds against them. Ground fire from both sides of the lines
was intense beyond anything pilots had seen before. Put all these factors
together, and the consequences are clear: in the last months of the war
more planes will be lost, and more pilots will die.

Billy Mitchell—by then he was General Mitchell, C.O. of a force of
British, French, Italian, and American squadrons—was much pleased
with the performance of his command: "Our air force," he wrote of the
St. Mihiel operation, "by attacking their transportation trains, railroads
and columns on the roads, piled them up with debris so that it was impossible for many of their troops to get away quickly, resulting in their
capture by our infantry. We had forced them to measure strength with us
in the air with their main forces, and if they did not come up and attack
us, we intended to destroy Metz, Conflans, Diedenhoffen and even
Treves." The whole dream of bombers' war is there: pile up the debris,
measure strength against strength, destroy cities.

Mitchell goes on to describe a raid on Conflans flown by French
bombers under his command. It's a harrowing tale. Eighteen planes—
two-seaters and three-seaters—take off, fail to connect with their protection patrol, and go on anyway, under fierce attack both from ground
artillery and from German fighters. They all reach their target, unload
their bombs, and turn for home. Mitchell describes the journey back:
how more German fighters arrive, and how the bombers begin to fall. A

three-seater is shot in one engine, slips down, is attacked by three German planes, is shot to pieces, and disappears in flames; a two-seater
catches fire, dives, loses a wing, and crashes; another bomber is hit in
the gas tank, catches fire, but holds its position in the formation, "leaving behind it a trail of fire about twice as long as the ship itself," until
pilot and observer are burned alive and the plane "dives to its doom."
(Mitchell is a vivid writer when the subject is havoc in the air.)

Of the eighteen planes that set out, only five reach their home field.
Mitchell sums up: "Most of the crews were wounded and their planes
perforated in all parts by bullets. They had never once broken their formation or failed to obey the orders of their leader [that's Mitchell]. They
furnished an example of military precision and bravery which is required
of all airmen."

As the numbers of men and planes lost increase, squadron historians
report those losses with a grim pride, as though the one-day losses
were proof of their squadron's commitment to the war. In late August
the two American squadrons flying Camels with the RAF—the Seventeenth and the 148th—do a low-bombing mission together. They're both
pursuit squadrons, but this time the 148th will be doing the bombing,
and the Seventeenth will fly protective cover for it. It's a foul day—rain,
low clouds, and high winds blowing toward Germany—but the planes
take off in the late afternoon and fly along the Bapaume–Cambrai road.
Two of the Seventeenth's planes turn back—engine trouble, jammed
guns—and the rest continue their mission. Just over the lines they see
Fokkers attacking a plane of the 148th; they dive down to protect the
victim, and as they do, more Fokkers—several flights of them—drop
through the clouds above. It's a trap. Two hours later, two of the Seventeenth's Camels return to their home field. After a while another limps
in. Nine Camels have been shot down: six pilots are prisoners of war;
three are dead. The squadron's historian calls it "our most tragic day."
But the Seventeenth has done its job: at least five Fokkers have been
shot down, and the 148th has unloaded its bombs and has not lost a
plane.

———

It's mid-September, and the First Day Bombardment Group has finally
been put together at Amanty: three squadrons at first—the Eleventh, the

Twentieth, the Ninety-Sixth. On September 18, the Eleventh flies an
attack on Mars-la-Tour. The weather is unflyable by any reasonable
standards—huge clouds are massed in the way—but seven planes take
off. Because the odds are against the mission even finding the target,
let alone bombing it successfully, the squadron's C.O., Thornton Hooper,
insists on leading the flight. They can't fly either above or below the
cloud barrier, so they plunge through it. In the turbulent air there one
plane stalls and spins down—and goes home. The other six search for a
hole in the overcast through which they can bomb their target. As they
emerge from a pile of cloud, they are jumped by eleven Fokkers. Two
DH-4s go down in flames, then three more fall. Only one is left flying.
The pilot dives back into the cloud cover, gets lost, and flies home on his
compass, arriving at Amanty as night is falling. On one flight the Eleventh
has lost five planes and ten men, including its C.O., who is shot down,
wounded, and becomes a POW. The mission has been the disaster that
he predicted.

Other squadrons had their bad days, and pilots who survived
remembered them. The Twentieth flew a raid of seven planes on September 26 and lost five of them over the lines; one of the two that made
it back to their field carried a dead observer. "Our most disastrous raid,"
a squadron pilot called it. And there were many others; if you were in
combat, you'd have a worst day.

Those were the extraordinary days. There were also the ordinary
ones, with their ordinary deaths in ordinary raids. There are enough such
days in the last months of the war that survivors begin to record deaths
collectively, in paragraphs of names that are like elegies, or funeral music.
It's bound to happen when you've been in a flying war for a while: you
get the feeling that you know a lot of pilots now, but many of them are
dead.

Lance Holden began counting in mid-August, when he'd been at
the front with the Ninety-Fifth for a month:

> Out of the 9 that came out with me to the group—4 have al-
> ready been killed. Bruce, Whiton, Beauchamp, Sands—over
> 33⅓ in a month. The 27th has lost 17 or 100% in 2½ months.
> Our losses are 12 in 3 months.
>
> What a joke this casualty list is that appears in the papers.

I wonder what America would say if they really knew the extent of casualties.

He returns to the subject in late September, after the St. Mihiel offensive is over: "Our squadron has lost 3 men in this sector . . . Heinrichs and Bill Taylor were lost . . . I saw a plane burning on the ground and 2 days later found it was Bill—shot down in flames. Heinrichs was last seen 10 kilms in Germany under 6 Fokkers. Sumner Sewall was shot down with his gas tank afire."

And again in October: "Lots of friends have gone lately—Woody and Walt Avery from our tent. Think of Walt—one of the best pilots I ever saw . . . Then there is Philbrick and Rheinlander. Worst of all Bob Converse and Wiss Morris." Holden has been at the front for two and a half months, and thirteen of his friends are dead or missing. It's not surprising that he draws a grim conclusion that he had not drawn before: "How can one help being an utter fatalist . . . It looks like certain death. Just a question of time."

Holden wasn't alone in his fatalism. Harvey Conover's journal entry for September 29 begins with an exuberant account of the work his observation squadron is doing in Souilly:

We were occupied chiefly with contact patrol, flying low just ahead of our barrage, noting the position of our troops, and that of the enemy. The sight is most magnificent: watching our men fighting their way from shell hole to shell hole, shells bursting all around you, and machine guns tack-tacking below you. It makes you want to yell to the men to give them hell, and it is more exciting than anything I have ever participated in.

But in the next paragraph he turns away from war's excitement:

There is a dark side to everything, however, and the bad part of this game is the large number of your friends who are killed. It is terrible to look back over the last year and remember your countless friends who have been killed, and it has now become so common that you accept the news of the death of a friend as you would the outcome of a baseball game. You say, "Oh is that so?" and straightway forget it. You can't help wondering, however, when your turn will come.

And there's Walt Avery. In August he wrote in his diary his own accounting of losses:

> Six of the fellows of the 27th were shot down today, and Winslow of the 94th is missing. Of the three Salmsons not escorted, two are missing. Buckley and Archibald had a fight against eight Boches and just barely got away. Denny Holden had a bad fight, five bullets in his plane . . . Our squadron [it was the Ninety-Fifth, the best the Air Service had] is just a mob without a system or method in the air. With the crack Boche outfit now on this sector, none of us will last a month.

Holden, Conover, Avery—three seasoned, skillful pilots, naming their dead: you can see how each might keep his own score of lost friends and become in time fatalistic about his chances of surviving.

Experienced pilots took fatalism to be a normal state of mind, given the nature of combat work. "War flying," Rickenbacker wrote in his memoir,

> is much like other business—one gets accustomed to all the incidents that attend its daily routine, its risks, its thrills, its dangers, its good and bad fortune. A strange sort of fatalism fastens to the mind of an aviator who continues to run the gauntlet of Archy. He flies through the bursting shells without trying to dodge them, with indeed little thought of their menace. If a bullet or a shell has his name written on it there is no use trying to avoid contact with it. If it has not—why worry?

Easy to say, you might respond, in a memoir written after the war, when the Archie has stopped and you're at ease back home. But insofar as one can register attitudes, Rickenbacker does seem to be right (though most of the young pilots took evasive actions when the antiaircraft fire began); there wasn't much else you could do out there among the shell bursts and the bullets. There'd be casualties, and one of them might be you. You endured it all, if you could; if you couldn't, you'd become a statistic, or you'd be taken out of the lines—temporarily, or permanently. Either way, it was all part of the cost of war in the air. Billy Mitchell explained,

> Pursuit squadrons are essentially an offensive element, and to enact their role successfully, they must take and maintain the offensive. They should seek the enemy and wherever found, attack and destroy him. A man cannot stand this pursuit game very long at a time without becoming over-careful, and when this stage is reached, it marks the end of a good offensive pursuit pilot . . . When fatigue and the terrible casualties they must endure begin to affect their nerves, they must be taken out and allowed to recuperate.

They *must* be taken out, and some of them were. The war story we follow is the account of eager young men moving up into the Zone of Advance, more and more of them as the war surges to its end; we don't, perhaps, notice that there was another story—the counterflow of pilots away from the front, back to other, less fatal places. They withdraw from combat for many reasons: they're tired, they've "gone stale" (that is, they're no longer responding to the continuous demands of combat flying), they've "lost their nerve." Some go back because experience has proved them inept at the game, others because their bodies can't bear the stresses—they grow dizzy in the air (Avery mentions a friend called Hunty who gives up flying altogether "on account of dizziness" and becomes a ground instructor at a flight school). "It is queer," Holden writes in his journal, "how the game reacts on different fellows. How they look at a chance to get out," and he names two pilots from his squadron who are going back to the States. He doesn't see how they could do that—just walk away from their war.

Fatalism, dizziness, staleness, loss of nerve—to the doctors of the American Air Medical Service these reactions to flying seemed to constitute a morale problem that was endemic wherever men flew. In August 1918 a party of thirty-three doctors and fifteen laboratory personnel came to France and England to examine the condition of American fliers there and to write a report of their conclusions. That report is a serious attempt by serious medical men to understand the physiology and psychology of the young Americans who flew and to determine their current state of mind. They concluded that yes, their morale was low, and yes, they had acquired a fatalistic attitude of mind. Fortunately, the doctors wrote, these conditions could be treated; they recommend exercise and rest and in extreme cases the grounding of the pilot.

All of the doctors who wrote that report had flown at least once, but none of them was a pilot, and that was their limitation: they simply didn't know what it was like to be up there at the controls, day after day after day, and no lab test would tell them. Most of all, they didn't know how the relentlessly mounting lists of casualties affected pilots, how the numbers of their familiar dead weighed on them, lowered their morale and fed their fatalism, and dampened their eagerness to fly on into the war's last great battles. How the dying changed them.

The young pilots didn't show that change much in their letters or in their behavior but masked it in toughness and the plain naming of the dead. But sometimes the mask would slip when an old friend was killed, and the survivor would recall the story of his friendship—"he rowed on the crew with me at Choate," "I knew him at St. Paul's and Yale," "he played quarterback for Dartmouth," "we were in Law School at Harvard together"—which would be a history of himself when young, before the dying began.

Such losses seemed to require some formal expression. But what? In war movies, pilots who survive make a great show of *not* grieving; they gather in their squadron bars and drink, as though nothing has happened. But in the real life of flying they did mourn for those dead comrades, though not emotionally, not out loud.

Pilots' letters and diaries record two ways in which a sense of loss could be expressed in a ceremony appropriate to men at war. One ceremony was already a traditional part of service life, a military funeral— formal and solemn and public—with marching men in uniform, perhaps a band, an honor guard to fire a rifle salute, the dead man's friends as pallbearers, and, most moving of all, squadron planes circling above, dropping flowers on the grave. Such funerals were most ceremonial when the dead man was one of the flying great—Lufbery's is described in many pilots' letters and memoirs—but it wasn't only the heroes, nor only the combat dead, who were honored this way: student pilots killed in accidents were often given the full military treatment. Ceremony humanizes—is that it?

The other ceremony was private and unofficial and not at all formal. When a pilot died, someone—a friend, a tent mate—assumed the task of sorting the dead man's possessions, dismantling his life as a flier, now that it was over. There won't be many personal items—a few photographs, a watch or a fountain pen, some letters from home, perhaps—for the folks at home to cherish. The rest—flight gear (a warm helmet, goggles, a compass), flying clothing, a comfortable cot, bedding, perhaps a few books—will be considered free property, to be shared out among whoever is on hand. Taken together, the whole collection will amount to at most the contents of a footlocker; a pilot on combat duty doesn't accumulate much—not enough, you might think, to define a young man's life, but all there is. And the sorting, like the military funeral, will be a reassurance that a man you lived with and flew with has been treated with due respect, which is all you can do.

SIXTEEN

ABROAD III: END GAMES

General Mitchell saw what fatigue and heavy losses did to pilots' nerves, how they lost their will to fight and how that endangered the lives of the men they flew with. When that happened, they'd have to be taken out of combat and allowed to recover. In some squadrons regular periods of rest and rehabilitation were an expected part of a pilot's schedule: George Vaughn, flying in the Seventeenth Pursuit Squadron with the RAF, wrote home in October 1918 that he'd been back from his last leave for two months and should be getting another in a month—three months of combat, then two weeks in London—"provided we haven't won the war by then." In American squadrons the rest periods don't seem to have been that predictable; your C.O. would simply order you to take a week out of the lines if he thought you needed it.

Mitchell was aware enough of the problem to organize a country rest home just for pilots. He had become acquainted with two aristocratic French ladies who lived in Voltaire's old castle near the Swiss border and arranged with them to take in young men who needed the rest. The plan didn't work, though; Jim Knowles remembered why: "There was no liquor allowed so no one ever went to the rest camp. Finally, Mitchell ordered Buckley and I to go down there. We stayed for two days and then headed for Paris. I don't know of anybody who went there after that. It was supposed to be a nice quiet place to rest but we were having too good a time. We didn't want any quiet at all."

What they wanted wasn't quiet or rest but release from stress. For that they needed a party, booze, girls: they needed Paris. By now they knew their way around there; they'd be sure to run into old friends at the Café de la Paix or the Crillon. They'd be the veterans now. They'd know the tricks for getting into Paris without a pass and for getting out of Paris without detection when they'd overstayed their leave. Knowles had another dodge for getting to Paris without a pass or permission:

> If you were scheduled to fly the morning patrol you would fly at 5:00 a.m. or 6:00 a.m. and you knew you didn't have to fly another patrol until twelve hours later until 5:00 p.m. or 6:00 p.m. Paris was only a half-hour away . . . you would get into your plane and fly into Orly. The fellows there were always kind about giving you a truck or a Fiat. We'd go into Paris and sit around the Cafe de la Paix for a couple of hours, return to Orly, and fly back to the front a little bit fried and go out for a two-hour patrol.

It would all be a game, pilots against the authorities, a sort of reverse of the eagerness they had felt back in the days before they'd even seen the front—an eagerness now to escape the fighting, however briefly, and get back to where the parties were.

And where the girls were. For some of the pilots, who had been in and out of Paris a lot, there'd be one special girl, whom they saw whenever they got to town and stayed with while they were there. Harvey Conover writes in his journal of three "most enjoyable days" that he spent with his girl in October. He doesn't name her; he simply refers to her as "ma femme," his regular companion. He wasn't supposed to go to Paris at all, he writes, but to "some rest home in a nice pine atmosphere" (clearly that's Mitchell's two aristocrats in their castle), so he's "a bit out of favor" with his colonel. That doesn't bother Conover—he had his three days.

Minor Markham, in his old man's recollections of his flying youth, fondly recalls a girl called Coco. Markham was flying with a French observation squadron at Luxeuil when their attachment began:

> At the officers' mess in the evening there were occasional women guests. Among them was an attractive girl known as

Coco who had been the mistress of the squadron commander until his recent transfer to another station. One day one of the older officers asked me:

"Why don't you take on Coco? She is lonely and she likes you."

Although my French was improving I did not want to take the risk of being turned down in what I thought might be a delicate negotiation and I asked him if he would arrange the matter for me.

She is willing, and they meet that evening in a small inn in Épinal. Just as they are climbing into bed, the air-raid sirens sound; they hastily throw on their clothes and spend the first night of their tryst in a crowded cellar. But the affair continues, and when Markham changes airfields, Coco goes with him.

The leaves spent in Paris sound more like binges than parties. Pilots who shared these binges explained and justified them. Lance Holden wrote in his journal on October 8, 1918 (it was his twenty-second birthday): "It never enters my head to plan of things after this war. Can you imagine a lot of boys—naturally wild or they wouldn't be in this game. With death almost a certainty. Then blame them for being wild when they're on leave."

Fifteen years later, in an article in *Liberty* magazine, Alan Winslow offered his own defense of the pilots' binges:

Generally speaking, I doubt if there is a sane war aviator alive today who does not feel that it was these occasional excesses which saved his nerves and enabled him to come through. A drinking binge, a party with a flock of snappy girls, or a quiet party with just one, were by no means the daily or nightly order of things, as some authors have misled their readers to believe; but they were not too infrequently part and parcel of a war aviator's life.

Thank God these occasional excesses were possible. Had it not been for their existence, shattered nerves would have meant the death in combat of many a pilot, and others would have returned home in an abnormal state, physically and mentally.

Winslow was the anxious young man who had tested his acrophobia on the window ledge of the Biltmore. He knew something about nerves.

Not all the binges were in Paris. Even during those last hard-fought months of the war a pilot might get a leave long enough to get to Deauville or even the Riviera. Failing that, he and his friends could have a night out in one of the towns near their airfield. Pilots of the First Pursuit Group could walk into Toul or drive the eighteen kilometers to Nancy and hang out at the Café Liégeois, where they would find pilots from other squadrons and perhaps French officers, too, and spend afternoons and evenings eating, drinking, and talking aviation.

Or they might have a party at their own field. The historian of the 135th Squadron quotes the diary of a squadron pilot, William Lynd, for October 26, 1918. That evening the squadron gave a dinner dance in its headquarters building to welcome a new squadron of SE-5s to the field. Refreshments consisted of

> twelve dozen quarts of champagne and a keg of white wine and beaucoup red wine. The results were more hilarious than expected; in fact it was just about the most complete party I have ever seen, with about twenty nurses present, and some of the Y.M.C.A. people, who participated as freely as anyone. Capt. —— got as drunk as possible and I put him to bed. He insisted on taking a girl with him, but that idea was frustrated by strenuous efforts on my part. Lt. —— went clear out, right on the floor, and he was put to bed through the window, and everyone else was just about as bad. Maj. —— was one of the worst of the lot.

Lynd concluded, "Candidly I think this party is a disgrace to the American Army," to which the editor of the history added, "But it must be admitted that the above notes are slightly Puritanical in nature and cannot be relied upon as a general consensus of opinion."

Other binges were more informal, spur-of-the-moment occasions. Jim Knowles recalled the night before the St. Mihiel attack. He and his friend Russ Hall were in the Ninety-Fifth Squadron hangar, shooting craps and drinking heavily. From time to time Waldo Heinrichs would come by the game and urge the players to quit and get some sleep: "We're going into battle in the morning." But the game went on, and the players continued to drink. The next morning Knowles and Hall took their hangovers on patrol, and each got his Boche; the sober Heinrichs was shot down, wounded, and spent the rest of the war as a POW. At least that's the way Knowles remembered it.

The doctors in the Air Medical Service took a different view on pilots' getting fried. The service's end-of-the-war report reads,

> The alcohol problem, despite the opinion of many aviators to the contrary, is a grave one. All the belligerent nations found that in order to save men from drunkenness, from the inefficiency that comes from partial intoxication, and from venereal diseases that come from lack of self-control when under the influence of alcohol, it was necessary to reduce, and if possible, eliminate the use of alcoholic drinks. Unquestionably a number of serious crashes in France among American fliers occurred on the day following an evening of excessive use of alcohol. Alcohol may falsify sensations and predispose to foolish action.

In a later passage the report considers the psychology of fliers and alcohol. Quiet, methodical men are among the best fliers, most able to adjust quickly to a new situation. "The nervous, high strung, or those bordering on the temperamental, are the least reliable; for though they often become good fliers, no great reliance can be placed upon them. They are liable to become psychotic under stress."

The doctors conclude:

> It is often claimed by aviators that a man can fly better when slightly under the influence of alcohol, and that a man who is not afraid, or too good, to drink is a better aviator. The latter observation should not be limited, perhaps, to aviators; but its truth or fallacy need not be discussed here. The former statement bears some relation directly to flying, and there is an element of truth in the observation. It is a fact, acknowledged by psychologists, that alcohol in moderate doses tends to remove inhibitions that interfere with a man's efficiency at the time, and thus increases his activity along directed lines.

Mild intoxication will remove "the slight fear or consciousness of him-self in the case of the aviator"; he'll be more able to give his entire atten-tion to flying the plane, less awkward and more free and skilled at flying it. That sounds like a description of the necessary wildness that pilots write about in their journals. But, the doctors warn, there are two dan-gers: drinking excessively will remove inhibitions "to the point that the flier becomes reckless, and wanting in good judgment. He may also lose control, both motor and mental."

The passage concludes with a firm judgment: "There is, therefore, nothing in the special claim of aviators, distinct from any other group, for the use of alcohol." Which covers the physiology of flying and alco-hol well enough, but doesn't address the morale question—why pilots sometimes drink too much and what to do about it.

———

Not all the journeys pilots made on the ground in their spare time were toward Paris. They had reasons for heading in the opposite direction, through the devastated towns, past abandoned trenches and their own artillery batteries in action, through infantry units on the move, to the very edge of the fighting in progress.

Some of those journeys to the war would be necessary actions. The flying game is full of uncertainties; many combat deaths are not wit-nessed, or only vaguely by troops on the ground, who have their own problems. A plane might fly off on a patrol into the smoke and flame and confusion over the lines and simply vanish. The squadron opera-tions report would describe the event in the barest terms: "Lt. —— did not return." And the squadron members would wait for news—from the Germans if the plane had gone down on their side of the lines, in a note dropped by a German pilot: your men are alive and are our prisoners, or your pilot is dead and has been decently buried. Or from infantrymen in the advance who saw a plane falling in flames at such and such a map location and report it. Or, eventually, from the Red Cross. If the plane is one of yours, and the men in it are your friends, "Missing in Action" is a painful uncertainty. You want to be sure.

On the first day of the St. Mihiel offensive three planes of the 135th Observation Squadron took off to track the progress of the Allied attack and disappeared. Other pilots in the air at the time reported seeing planes land or crash between the shifting lines, but none could identify any of them. Two days later word came to the squadron that a plane that had been hit by an American artillery barrage on the first day of the attack and had gone down in flames belonged to the 135th. Squadron pilots thought it must be the plane Jim Bowyer had flown, with Art Johnson as observer.

A week later, when the force of the offensive had eased a little, a group of fliers determined to find the wreck. They drove to a point north of Flirey, a village east of St. Mihiel, parked, walked across the fields as the map reference directed, and found . . . almost nothing. The force of the crash and the fire had consumed everything but the plane's engine. Searching around, they found a piece of a Sam Browne belt with Johnson's name on it and the buckle from Bowyer's flying coat. There was nothing to bury, but now they knew.

There's another reason to journey up to the front lines. In the confusion of combat in the air, the victories are as uncertain and unwitnessed as the deaths. A pilot attacks an enemy plane, fires, and swoops past it, the enemy dives or spins out of sight into the smoke, another enemy plane appears out of nowhere, and a new fight begins. Did the first Boche go down? Or was the spin simply an escape route? The evidence will be on the ground, somewhere. And so pilots go out in search of confirmations.

Josiah Rowe was a latecomer to the 147th Pursuit Squadron. He joined the squadron in early October 1918 and had not yet flown over the front when he was sent up to the lines, not in a Spad but in a Fiat touring car to search for evidence of victories that pilots had claimed but that had not been confirmed. His long letter to his mother about the search is an account of what he saw: first the wonderful French roads, and the mass of the traffic that carries all the stuff of war to the fighting men—the food, the clothing, the munitions, the equipment—trucks by the thousands driven by men of every race and ambulances driven by Red Cross girls, in endless, honking movement; then the construction work on roads and bridges and the artillery batteries firing beside the road; and the camps of soldiers waiting for the next attack or recovering from the last one (Rowe pities and envies them); and the annihilated little villages and blasted towns; and the barren desolation of what had been Dead Man's Hill, scene of terrible fighting for Verdun in

1916; and abandoned German trenches filled with abandoned weapons and equipment; and Verdun itself, one side of the city completely demolished, the other side only partially wrecked.

It's all vividly observed; this is Rowe's first look at what modern war does to the earth and to human habitations, and his responses to what he sees are fresh. He says nothing—not one word—about the wrecks he was there to identify. Only at the end a brief tally: they have brought back five confirmations of five victories by pilots of the First Pursuit Group. But victories of one man over another man aren't Rowe's subject: it's the immensity of the war, and of its destructiveness, that he has seen and felt.

For squadrons in the combat zone, No-Man's-Land was a convenient scrapyard in which to search for useful salvage. A plane that had made an emergency landing would probably be damaged, but perhaps it could be repaired and flown out. Even if it was beyond repair, it might yield parts that could be taken back to the field for spares—instruments, machine guns, bomb racks, maybe ailerons or a rudder, even controls and seats might be used again. The keenness of combat squadrons for salvaging runs is a reminder of the enormous and continuous demand for materials of war that those squadrons felt and of the scale of the wastage. There never seemed to be enough of the stuff men fight with.

German wrecks, if they were brought down inside Allied lines, were also fair prey for stripping. When Sumner Sewall shot a Rumpler down, he wrote excitedly home about all the instruments he got out of the wrecked plane: "I am just like a kid with a lot of new toys. I got a beautiful compass, an altimeter which runs up to 8,000 meters, a great little do-hickey for registering speed and then, of course, his camera and lens." It makes you wonder what kinds of instruments the French put in their Spads. When Walter Avery shot down the German ace Carl Menckhoff, he took the gun sight out of his enemy's plane and mounted it in his own. He flew with it and shot down other Boches, until Waldo Heinrichs borrowed the plane for a patrol and was shot down and captured. "There goes my Menkhoff sight and my pistol," Avery wrote ruefully in his journal.

Enemy instruments are spoils of war; American pilots appropriate them for their own use as a matter of course. But the other spoils—the odds and ends of military gear and personal possessions that strew a battlefield after a battle—are out of reach of men who do their fighting in the air. It's a disadvantage they feel, never getting close enough to the war below them to share in the loot. And so, if there's a lull in the fighting, or the weather is unflyable, it's tempting to commandeer a car and drive up to yesterday's front line to look around for something to take home, as physical proof that you had been there.

It was easy to arrange; you simply "got the Cadillac" (every squadron seemed to have one), filled it with your buddies, and set out through villages where a day or two before you had been strafing German troops, up to where the abandoned trenches and dugouts stood, empty of men but full of the flotsam of the things a retreating army leaves behind. Among the objects that various souvenir-hunting pilots collected were a Boche helmet, a canteen, an ammunition pouch, German officers' swords, pistols, Hun shell cases, a rifle and bayonet, another rifle with a crown engraved on it under which is written, "Danzig, 1916," postcards, picture-show tickets, a large gilded eagle from an officer's helmet with "Mit Gott für König und Vaterland" stamped across it, the gun sights for a Maxim machine gun. (Some trophies they reject. When one of the guys souvenir hunting with Holden picks up a Boche helmet, flies swarm out of it; the Boche's head is still in it.) They also carry back more utilitarian objects: wicker chairs, a huge mirror, boots—enough stuff to fill a two-ton truck. Everything on a battlefield is yours after the battle, if you want it.

One other motive drew the young pilots to travel up to the front lines—a desire to see what a battlefield looked like, up close. In some, it was simple curiosity: they'd seen the war zone from the air; they'd like to see it on the ground.

But for some of the young men who travel through those scenes, the feeling is deeper than that; call it a need—as strong as their eagerness to fly into danger—to witness what the worst destruction in human history has done to human beings, and to their habitations, and to the surface of the earth, as though what had happened down there on the ground were *essential* war, more real in its mud and wire and desolation than war above it in the air could ever be.

Henry Sheets was an observer with the 135th Squadron on liaison duty with the Eighty-Ninth Division at the front on the first day of the St. Mihiel offensive. That morning he had watched the troops go over the top at 5:00 a.m. and later had moved up to Flirey, which had just been taken. In the afternoon he followed the operation from division headquarters for a while, and then, when there seemed nothing further for him to do, he decided to take a walk out to where hand-to-hand fighting had been taking place since the five o'clock beginning, past the American trenches and on into the old German trenches.

"I'm not sure," Sheets wrote in his diary, "whether I'm glad or sorry that I took this walk today":

> Never have I seen a more gruesome sight. Never have I felt such absolute solitude as I felt out there in a drenching rain, in that slimy mud, miles, it seemed, from any living human being, but completely surrounded by many, many dead with their mud stained gray-black faces, with their hair and clothing streaked with mud and blood, with their bodies in all sorts of grotesque poses—partly supported in a semi-sitting posture by barbed wire or lying in the mud, face up, staring ahead, with that horrible vacant stare, at the rain soaked sky.

He hears the sound of hand-to-hand fighting nearby and feels relief to know that there are living people within earshot. At the same time he realizes that if he can hear fighting, he shouldn't be out there alone, and he heads back for Flirey.

The diary entry continues, as Sheets tries to describe his feelings as he leaves the scene: "There was the impulse to run, very much as I probably had that same impulse as a small boy when I became frightened by some imaginary spook in the dark. There was nothing to fear except the utter horror of the desolate scene. I got out of there, but I did not run. There were too many dead, too much mud, too many shell holes, too much wire, too much desolation."

Still, in the end he's glad he went. He's been present at the D-days of two great battles—at Château-Thierry in the air, and now at St. Mihiel on the ground—and he's proud of the earth-and-air completeness of his witness.

SEVENTEEN

THE LAST BATTLE

September fades, and the war grinds on, like a great iron machine, toward its necessary end. The St. Mihiel salient has been straightened, and the armies gather for what will be the last offensive, the battle that will be called the Meuse-Argonne—"Meuse" for the river that runs south out of Germany past Verdun, "Argonne" for the dense forest that lies to the west of the city. Experienced American squadrons are in place along the front—some forty-five of them. Most of the pilots in those squadrons have flown enough in combat to know how to do the pilot's work and what the odds are, but there are also the new, untried ones, who have moved up to replace casualties in existing squadrons or to establish new ones. Josiah Rowe, new to the 147th Pursuit Squadron in early October, writes home excitedly that the pursuit group he's now in scored 103 victories in September alone! And he's one of them!

Pilots who are already there are less keen. Their squadrons have flown their missions in the St. Mihiel offensive and have taken heavy losses; they know what this new offensive will be like. A few days before the Meuse-Argonne fighting begins, pilots of the 135th Observation Squadron, grounded by the weather, visit their friends in the First Day Bombardment Group at Amanty and find them in a "deplorable situation." As Percival Hart, the 135th historian, explains, pilots of the group are being assigned to bomb objectives twenty or thirty kilometers over the lines, and on every flight they are attacked by swarms of Fokkers from the Metz Home Defense Squadrons:

> On several occasions some of our planes had seen these combats from a distance and had counted as many as sixty ships in the engagements. It turned out that from six to twelve were usually Liberties [American-built DH-4s with American Liberty engines] from these Day Bombing Squadrons and the rest Fokkers. The Liberties were generally cut off from home after they had dropped their bombs, and had to fight their way back, with frightful casualties. The 96th Squadron alone had thirteen men killed from September 12th to September 16th.

With odds of five to one or even ten to one, it's not surprising that the morale of the bomber pilots and observers was low—"scraping bottom," Hart says; each of them expected that it would be his turn next to "go West."

The pilots of the 135th return to their field wrapped in gloom; pursuit pilots are getting all the glory, while bomber pilots are taking most of the grief. No observation squadron has taken such losses in such a short period, although, Hart adds, the First Observation Squadron, with a total of nineteen men killed in action, led every other American squadron in casualties.

In the week leading up to Meuse-Argonne, Roland Richardson, of the 213th Pursuit Squadron, recorded flying conditions: rain, mist, low cloud, the kind of weather that sends pilots back to bed. But once the fighting starts—on September 26—they fly anyway. Richardson's notes begin to read, "Went up, saw nothing" (September 28), and "Clouds low, saw nothing" (September 30)—inglorious, dutiful flying, which he had to do because everybody did it, because the new drive had begun.

The weather in October was more of the same, and pilots wrote about it in their journals—gloomily, because it kept them grounded and stuck in the French mud. Those entries are a bit monotonous—a flying story without the flying—but they make that time damply real. Percival Gates spent the first half of October with the Twenty-Seventh Pursuit Squadron at Rembercourt. It was his first experience of over-the-lines duty, and he kept a careful record of his days there. Almost every entry begins the same. October 4: "It was a pretty poor day this morning so we did not have any patrols"; October 8: "It was rainy all the morning so we just sat around"; October 9: "It was too rainy to fly this morning so I helped Kelton censor mail"; October 11: "It rained all day today so we did not have any patrols"; October 13: "It has been raining all day to-day"; October 14: "It was rainy this morning so I did not have to get up early"; October 15: "It is still raining so our early patrol did not get off"; October 16: "It rained all day today . . . We did not have any flying."

The search for the Lost Battalion is a foul-weather story from that rainy month that became a part of the air-war myth. At the end of September and in early October the Fiftieth Observation Squadron was flying infantry liaison missions over the Argonne. In that dense forest, in low clouds and haze, locating advancing American troops was difficult, often impossible. One unit in particular, the Second Battalion of the 308th Infantry, was in trouble: the troops had moved forward and had lost contact with other units in the line. They were at the bottom of a deep ravine surrounded by German troops occupying the hills on either side and could only communicate with their own forces by carrier pigeon. The Fiftieth was ordered to find them and if possible supply them. Over several days planes were sent out, flying below a thousand feet, at about the height of the hills above the ravine, from which enemy machine guns fired at them at close range. The planes carried at first chocolate and cigarettes and later ammunition, food, and medical supplies, only part of which reached the surrounded troops. Finally, on October 7, the battalion—what was left of it—was found and relieved.

Squadron histories are essentially mythologies; they organize actions and out of them compose a story expressing meaning and values. The Fiftieth's historian (he was the squadron's commanding officer, Captain Daniel Morse) makes the search for the Lost Battalion a brave and successful collective effort, in which nearly two dozen pilots and observers flew, three planes were shot down, two men were killed, and a third was badly wounded. His account ends with this assessment: "Naturally, we felt much relieved by the relief of this battalion and also elated by the part the 50th Squadron took. Those who will forever be honored by their part in the heroic work of dropping provisions on that history-making day were . . . ," and he names the pilots and observers, and notes parenthetically after some names "killed," "wounded," and "shot down." Of the two men who died, he says only that Lieutenant Harold Goettler and Lieutenant Erwin Bleckley flew two missions and did not return from the second and that both "received posthumously the Distinguished Service Cross for their heroism." (Both medals were later upgraded to Medals of Honor.)

Why, one wonders, were those two men, among all the pilots and observers of the Fiftieth who flew in that search mission, chosen for special honor? Because they were the ones who died? Or because, having tried once to find the battalion and failed, they flew back into that fierce ground fire to try again? Whoever decided on Goettler and Bleckley must have seen in their second effort an act of self-abnegating courage that merited recognition, even though it had no evident effect on the mission or on the war.

With such weather to fly in, it's not surprising that most of the missions flown that fall were low work—and not only by bombing and observation squadrons but by pursuit squadrons as well. Looking back on that period, Jim Knowles, an ace with the Ninety-Fifth, recalled that from the beginning of the St. Mihiel attack on, "low flying on the offensive" was the order: "This was also done through the Argonne-Meuse attack, and at no time did any pilot in the Group fly at more than 600 metres, except in a voluntary patrol. Ground and balloon 'strafing,' and attacks on enemy reglages and observation machines constituted the day's work."

Continuous low work is stressful: pilots recognized that, and so did the doctors in aviation medicine departments. One of them, attached to the RAF, wrote about such stress in an article in *The Lancet*, published while the Meuse-Argonne offensive was going on:

> During the last few months great attention has been paid to low flying (at 500 feet or less) attacking the enemy with machine-gun fire in his trenches, whilst marching along the roads, in rest billets behind the lines, &c. The strain of this kind of flying is great, as the machine is subjected to a tremendous amount of machine-gun fire, and, when working in conjunction with an infantry attack, is continuously in, or very near, the barrage fire put up by the artillery. A hit that might only temporarily disable the aeroplane and give the pilot time to recover

from it flying at a height is probably fatal when so near the ground.

There were high-barometer, high-altitude days, too—days that were clear enough to launch the many-plane flotillas Billy Mitchell wanted for what he called "America's Greatest Battle." Eddie Rickenbacker was there and described what it was like in the air that October as the enemy responded to the numbers of planes in the American offensive, "filling the skies opposite us with the best fighting airmen in the German service." On the tenth he took off with fourteen Spads from his own Ninety-Fourth, accompanied by eight planes from the 147th on one side and seven from the Twenty-Seventh on the other: "I pushed my Spad No. 1 up several thousand feet above the flotilla to watch their progress over the lines from a superior altitude. The enormous formation below me resembled a huge crawling beetle, Coolidge and Chambers flying in exact position ahead of them to form the stingers. Thus we proceeded swiftly northwest in the direction of Dun-sur-Meuse." The formation was attacked by eleven Fokkers, there was a fight, and Rickenbacker shot one down. Forty planes were in that fight, and the object of it all was a single enemy balloon, which the German ground crew quickly pulled down.

Men who flew in those vast operations remembered them all their lives. Charles D'Olive, a Spad pilot with the Ninety-Third Pursuit Squadron, looked back forty years later at what he described as "the biggest flight of all time up to then," on October 18:

> Every plane that we had that had a gun on it was on that one flight. There were 276 of them . . . Our whole squadron was there and the three flights were stacked up. Then the 94th was over here and some others all over the place . . . Everywhere you could look—down, up, or sideways—you could see these little black devils coming. They were all over. I saw on that day three burning airplanes in the sky at one time.

More planes in the air meant more and larger missions, more and larger fights, more combat victories, more balloons shot down: Mitchell must have been pleased. It also meant more losses: more planes shot down by the Fokkers, or by enemy ground fire, or by friendly fire—the gunners down there were nervous and hasty, and the air was full of artillery shells—and more emergency landings, and more crashes.

To a big-picture military historian the loss of a single plane is simply a unit in the total cost of an action, but to the pilot who goes down, it's a sudden shock, unimaginable and personal. Decades later, old pilots will still remember the moment when the bullets hit their plane, and it ceased to be a flying machine and became a cripple. I quoted Charles D'Olive's awed description of "the biggest flight of all time" but stopped at the end of his vision of the huge flotilla he was flying in. At that point he turned to his personal story—what happened to *him* in that operation. He's just mentioned seeing three planes burning in the sky at the same time; the sentence continues without a pause: "and I got shot down on that flight," as though it's a detail he just remembered, an afterthought:

> I had shot a guy with Bill Goulding and like a damn fool I was sitting there watching him go down, which was error number one. You know how you sense there is somebody in a dark room or somebody looking at you? Well I looked up and here came this devil. He had black streamers off the tips of his wings and off the tip of his rudder and he was right there. All I could do was turn sideways. He shot three times—Put—Put—Put. My gas pressure went and I forgot about completing the turn.

His gas tank has been hit, and his engine has lost power; he rolls, losing speed, and switches to his auxiliary tank. When he comes out of the roll, the German plane has overshot him and crosses in front of him. D'Olive fires but misses, and the German withdraws, leaving his victim still flying but trailing a tail of gas, "like an exhaust . . . like when you blow a cylinder on a locomotive," he says, "with this vaporized gas going back."

Being a pilot, he remembers the damage to his plane exactly:

> What had happened was, he hit the wing and one bomb that had stuck on there [the Spads were armed with four twenty-pound bombs in racks hung on the belly of their gas tanks]. He

had them lined right up. The one that hit the bomb was either an explosive bullet which those guys had, they had an explosive machine gun bullet, or it hit in such a way that it fragmented. The gas tank looked like it had been shot with buckshot. I went down and landed in a little advance field that I never knew existed.

This is a story remembered more than forty years after the event. It's different from a spontaneous letter or a diary entry; D'Olive has had time to reflect on his follies and mistakes. And yet how sharp and immediate the details are—the black streamers on the German's wings, the sound of his machine guns, the look of the trail of vaporized gas. But one moment in the action still puzzles him: after the German plane has crossed in front of him and D'Olive has fired at him, the German (D'Olive calls him "the kid that was shooting at me") pulls up on D'Olive's left, waves at him, and grins. And then flies off, leaving D'Olive wondering why the German didn't finish the job: "The guy was either out of ammunition or he thought, what the hell, the war is over, why kill this poor devil? He saw that gas was coming out of there but he just pulled up, looked back and waved." D'Olive has no answer to that question, but that doesn't keep him from asking it, forty years on.

If getting shot down is a shock, unimaginable until it happens to you, being wounded is worse and stranger. Harvey Conover was on a contact patrol on October 27, looking for American infantry on the right bank of the Meuse. The troops on the ground had not set out signal panels to identify themselves, and Conover had to descend to just above the tree-tops to locate their positions. He found them stopped by "murderous machine gun fire," and so, being the aggressive pilot he was, he began diving and firing on the machine-gun nests. He had a great time "shooting at the pigs," he wrote in his diary,

until, while I was in a low right hand bank, I was surprised by a crash. My left leg flew off the rudder and my goggles were covered with blood. The cockpit filled with smoke, and we started to spin for earth. It happened so quickly that surprise held me motionless for a second. However, I managed to get her out just above the earth and to poop over to our side. I landed

just behind our trenches between two rows of barbwire near
the village of Consenvoye. The bus stopped rolling about two
feet behind a shell hole, and I had miraculously landed on the
only smooth place north of Verdun.

What strikes me most about Conover's account of being wounded is
his first reaction: not pain, not anger, but *surprise*—he uses the word
twice. Something violent is happening—his goggles are bloody, his left
foot has flown off the rudder—something new and incomprehensible that
wasn't supposed to happen. And his world is changed.

Conover didn't write the story of his wound into his diary until the
end of November, a month after it happened. In the time between he
has been picked up by French stretcher bearers and carried bleeding to
a car, stuck in the backseat, and bumped through military traffic to
Verdun, where he's shifted to a Ford ambulance and driven to a field
hospital, where he's given a cup of hot chocolate and an anti-tetanus
shot and loaded into another ambulance with three other wounded men
and jostled along for another hour to a hospital at Souilly, where a surgeon removes shrapnel from his leg. Eventually, he's loaded on a train
for Bordeaux and, finally, on November 28, is put aboard a hospital ship,
the SS *Sierra*, and sent back to the States to be rehabilitated and turned
back into a civilian. His war is over.

In the long months of the Meuse-Argonne fighting, many pilots
become casualty statistics: dead or wounded, or missing, or shot down
and captured and made prisoners of war. If you read their letters and
journals, you're bound to take some of those losses personally. You've
followed these young men from college to flight school to a squadron at
the front; you've felt their eagerness and witnessed their triumphs and
mistakes. And now, suddenly, their war stories end, or are interrupted,
and you feel their absence. Having come this far in the company of
these pilots, I could make my own muster of the lost—the ones I'd like
to have flown with. That muster would include:

Walter Avery: He had predicted, back in August, that he and his
mates wouldn't last a month. In fact, he lasted two. Ham Coolidge witnessed what happened then and told the story in a letter home. He and
Avery had been attacking enemy balloons, and Coolidge had just seen
his target burst into flames:

My companion, a boy from another squadron, was ahead of me and about to attack another balloon, when I suddenly saw a formation of seven Fokkers above. My heart stood still. He never saw them, Mammy; it was hideous. My shriek of "Look out Walter!" never got beyond my mouth because of the roaring exhaust. In a second they were upon him. Just a glimpse of the poor boy in the midst of those devils was all I could catch before the whole mess went circling to the ground. When I reached the spot they were careening around like a flock of buzzards over a freshly killed prey.

Avery didn't die; he was wounded in the jaw, taken prisoner, and spent the rest of the war in a German POW camp.

Ham Coolidge: He lasted until nearly the end of October. The Ninety-Fourth's daily squadron report for the twenty-seventh is, as usual, terse: "Protection Patrol . . . Eleven (11) Planes . . . Captain Coolidge and Rickenbacker . . ." followed by the names of the towns they'll fly over and the names of the other pilots in the flight. And at the end: "Captain Coolidge, has not returned." For details, one must turn to another pilot of the Ninety-Fourth, Joe Eastman. His diary for that day reads, "We learned that during the period of this afternoon we lost our right good comrade Ham Coolidge. He was struck by a direct hit of a hun archie which carried away his wing and set him in flames. We like to believe that he was killed instantly by the explosive."

Eastman had noted Coolidge's attitude toward antiaircraft fire in a diary entry back in September. The two of them were on a patrol at a low altitude over St. Mihiel when the German gunners below opened up on them. Eastman at once began evasive action, dodging and climbing; whereas Coolidge, "apparently contrary minded, let them pop—he slowly losing altitude in a comparatively straight line over the hun city towards our lines."

That time Coolidge escaped the antiaircraft fire and landed safely; this time the gunners won: in the margin of his diary Eastman drew a burning plane and a crude grave.

He then added his tender recollection of his friend—"he was the one man I've seen in the army who had an evening practice of kneeling by his cot in prayer"—before he went on to record Coolidge's combat

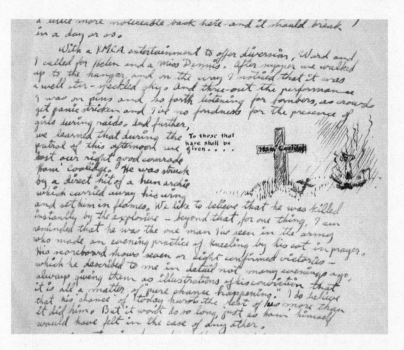

record and how Coolidge felt about it: "His scoreboard shows seven or eight confirmed victories—which he described to me in detail not many evenings ago, always giving them as illustrations of his conviction that it is all a matter of 'pure chance happening.'"

Kenneth MacLeish: His story is from the other end of the front, the English end. MacLeish was one of the eager, restless ones: he enlisted in the Navy with the First Yale Unit, but he flew with everybody, in a long series of moves—some voluntary, some under orders—aimed at getting to where the action was. In April he was flying Camels with the Royal Naval Air Service; in May he was on seaplanes with the U.S. Naval Aviation Forces; in June he was at the U.S. Air Service school at Clermont-Ferrand, learning to fly day-bombing machines. By July he was with the RAF's 218 Squadron near Calais.

The movement wasn't over yet; in August he was sent to a desk job in Paris and then to the Navy's testing and repair base at Pauillac, followed by an assignment to a testing job at Eastleigh in the south of England. After that he was at last returned to the front (by then it was

October) to rejoin the RAF's 213 Squadron at Dunkerque. His eagerness to return to the front was intense; on October 11 he wrote to his sweetheart back home, "I'm going out to the front to make one last try at really doing something. If luck is with me, all well and good, if it isn't—if there aren't any Huns in the sky, or if I don't come through with a punch, then I'll give up and try my hand at something else."

On the thirteenth he ferried a new Camel across the Channel to the Dunkerque station and the following morning flew an early bombing mission that turned into a fight with a German patrol and got his Boche (or half of one; another pilot was also in on it). In the afternoon he took off on another patrol, again engaged a flight of Fokkers—and disappeared. The squadron log reads, "Lieutenant MacLeish was last seen attacking about seven Fokkers single-handed." No trace of plane or pilot was found until late December, when a Belgian farmer returning to his war-ruined farmstead found the decomposing body of an American naval aviator and the wreckage of a Sopwith Camel. He gave the body a decent burial and notified 213 Squadron, RAF. In the confusion of the postwar period, American headquarters was not notified of the discovery until late January. A Yale classmate of MacLeish's was sent to investigate, and found the grave, but no sign of the wrecked plane. Perhaps local scavengers had dismantled it and carried the parts away.

———

Pilots' stories of their wars and their losses tend to be plain-language stories. But there was one group of storytellers who needed the big words of war to do their job: they were the senior officers up the chain of command who awarded the medals and wrote the citations. It's the big words that justify the awards: "extraordinary heroism in action," "distinguished and exceptional gallantry," "valor," "the highest possible contempt for personal danger," "devotion to duty." Such words are dictated by the congressional act that established the Medal of Honor, for reasons that seem obvious; in the anonymity of modern war (the act was passed during the American Civil War, which was America's first modern war), it was necessary to have a way of affirming that war could still be individual and heroic and worth fighting.

The awarding of medals to American pilots in the First World War seemed to increase in the war's last months. No doubt that was partly because there were more pilots flying more missions then, but perhaps it also had to do with the increasing costs in lives lost: the more dead pilots, the greater the need to praise their individual actions and to elevate those actions where possible with a high-ranking medal.

Those pilots who lived to see their medals were pleased to have them. Lance Holden notes in his diary who in his squadron has a Distinguished Service Cross (Rickenbacker and Doug Campbell), and who has been recommended for one (Ted Curtis, Harold Buckley, Jim Knowles, and Sumner Sewall), and dreams of getting his own. He writes in a letter on November 1, "Wouldn't you be tickled to death to hear I was an ace, and a captain with the D.S.C. It sounds wild but it may come true—I now have 3 official balloons . . . Now if you look at some of the fliers who have been given the D.S.C. you will see their citations are not so impossible of attainment."

There's one resonating word in that passage: "ace." It's a pilot's word, to be distinguished from the windy language of the medal citations. "Ace" names something tangible: there are wrecked planes and burned balloons out on the battlefield to prove it. A medal would be nice, and so would a captaincy, but to be an ace is what Holden wants most. And time is running out, the war might end any day now, and Holden feels a tense urgency to add to his score while he can. On November 3 he gets another balloon, and the next night another, and writes in his journal, "At last! at Last! I am an Ace!!" He's accomplished his dream, a week before the Armistice; it was a close one, and you can feel his relief.

Another pilot of the First Pursuit Group made his name attacking balloons in those last months of the war. Frank Luke, a roughneck from Arizona, joined the Twenty-Seventh Squadron at the end of July and in the next two months destroyed fourteen enemy balloons, more than any other American pilot. He also shot down four planes. Luke was a difficult person by all accounts, solitary on the ground and independent (some would say insubordinate) in the air, likely to fly off alone, or separate himself from his assigned patrol over the front and go balloon hunting on his own or with his one squadron friend, Joe Wehner.

The record of those two pilots during the Battle of St. Mihiel and the first days of Meuse-Argonne is remarkable. Flying together, they shot down balloon after balloon—two on one day, three on another—and sometimes a Fokker as well. Luke would sometimes announce in

advance the time and place at which he would burn a balloon, and spectators would gather back at the airfield and at the promised time would see flames rise over the front. Luke's combat report for September 18 tells a typical story: he and Wehner take off to go hunting, burn two balloons near Labeuville, get in a dogfight with an enemy formation, in which Luke shoots two Boches down; the two pilots lose each other, and Luke flies home to the airfield alone, shooting down an enemy observation plane on the way. His report is careful to give Wehner credit in the two balloon burnings. But by then Wehner is dead, shot down in flames during the dogfight, apparently.

Nine days later, in disobedience of orders, Luke flew off alone, dropped a note to a balloon company along the way predicting burning balloons at specified map sites, and disappeared. At the appointed time, the fires burned. But Luke was wounded, had to make a crash landing, and died at the scene.

Such a story is the kind that pilots would tell and retell (it's in the memoirs of both Rickenbacker and Mitchell), the kind that would enter the myth of the war, embellished, contradictory in details, but essentially the same—the story of the Balloon Buster who wouldn't take orders. That story might begin with his Medal of Honor citation (he was the first American aviator to receive that medal):

> After having previously destroyed a number of enemy aircraft within 17 days, he voluntarily started on a patrol after German observation balloons. Though pursued by eight German planes which were protecting the enemy balloon line, he unhesitatingly attacked and shot down in flames three German balloons, being himself under heavy fire from ground batteries and the hostile planes. Severely wounded, he descended to within 50 meters of the ground, and flying at this low altitude near the town of Murvaux opened fire upon enemy troops, killing 6 and wounding as many more. Forced to make a landing and surrounded on all sides by the enemy, who called upon him to surrender, he drew his automatic pistol and defended himself gallantly until he fell dead from a wound in the chest.

There's more than a combat report here: there's a drama, starring a flamboyant hero. What Luke did on that last flight was skillful and effective, any pilot would agree on that. But the citation version is not addressed to pilots; it's for the admiring folks back home, who need to believe that their men at war are heroes and that war itself is a brave business.

————

By October 1918, men at the front knew that the war was nearly over. All through that month rumors of peace talks were in the air. Roland Richardson, that careful recorder of the daily details of his war, reported the peace rumors as carefully:

> *October 2* (in a letter): Say doesn't the news look good though. Bulgaria out and internal trouble in Germany and the Allies pushing on every front . . . We may get home by Christmas you can never tell.

October 10 (diary): War news sure looks good today . . . We may get home yet, who knows.

October 12 (letter): It isn't as bad as you think, especially with all the good news about peace that is going around. President Wilson is certainly on the job.

October 13 (diary): Good news. Germans accept our peace terms. Gee but that does sound good. [They hadn't, quite, though negotiations had begun.]

October 20 (diary): The news isn't as good as it was. Suppose the war will last all winter.

For Richardson, the end of the war will be good news: he can go home then to Cincinnati. Other pilots regarded it with less enthusiasm. In mid-October, Ham Coolidge wrote in a letter, "Gosh, one doesn't know what to think these days with all this peace scare flying around; in fact they told me this afternoon that orders had been received in the trenches to stop firing. I was able emphatically to contradict that rumor this evening however."

A few days later Jerry Hughes, the younger brother of the combat-experienced George, wrote home to his mother from the Third Aviation Instruction Center, where he was close to completing his flight training. There had been delays in the program, and he was worried that the war would be over before he reached the front. So it was with relief that he wrote, "The 'peace scare' does not seem to have upset anyone. Things are going on just the same." Ten days later he wasn't so confident: "If Germany quits cold now, it will spoil the whole war for us. After training for a year and a half for the big game—and then to be left sitting on the bench."

"Peace scare" seems an odd phrase for men in combat or on the way there to use. But it's entirely understandable if you think about it in their terms. Peace will mean the end of the game they entered when they enlisted, the game that would change them from college boys into older, different people.

Some of them—the more sensitive ones—feel that change early in their flying lives. Alan Nichols hasn't even reached the front when he writes to his father: "Jack and I had quite a time discussing what a wonderful eye-opener this war has been for both of us. And what innocent babes we were when we left home! It certainly has made a wonderful difference in my life . . . everything has been touched, broadened, and remodelled."

Not only has his sense of his present self changed; so has his future: "One of the biggest effects on me has been on my ideas for the future. Altho I am not in the safest sport in the world, I have never given up the idea that some fine day this will all be over and I again be put back into a civilized life to see what I can do. So I've done a lot of figuring on what I'm worth or good for." The flying life, he says, has given him "a terrible wanderlust," and he no longer thinks he will ever stay long in one place: "I thot I had my life all fixed, and pictured my self a spectacled City Manager. That has gone like a puff of smoke." He's not yet twenty-one, and his future seems wide open and full of options. He runs through a list of careers: engineering, geology, forestry, aviation, automobiles. They're all possible—anything but that city manager with his glasses.

Such existential questions about life after the war—what will I do? who will I be?—occur less frequently once the young pilots reach the front and plunge into the immediate demands of the last battle. Their thoughts then are with the next mission or the last one, and with their victories and their losses. If they think of the life they'll live after the war, it's in simple, practical terms, as when Ham Coolidge, hearing a rumor of peace, writes to his mother, "Well, Mammy, if it *should* be true don't forget to tell dear old Anna to have my tuxedo pressed, my citizen clothes taken out of camphor, and the sewing machine removed from my room!"

The letter is dated October 13. Two weeks later, he was dead.

EIGHTEEN

NOVEMBER ELEVENTH

October becomes November: the war is ten days from its end. Pilots at the front don't know that, of course, but rumors increase and begin to contain reliable-sounding details. Joe Eastman writes in his journal on November 4,

> This evening we have reported telegrams of the assassination of Wilson and the Kaiser's abdication. Austria is said to have signed armistice which with the one with Turkey gives us the immediate use of all military points, transportation and u-boats, etc, . . . Also, we hear from the office of C.A.S. [Chief of Air Service] that we have submitted terms to Germany for armistice . . . What is rumor and what is fact is not known.

And on the next day:

> One treads ground seething with rumor and breathes air that sizzles for momentous wire and radio sensations. "Rummy" [a friend from another squadron] dropping on our field at noon says a French mechanic told him Germany has accepted our armistice terms . . . Followed shortly by Davitt [one of the Ninety-Fourth's pilots], who can always burnish up a tale—Ludendorff is captured disguised in a private's uniform.

In the evening he hears another rumor that disconcerts him: gossip has it that General Mitchell "thinks we'll be at it to Spring at least. Hang it!"

Squadron commanders worry about flying in this atmosphere of rumors. Eddie Rickenbacker calls the pilots of the Ninety-Fourth together to give them some advice (Joe Eastman is there, and records what his C.O. says): "His idea is to have us use our heads in the air, for flights to cooperate with flight leaders and work by pre-arranged plan as far as practicable—and for us all to unite in keeping the fair name of the 94th ahead of all others, as it has been from the first—the pending conclusion of hostilities notwithstanding."

It's good advice: be careful in these last days of combat—no more one-against-seven adventures—but also be professional, protect the reputation of the squadron, now that it is about to pass into history. It's a speech heavy with the sense of an ending.

While the rumors circulate, the ordinary war goes on, in lousy weather. On six days the weather keeps Richardson's whole squadron grounded; on three Richardson gets into the air but has engine trouble and turns back. (He's not malingering: Spad engines were notoriously untrustworthy.) On one flight the pilots of his patrol bomb a town held by American troops. On another they get a Boche, and lose one of their own. It's not an impressive record, but not an unusual one, either: just ten ordinary days in a pursuit squadron at the war's end.

Ordinary in other ways, too: ordinary illnesses. In the last week of the war half the personnel of the Eighty-Eighth Observation Squadron catch the flu, and as a result, Kenneth Littauer says, "not much work was done." And ordinary accidents, just as many as any other time. On the fourth—a day on which Richardson goes back to bed—Gustaf Lindstrom, an observer with the Ninetieth Observation Squadron, and his pilot, Leland Carver, volunteer to fly an early morning mission, even though the fog is heavy and the ceiling is almost on the ground. At fifty meters they can't see the ground, so they come back down. A couple of hours later they volunteer again, and this time visibility is slightly better. They're flying at two hundred meters, just below the cloud cover, when their engine cowling comes loose and blows back into the landing wires, disabling the controls. Carver cuts power and heads for the ground, but he's "lost the stick" and can't level the plane out as it reaches the ground. They crash head-on into a shell hole. Carver's leg is broken, and Lindstrom is knocked silly.

An ordinary crash that sends Carver to a hospital for the customary treatment. But for Lindstrom it means four days of rest leave in Paris that are extraordinary days. He arrives there on November 7 and sets about doing what one does on leave in Paris—goes to the Folies Bergère, eats well, and wanders the streets just taking it all in. On the ninth he writes in his diary, "In the afternoon we strolled about the boulevards to look over the city and see the crowds. The crowds were very large and everyone appeared to be happy as the war seems to be about over."

And on the tenth: "Today was a beautiful day, the sun shone but it was very misty. People all over town were buying flags to get ready for the big celebration of peace with victory . . . The city certainly has livened up, the lights are gradually coming on, the people are all happy and preparing for the morrow, when peace is expected."

The war is about to end, and Paris is happy. But not all the pilots at the front are rejoicing. Those who have just arrived are eager and anxious; they haven't flown over the lines, or have, but haven't seen any action there—there's a war right in front of them, but they aren't in it yet, and it's threatening to end. Before that happens, they must do something belligerent: fly patrols, go on bombing missions, do some artillery ranging, strafe a trench—any work that will feel like the real thing.

Some of them manage to do that, and their jubilation is loud in their letters. Josiah Rowe writes to his mother on November 8, "Well, thank heaven, I'm not a rookie any more." He's flown one patrol over the lines; he's seen the devastated countryside, and the artillery flashes, and the black smoke of the antiaircraft bursts, and the Huns in their trenches below, and the Hun patrols hovering above. There's no fight, though, no action at all; the squadron operations report makes it sound entirely humdrum: "No combats or enemy troops fired upon. Nothing to report." But that one patrol has changed Rowe; he's been over the lines, into the war. He's a real pilot now, and he's content.

———

Wars seem easy enough to get started: you just invade somebody else's territory. They're more difficult to get stopped. Spike Irvin, the efficient sergeant major of the 148th Pursuit Squadron at Toul, filled a week's entries in his diary with a day-to-day account of what he heard as the Great War wound down:

> *Tuesday, Nov. 5*—Italians annihilate Austrian Army . . . Armistice made with Austria.
>
> *Thursday, Nov. 7*—German delegates leave Berlin for West to ask General Foch for terms of the Armistice. Wild peace rumors today.
>
> *Friday, Nov. 8*—Germany's ten-man delegation met General Foch yesterday at French outpost . . . Foch states terms . . .
>
> *Saturday, Nov. 9*—All stand by waiting for Peace with hopes that the Germans will accept the terms of Allies. Rumors that the Kaiser has abdicated.
>
> *Sunday, Nov. 10*—Kaiser abdicates and flies to Holland . . . A Revolution starts in Germany.
>
> *Monday, Nov. 11*—THE WAR IS OVER! Armistice signed. Hostilities cease at 11:00 A.M. . . . Much rejoicing.

Like most war news at the front, the sergeant major's calendar was mainly rumors and hopes. Nobody *knew.*

Joe Eastman got what seemed the first certain news that the end of the war was in sight late on November 10. He had been out on a solitary solo flight over the lines, and when he returned at dusk, his friend Ward Fowler was on the ground waving a copy of *The New York Herald* with the headline "Kaiser Abdicates—Revolutions in Germany." As he climbs out of the cockpit, Eastman thinks, "There will be very few more trips before the end of the war."

Some time after dinner he hears a great clamor outside his tent: a parade of enlisted men has formed, drumming on a tin pan, tooting a bugle, and cheering. Jimmy Meissner of the 147th runs in, crying, "They've signed an Armistice, official wire up at the Operations from C.A.S. All hostilities to cease tomorrow at 11:00." Meissner invites the pilots of the Ninety-Fourth to the Ninety-Fifth's bar, and they flounder there through the mud. The party has already begun: from all the hangars on the field landing rockets and red and green flares shoot up, and the din is a composite of New Year's Eve and a battle. There are cowboy yells and revolver shots, and somebody has got hold of a machine gun, which he fires a few inches from the revelers' heads. Many toasts are drunk, while outside the tent a delirious band plays. Eddie Rickenbacker leads the drunken pilots in a swaying snake dance, which dissolves into a series of wrestling matches, rolling in the mud underfoot and smearing the wrestlers' faces with the stuff (Eastman complains that his fur coat is ruined). There is little peace, Eastman says, for well into the evening.

Eleven o'clock the following morning was different. Pilots in their letters and diaries tried to describe their feelings at that solemn moment. Percival Gates was at the same field as Eastman, with the 185th; in a letter to his mother that day he wrote, "This is probably to be the greatest day in the World's History. For this morning at 11:00 for the first time in over four years all the noise, guns, and fighting at the front stopped. Up to the last few minutes there was a great roar of artillery fire as if everybody was trying to get rid of all his ammunition. Then suddenly all the noise stopped and a great shout rose from all over the camp."

And John Gilchrist, an observer with the 104th: "All night long artillery on both sides seemed to be firing. In the morning there was a heavy ground mist and no flying . . . At eleven a.m. firing ceased. Because I had heard so much of it in the last two months the quiet seemed uncanny." It's the silence, as though overnight the world had been drained of the noise of war.

With no flying to be done, pilots were free to leave their airfields and look at the French people's reaction to the peace. George Vaughn and some friends went into nearby Toul "to watch the excitement." He wrote, "I have never seen anything like the changed general atmosphere about the place. Everyone was wearing a broad 'won't come off' smile, and big ribbons or flags of their national colors. Flags were everywhere, in every conceivable place, and every motor car or truck carried large flags down the streets. In the square an American band was giving a concert."

After dinner they drive to Nancy and find the effects of the news even more marked: people of all nationalities parading up and down, singing, shouting, and waving flags. But what most impresses Vaughn is that the lights of the town, "which have been dimmed and shaded since the beginning of the war, were all blazing away at this full power. It is so long since I have seen a city with its lights really going." In the morning, silence after the roar; in the evening, light after the long darkness. It all seems a world they had forgotten.

Lance Holden was on leave in Paris when peace happened—"in a fine hot bath in the Continental when the riot outside let us know that it was all up with Germany." He went down into the streets, met an American friend, and wandered about, observing how the French celebrated:

> An American uniform meant cheers, kisses and hugs wherever it went. Such a crowd I never saw . . . It took a good half hour to worm our way across the Place de la Concorde to the Crillon—No one was going anywhere—just pushing for the fun of it.
>
> Then the guns began to boom which pleased everyone beyond words. By night fall the blue had been cleaned off the street lamps and Paris became what it must have been before the war—wholly fascinating and beautiful.

George Moseley was in London, on his way home to get married, when the war ended:

> The news that the war was really over seemed at first to stun everyone—they would not believe it, and then, as the tooting whistles and clanging bells gradually impressed the truth on the minds of everyone, all the pent up fears and anxieties which four years of war had caused were suddenly released, intoxicating all with joy. They yelled, laughed, cried and ran up and down the streets. The women kissed all the men and the men returned the compliment with interest. Autos drove around Piccadilly Circus with girls on top, hair streaming in the wind, waving and throwing kisses to all. Men were surrounded by circles of girls who would not let them out until the unfortunate or fortunate man, have it the way you wish, kissed each of his fair captors. London went wild. Bedlam reigned.

The next evening Joe Eastman and his friend Ward Fowler drive two young ladies into Troyes for a final peace celebration. In Troyes, he writes in his diary, "the French were mad, flags in every window—streets barely passable for the mobs out rejoicing."

He doodles a sketch of the celebration in the top margin.

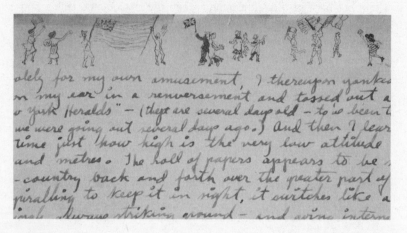

But after the peace, after the cheering and the flags and the bright city lights, the new peacetime seems a vacancy: the sky is empty now, and so are their lives. The introspective Eastman feels it. "So this is France," he writes:

> I mean—so this is our reception of Peace. As a matter of fact, I don't think that the thing has quite sopped into our heads. What tells me more than anything else that it is coming to me, is a sinking feeling not unlike the hopeless dawning of the responsibility tied with a college diploma. It's all over. What now? No matter what the life one quits, I don't believe it can be done entirely free of reluctance.

NINETEEN

AFTERWARDS

Joe Eastman asked, "What now?" It was a question everyone in the Air Service asked: the pilots at the front, the *embusqués* behind the lines, the students still in flight training, and all the ground personnel—the mechanics and the armorers, the cooks and the truck drivers—who kept the squadrons in the air. And in the trenches, the troops who had fought the ground war. Eventually, they would all go home, but it would take time to gather the necessary transport ships and marshal the troops at ports of embarkation. It had taken a year and more to get them to the war; how long would it take to deliver them back where they had come from?

The answer is months. In the meantime, the Air Service found itself in a new, peacetime kind of muddle. On November 11, forty-five Air Service squadrons were at the front and operational (though not all of them had yet flown in combat): some twelve hundred pilots and observers and gunners, trained and equipped to confront their enemies in the air. And now the sky is empty.

What will all those pilots do with themselves? The squadrons will go on functioning, in a desultory way; new young men will arrive at the airfields, and will be ordered to fly, and occasionally given some training; old hands will fly when they feel like it—out over the now-silent No-Man's-Land, tourists now, seeing the front clearly for the first time without the blur of smoke and the distractions of antiaircraft shells, and reflecting, perhaps, on the devastation and the carnage of the worst war in history.

Some take their release from war more cheerfully, even joyously. Bogart Rogers writes to his "Dearest Isabelle" in late November: "I've never enjoyed flying more than I did this morning. It's a wicked old game. Once it gets hold you're gone, never will be able to get away from it. If you'd ever flown, you'd understand the feeling, dear. There's nothing else like it and there never will be."

And in another letter: "I've always maintained that with the elements of danger removed this would be a very nice war, and so it is."

Some fly with a new recklessness, now that the shooting is over. Two days after the Armistice, Joe Eastman goes out hedgehopping and is "fiendishly tempted to cut my wing between church spires, etc—and wonder why, when courage of the unreasoning variety might have helped win the war—I was thoughtful, and now when recklessness can only break my neck—I take huge pleasure in it."

A week later he goes hedgehopping again. "A fever for playing around at low altitudes has somehow possessed me," he writes, "possibly to compensate for the stimulant of uncertainty that was cut off November eleventh. The boys who met their boches tell me that I don't want to live thru the war, or perhaps think I am aiming to impress them that there's a regular devil 'mongst us—which naturally kids me beyond words."

There's a note of bravado in that passage, but there's also an anxious young man worrying about what the other guys think of him. Anxiety was always there in Eastman's mind, right from the beginning of his war adventure, when he brought too many suits of long underwear on the cross-country journey. When he began flying patrols over the lines, he was the one who listened closely to the sounds his engine made, and looked nervously around for a place to land, and more often than not turned back.

From the time he joined the Ninety-Fourth at the front in March, Eastman's diary is full of troubles with the planes he flies: engines knock and oil pumps fail and connecting rods make sinister noises; by the first of June he has made eight forced landings. He goes on flying, gets into dogfights, and returns to his field with bullet holes in his plane, like any other pilot in the squadron, but he worries about the existence of courage in a nervous temperament. In late September, after a flight in which his engine spouted steam "like a peanut stand," he reflects on what a difficult thing it is for him to distinguish between mere nervous apprehension and sound judgment: "I can't make out if this is yellowness or idiocy. Whatever it is, it's certainly annoying."

As the war neared its end, Eastman looked back on his time at the front and considered what kind of a record it made: "It seems almost unbelievable that tho every patrol I've been on to come anywhere near boches has combatted—in my seven months I've had only about five fights—one, more of a flight than a fight. Something must be done about this."

And so, on November 7, when a man might be forgiven for being cautious, he volunteers for a mission to the Mézières railroad station the next day. But by then the ground troops have taken Sedan and cut the Mézières line, and there's no reason to go there. "Still full of splendid ideas about doing my little wallop," he tries to go on a volunteer patrol but is persuaded by Rickenbacker to wait for a scheduled one. He does, and takes off . . . and you can predict what happens: an air line breaks, the engine stops, and he has to make another emergency landing.

You can see in this story of poor Eastman two separate narratives. One is the external story of an extraordinary run of bad luck with temperamental, rough-running planes—a curse, Eastman calls it, and a jinx. The other story is internal, a confessional narrative of a fidgety worrier who wants to do his duty but listens to his engine. Eastman was aware that his record exposed him to the doubts and suspicions of his fellow pilots, and even the charge of cowardice.

A month after the Armistice, Eastman stands at a window of the château where he's billeted and notices that the mist has risen from the hills and that it's flying weather. It's getting late, and anyway there's no reason to fly. And as he stands there, idly musing over the commonplace prospect of flying at all, he lays his hand upon his heart and finds it "fairly jumping out my ribs! *I was afraid to fly!*" He heads for the airfield and orders his plane prepared for a flight. By then it's nearly evening; candles are burning in the barracks, and the far end of the field is indistinct in the dusk. He takes off, grazing the end hangar by a "disagreeable margin." It's not really much of a performance, he thinks; the Balloon Busters used to do this every night. Yet, as the darkening country and

illuminated barracks rolled beneath him, he writes, "I was not unconscious of rabbit-headedness. And as it was actually turning to night
I was content with playing around less than fifteen minutes before
making a two-trial landing. Obviously I'm an excitable specimen, for I
climbed out of my teddy-bear [his fur-lined flying suit] in the customary
state of shakiness." And he draws his conclusion: "I know of no greater
moral satisfaction than comes of putting on the gloves with one's own
skeleton-in-the-closet."

Eastman has been doing that for all of his flying life—putting on
the gloves with his nerves and his anxiety: in short, with his fear of flying. He does so by flying, and so dispersing any possible charge of cowardice: a coward *flees* from what frightens him; Eastman *confronted* it.
I reckon that takes a high degree of courage, and as I read his honest,
confessional diary, I feel admiration and affection for the troubled
young man who wrote it.

———

The shooting has stopped, and the Boches have gone, but it's still possible, and necessary, to take chances, and so prove that you're not rabbit-
headed. It's not only the new men at the front who feel that urge; Temple
Joyce, still stuck back at Issoudun in a test pilot's job, relieved his need
for excitement in his life by flying three hundred consecutive loops (for
a while it was a world record).

"What now?" was a hard question not only for the pilots; commanding officers and their superiors, the colonels and generals who made the
big decisions, faced it too. What do you do with a bunch of trained
combat pilots when there's no more combat? Bogart Rogers's 32 Squadron, RAF, was entered in a wing aerial firing competition; pilots of the
135th Observation Squadron were ordered to ferry planes to Colombey-
les-Belles, where they were burned like any household rubbish. (You
don't think of flyable combat planes as a disposal problem, but of course
they were.) The pilots of the 185th stopped flying to paint their planes so
they'd be sharp-looking when they were turned back to the Air Service.
It was all busywork, anything to keep them occupied.

Some of the pilots of the Ninety-Fourth were sent to Issoudun for
medical examination: the doctors at the research laboratories there

wanted to observe the effects of extended combat on men who flew. The pilots managed to spend six days in Paris on the way, and when they finally arrived at Issoudun, they flunked all the tests.

Back at the airfields along the front, pilots found ways of passing the time on the ground. Some toured the battlefields. Jerry Hughes, who had come to the 258th too late for the fighting, borrowed one of the squadron's Dodges and drove to Verdun, just to look at the war world that he had missed. Great piles of rifles and machine guns and other implements of war were stacked high in one of the town squares. He helped himself to a Springfield rifle and a Browning automatic rifle (both American weapons) and carried them back to the States when he went home.

Late in November, Hughes's C.O. suggested that Hughes and a pal drive to Metz for a look at the town before the French army reoccupied it. They went and the next morning watched General Pétain, on a white horse, lead his troops into the ancient fortress. Afterwards there were wild scenes in the streets. They saw Nungesser, the French ace, drive by, waving to the excited crowd. One unfortunate incident marred the festivities. Hughes describes it:

> During the celebration, French SPADs were circling the city and diving down close to the buildings. Suddenly one pilot came in too low and struck some wires. His plane plunged into the middle of the main town square. We were standing on the edge of the square and saw the plane smash into the crowd. Several people were badly injured. I'm not sure if any were killed. The report was that the pilot, although badly hurt, came out alive.

They've had enough of Metz and go back to their squadron and the mud at Manonville.

Some pilots pass the time wreck hunting, or grave hunting, trying to bring the war stories of fellow pilots to a final conclusion. Bogart Rogers and two of his friends take their C.O.'s car and go looking for the grave of a fellow American from their squadron, Alvin Callender. They find the grave without much trouble, and the wreck not far away. The plane, Rogers writes in a letter to his sweetheart, had simply been shot to pieces, holes everywhere, some from explosive bullets; he thinks it probable that Callender had died in the air or was at least unconscious when he crashed. They have brought a cross made from a four-bladed propeller, and they set it up; then they lay sod over the grave and build a border of bricks around the edges. "It was a solemn party that came home," Rogers writes. And so it would be; it's not often that a pilot confronts his own dead so closely.

One way of escaping from the boredom of waiting is to move up into Germany with the Allied occupation forces; it won't be combat, but at least it will be active duty, and they'll fly. Squadrons along the front are eager to go, and some do; the Eighty-Eighth Observation Squadron (Fletcher McCordic's unit) moves up to Trier, in western Germany, in December. Percival Gates thinks his 185th might go to Germany and stay there until everything is over, but it doesn't happen. He volunteers to be assigned separately to the Army of the Rhine, but is turned down.

At Toul, Hobey Baker and the 141st Pursuit Squadron (of which he's now the C.O.) wait for orders. If they're sent to Germany, Baker can continue his flying life. I can imagine how that appeals to him. For a decade he's been a star—on football and hockey teams at Princeton and as a fighter pilot (he's shot down three Boches). Going home would mean settling down in some boring job on Wall Street. Occupation flying would be better than that.

Baker's after-the-war story is the sort pilots tell for the irony of it. In December he receives orders to return to the States and is scheduled to leave the next day for Paris and home. He decides to have one last flight in a Spad. And crashes. And dies. Because of the last-day timing, and because he was Hobey Baker, the story is told and retold and enters the myth.

Colonel Frank Lahm was in an Avro approaching the Toul airfield when the crash occurred. He describes it at length in his diary:

> We were just coming in for a landing when a Spad started out, giving us a little bump from the wash of its propeller as it left the ground. I landed, stopped and was about to take off again when Krout [the other man in Lahm's plane] said, "The Spad crashed." I looked round and there it was, lying on the field, not far from us. We taxied over, I helped to get the pilot out—had to use an axe to get his feet loose. He probably died as he was laid on the stretcher. His face was badly cut up, and it was not until someone said, "It is Capt. Baker," that I realized it was Hobey Baker . . .

He pauses in his account to summarize the reputation before he completes his version of the accident and the ironic last-day occasion: "He was anxious to get home—finally, yesterday, his order came, he was going out for a farewell spin in his Spad, shot up, motor evidently died and he was too low to recover so crashed on the field."

Forty years later, Charles D'Olive told his version of Baker's death in an interview, beginning with the validating fact that he had four or five pictures of the crash: "He had orders to go home," D'Olive recalled, "on the first of December, and he was flashing them around. We all told him, 'Don't get in another plane.' He said, 'I agree, but I just want to fly down to Nancy to get some new pink pants.' We were all inside when he took off and when his engine quit over the edge of the field he pulled

a fool stunt and tried to turn back. The SPAD stalled and he hit nose down. He split his head open on the gun butts."

In February 1919, Fletcher McCordic, the reliable man, the protector of the Eighty-Eighth, is with his squadron at Trier as part of the occupation force. In a letter home he writes that the squadron is getting a single-seated Fokker D.VII into shape and that he expects to take a hop in it soon. Two days later he gets his turn. Here is the Air Service special report on what happened on that flight:

He stunted over the field for about fifteen minutes, showing perfect control of the plane, and then flew north over Trèves [the French name for Trier] disappearing in the direction of Coblenz. The motor seemed to be turning up regularly. At 14:15H he was seen flying low over a forest just east of Waldweiler. His motor was turning up very irregularly and he was evidently trying to glide to an open space north of the woods. Seeing that he did not have enough altitude for that he banked up to turn to a little clearing of stumps on his left. It is impossible to tell from the account of a German that saw it whether he side-slipped and fell on this turn or went into a spin, at any rate he was just above the woods when he banked.

The report passes no judgment on McCordic's decision to try to turn at low altitude with a sputtering engine, but an old pilot can't help remarking that he made the same mistake that Hobey Baker made, and that many beginners made, and with the same result. Airplanes are unforgiving, even in peacetime.

———

The game of war is over, and the pilots who played in it look back and try to assess their performance. For some, that's easy; Holden has got his last balloon and is what he wanted to be—an ace; Harold Hartney is a major and commanding officer of the First Pursuit Group; Field Kindley has his twelve victories and is commanding the 148th. For most of the others, the summing up is less glorious. "Thank Heaven I have no regrets," Percival Gates writes on November 20. "If I did not get a Hun machine or balloon I got through and that is more than some of the others did. I never missed a patrol, and I never hesitated to volunteer when volunteers were called for."

It's an honorable record: he did his job; he didn't flinch. And now he's through. No regrets, and no nostalgia; his war is over.

For commanders, this is a time for another kind of summing up and tidying up—the final awarding of medals and citations. In the last week of the war and the weeks after, awards were distributed in a shower, a blizzard of honors. *Out of Control*, the First Pursuit Group's irreverent newspaper, kept score of the group's share: on November 7 it reported that of twenty-four DSCs awarded in a single ceremony, the First had gotten fifteen; and two weeks later it ran this headline:

AGREEABLE SURPRISE
Lt. Col. B. M. Atkinson and Capt Philip
Roosevelt Bring Bushel Basketful
of Croix de Guerres.

The list of fifty-seven pilots and observers that follows includes many names that a reader of this book will recognize: Eddie Rickenbacker is there, and Sumner Sewall and Jim Knowles. Some of the recipients are dead: Ham Coolidge and Quentin Roosevelt are on the list. Some are prisoners of war: Zenos Miller and Waldo Heinrichs and Walter Avery are all there. At least one, Doug Campbell, is back in the States. The dead and the living, the prisoners and the free, are all swept together into one basket, as though medals were perishable goods that had to be used up before they went bad.

Another basketful of DSCs—thirty this time—was distributed in December, at the Second Pursuit Group's field at Douilly. Lance Holden got one and wrote about it:

> You can't imagine what a relief it was to hear I had gotten the D.S.C.—With that blue ribbon on you can look anyone in the eye and tell them to go to ——! After being walked all over while a cadet by every embusque guy with a Sam Browne on— then when finally a Lieut., to be laughed at for wanting to get to the front and risk my neck—then to be stuck on the Defense of Paris—But now!—Well I wouldn't trade my 7 [victories] for most anything in the world.

The tone of that passage may seem surprising for the occasion; there's elation in it, and relief—at last Holden has got the recognition he deserved and wanted—but there's also resentment and anger at the muddle and the slights and offenses he endured. Holden is looking back at his flying career not as a story he's still living but as history. The war was an exciting, frustrating time to live in, but now it's over, closed like a chapter in a book. Now the completed story can be told and assessed. Now they can go home.

And most of them do. Bogart Rogers goes home to California and marries his Isabelle. Harvey Conover, who couldn't imagine drudging once more for the Butler Paper Company and living in a one-horse suburb with a wife to report to, does just that—returns to Chicago, marries a girl from La Grange, and settles down at an office desk. Roland Richardson goes back to Cincinnati, marries his sweetheart, and takes a job with the family business. The Hughes brothers, George and Jerry, return to

Long Island, where they buy and operate the Garden City Garage. Percival Gates returns to school, marries, and founds a felt company in
New Jersey: all solid, middle-class American lives, lives they'd probably
have lived if they had never flown, never seen the war. Most of them
seem content never to fly again.

But for others, the reluctance to leave the flying life remained com-
pelling. They responded to that reluctance in many ways. Some pilots—
especially those with wartime flying reputations, like Rickenbacker,
and Doug Campbell, and Sumner Sewall, and Walter Avery, and George
Vaughn—entered the new world of commercial aviation and prospered
as that business prospered. And returned to squadron reunions forty
years later, gray and balding and successful-looking, to reminisce about
the old days.

Some, who had been college boys when they enlisted, returned to
their colleges and rejoined the college flying club. In 1920 some of them
would fly in the first Intercollegiate Air Contest at Mineola, Long
Island, on May 7. Eleven universities and colleges sent teams of pilots to
compete: Yale, Harvard, Columbia, Princeton, Cornell, and Pennsylva-
nia from the Ivy League, and Wesleyan, Lehigh, Pittsburgh, Rutgers, and
Williams. Colleges that didn't have their own planes borrowed planes
from the Air Service.

The events were straight out of military flight training: a cross-
country race, precision landings, aerobatics, and an "alert contest," in
which the pilots lay down on cots on the field, feigning sleep, and at a
signal leaped up, dressed in flight gear, and ran to get their planes into
the air. Yale won the contest, Williams was second, and Columbia and
Princeton tied for third place. There were the usual, predictable accidents: the Lehigh contestant crashed on takeoff, injuring his passenger
but not himself. And an unidentified person in the group walked into a
whirling propeller and injured his shoulder. Just like the old days, they
must have thought.

Two days later *The New York Times* ran an editorial about the contest, headlined "Aviation Triumphant." "A year ago," the editorial began,
"—aviation was torpid then—who would have predicted that the colleges would soon be holding races in the air?" Back then, it went on,
economic prophets saw little hope for American aviation; Congress had
not appropriated funds for Army and Navy flying, nor had it offered aid

to American aviation manufacturers. Many were saying that the industry was dead, killed by the indifference of the government. But, the *Times* argued, the sight of those "college youngsters, . . . cleaving the air in ardent competition and complete masters of their frail craft," demonstrated that in fact aviation in America was flourishing. (It did not mention that many of the "youngsters" were veteran combat pilots, back at the colleges they had left for the war in Europe.) The Intercollegiate Air Contest was never held again. But it had made its point: flying would play an important role in the American future.

Other returned pilots satisfied their need to fly simply by flying on their own. In July 1922, Zenos Miller—poor old accident-prone Zenos—planned a transcontinental flight with his brother and a friend. They were about to take off when someone on the ground asked them to search for a plane that had gone down nearby. Zenos agreed, took off, and found the crash, with the pilot standing beside it. He returned to the airfield and circled, waving to signal that the pilot was not injured. Low and slow and in a turn, and so the inevitable happened: the plane stalled and spun in, and Zenos was killed.

Crashes weren't the only post-Armistice casualties. One other in particular stands out for the irony of it. George Hughes had been a serious, dutiful pilot throughout his career; he had accepted command responsibilities when they were thrust at him—one at the beginning, when he herded a band of students from Illinois to Issoudun without losing a one, and again at the end, when he took command of the new 258th Observation Squadron. He did his pilot's work without complaining (though he never expressed the joy in flying that other pilots felt); while he was with the Twelfth Squadron, he flew more patrols than any other pilot; he was shot down twice and had to crash-land. A strong, exemplary leader, you'd say, and you'd be right.

Four days after the Armistice Hughes's brother, Jerry, newly arrived at the front, went looking for George and found him in his bed, shaking uncontrollably. Now that the war was over and the pressure was off, his body had simply given up—a casualty of war as surely as any combat fatality. He spent a month in an Army hospital and another month in the muddle of waiting for transport before he finally boarded a ship for the United States in mid-January 1919.

Alan Winslow was a different kind of postwar casualty. He'd been the first American from an American squadron to shoot down a German plane; later he'd been wounded and made a prisoner of war. After the war he returned to Washington, where he held various government appointments before joining Pan American Airways in 1930. In the spring of 1933 he wrote his recollections of his war experiences in a series of articles for *Liberty* magazine under the anxious-sounding title "No Parachutes." His mind must have been full of those memories when he traveled to Canada that summer on Pan Am business. There, in Ottawa, he fell from his hotel window and died. It's hard not to see that fall as the last act of a tragic play that began fifteen years earlier when the young Winslow, on his way to enlist in the Air Service, climbed out another hotel window, at the Biltmore in New York, and lay down on the window ledge to test his fear of heights.

––––––

It's natural that after a great destructive event—a war, or a natural disaster, or the fall of a dynasty—witnesses should look back across the ruins and try to get the story right before they move on. In the days after November 11, some pilots paused in their postwar diary writing to count their dead. Joe Eastman stuck a loose, undated fragment of paper into his diary at the end of his wartime entries, headed simply "Killed." It contains the names of seventeen pilots, most of them from the Ninety-Fourth and Ninety-Fifth Squadrons, others not. It's not a unit roster; these are *personal* dead. Lance Holden made a similar list and put it in his scrapbook—an annotated list of twenty pilots killed, wounded, or taken prisoner. These lists are reckonings of the cost of the war in dead friends—to pilots, a more important part of the story than battles won or lost.

In the U.S. Air Service, looking back was also an official order from the Chief of Air Service, AEF to Colonel Gorrell, then Assistant Chief of Staff, who passed it on to every unit: each one would write and submit a history of its war—battles fought, production problems faced, lessons learned. The implication was clear: somebody in every unit must compile his unit's history; when that was done, they could all go home.

These histories got written—some brief, not much more than a compilation of operations reports; others more elaborate, describing major actions and tabulating the combat scores and the losses. What they had in common was an objective, nonjudgmental tone: this happened, and that happened—history at its most basic. These histories were gathered together under the direction of Colonel Gorrell into one vast bundle of documents and deposited (maybe "dumped" is a better word) in the vaults of the War Department in Washington, where it lay for decades, tattered and yellowing and largely unconsulted, Gorrell grumbled, "because of its inaccessibility."

Other versions of some squadron histories followed, unofficial stories written by squadron pilots or observers and addressed not to the generals and the colonels but to fellow fliers, to preserve memories of what it was like, in their own wars. They begin to appear surprisingly soon after the Armistice, usually privately printed, often without the name of either the author or any publisher, sometimes without even a date of publication, each volume one amateur writer's effort to tell his squadron's story before it faded: *A History of the 17th Aero Squadron* in December 1918; *History of the Twentieth Aero Squadron*, undated but probably 1919; *The History of the 50th Aero Squadron*, dated January 1920 in the anonymous author's introduction. And they continued to appear, some of them years later: Harold Buckley's *Squadron 95*, published in Paris in 1933; Percival Hart's *History of the 135th Aero Squadron*, from Chicago, 1939; and John Stuart Gilchrist's *104th Aero Squadron* not until 1968—fifty years after the war's last patrol.

Whenever and wherever they were written, each of these histories tells a squadron's story in personal terms. The pilots are men the author knew, and the details of their lives—the fields they flew from, the weather, the quarters, the food—are set down from direct experience. The stories of their lives in the air are just as individual and personal— what it was like to fly an observation mission over the lines at twenty-five meters, to make an emergency landing in a field full of shell holes, to attack a German airfield, diving and machine-gunning the enemy planes lined up to take off. You don't get that kind of detail, or the note of excitement in the telling, from an operations report.

Many of these unofficial histories begin with an "In Memoriam" page, like this one from the *History of the 17th*. This page is more than a table of casualties: it's a formal mode of grief for comrades who were young, and are dead:

> ## IN MEMORIAM.
>
> Lieutenant **W. C. Potter.**
> Lieutenant **R. P. Mathews.**
> Lieutenant **P. N. Rhinelander.**
> Lieutenant **K. G. West.**
> Lieutenant **S. P. Mandell.**
> Lieutenant **W. F. Frank.**
> Lieutenant **E. A. Parrott.**
> Lieutenant **C. G. Stephens.**
> Lieutenant **P. R. Perkins.**
> Lieutenant **L. B. Fuller.**
> Lieutenant **J. H. Weimer.**
> Lieutenant **E. Forbes.**
> Lieutenant **E. A. Taylor.**
> Lieutenant **H. C. Preston.**
> Lieutenant **D. B. Harris.**
> Lieutenant **G. B. Wiser.**
> Lieutenant **H. W. Wilmer.**
> Lieutenant **H. E. Turner.**

Another kind of memorial, the collections of dead pilots' letters gathered and edited by grieving family members, began to appear midway through the war, as early Lafayette Escadrille volunteers were killed. Victor Chapman was shot down on June 23, 1916; his *Letters from France* was published in May 1917. Norman Prince died on October 15, 1916; *Norman Prince: A Volunteer Who Died for the Cause He Loved* appeared in December 1917. Both books remember the dead man's entire life, beginning with his ancestors, and are illustrated with photographs, some of them family pictures from his childhood and youth. The tone is sorrowful and fond, as one would expect: a dear son is dead, and a parent who loved him looks back at the life that was lost.

Memorial volumes kept coming after the war, as though the war would only come to a close when all the dead were remembered, individually: in late 1918, Briggs Adams (killed in action March 14, 1918); in 1919, Houston Woodward (killed in action April 1, 1918), Kenneth Mac-Leish (killed in action October 14, 1918), and Ham Coolidge (killed in action October 27, 1918); in 1920, Richard Blodgett (killed in action

May 17, 1918); in 1921, Quentin Roosevelt (killed in action July 14, 1918) and Sidney Drew (killed in action May 19, 1918). The accumulative effect of reading these stories of life and death one at a time is indeed moving, more moving than any statistics could be.

A more intimate way of preserving the war story—or at least a part of it—was for one man who had been there to look into his memory and write what he found there. The stories he recalls won't be exactly what happened, or the whole of any action, but like the letters and diaries they will tell us what it was like to be there when it happened—how historical events feel when you are immersed in them.

The first personal narratives appeared surprisingly early, almost as soon as the war ended. The authors were the slightly older pilots, men who brought more experience to the telling. Most of them had risen in the Air Service to command positions and could see beyond the personal to wider understanding of the war in the air—men like Eddie Rickenbacker, whose *Fighting the Flying Circus* was published in 1919, and Charles Biddle, whose *Way of the Eagle* appeared the same year, and Hiram Bingham's more administrative account, *An Explorer in the Air Service*, published in 1920.

In the years just before the Second World War another group of First World War air narratives appeared, written by ex-pilots who were by then middle-aged men, remembering their flying days with a certain inevitable nostalgia, because they were looking back at themselves when young: among them Norman Archibald (*Heaven High, Hell Deep*, 1935), Charles Codman (*Contact*, 1937), and Harold Hartney (*Up and at 'Em*, 1940). And then, after a long silence, a third small wave of recollections of First World War flying, written by old men whose backward gaze was longer ranged now, a look through time's haze, perhaps, but with bright patches of memory, like sunshine through clouds, and sometimes the frankness that often comes with age, when reticence seems pointless. In a small town in Ohio, Curtis Kinney is in his eighty-fourth year when he writes *I Flew a Camel* (1972). George Vaughn is eighty-three when he writes *War Flying in France* (1980), and Minor Markham is ninety and living in Paris when he writes a memoir—never published, so far as I can tell—to which he gives two tentative titles: *Old Man . . . Mumbling* and *Survivor*.

Memories of old men have their own qualities. What they see when they look back is bound to be tinged with melancholy, and a sense of how innocent they were when they were young, and how ironic life is. So Vaughn writes in the preface to his book: "I hope that the reader will bear with me as I recall those long-ago days when we sincerely believed we were fighting the war to end all wars." And Markham puts that melancholy and irony into his two titles: he's only an old man mumbling, a survivor. Still, they remember, and they are moved to tell their stories because for them, as for anyone who has fought through a war, their war, in all its dark and shining details, is a shaping part of who they are.

All of these men, the young and the middle-aged and the old, have been combat fliers—a role that defined them and gave their existence meaning—in a war that was its own world. That turbulent world came to an end and receded into the past, into history and myth with all the other epic wars that have been fought since Greeks met Trojans on the plains of Troy—one more war story to be remembered, written, and told to all the rest of humanity. Eastman was right: no one who was there in that heightened world would leave it without reluctance. Out of that reluctance came the stories that have survived and become the myth that is what we know as the first war in the air, a part of the whole grand, terrible story of men at war.

I come to the end of this story of the flying game with a feeling of admiration for the men I have met here, but also with a certain sadness. Like old Nestor in the *Odyssey*, I look back on the war and think, "So many good men gone." How young they were, how promising those young lives that would not be lived out, what talents they had that their country might have used well in the years ahead. And what good guys they were—funny, risk-taking, good friends and good fliers. War is a cruel devourer of the young. And flying is a gamble that even the best pilots don't always win.

And yet . . . for the survivors their war has been a memorable, self-expanding experience in their lives. They have learned skills they're proud of and have found within themselves reservoirs of courage and endurance they didn't know they had. For most of them the flying game has been a sport, at least sometimes, that gave them a kind of pleasure—even joy—that they will not feel again. And it has been a game they won. All of that will remain part of who they are for the rest of their lives.

They have fought the war to end all wars, or so they think. But they're mistaken. Two decades later there will be another war, another fire beyond the horizon that will draw another generation of young men to its cause. It will be worse than their war was; vast flotillas of planes will drop their tons of bombs, annihilating civilian populations and devastating cities—Warsaw, London, Berlin, Dresden, Hiroshima—cities that had nurtured civilization. That war lies in the future, but it will come, humankind being what it is. It's only a matter of time.

NOTES

PROLOGUE: A FIRE BEYOND THE HORIZON
3 "There was no marching": Mitchell, 175.
4 "I pay my part": Rockwell, 97.

1. AN OCCUPATION FOR GENTLEMEN
7 "a great opportunity": Rockwell, 1.
8 "If I should be killed": Ibid., 7–8.
8 "These Sand Hills": McConnell, xi–xii.
9 "if a country": Bert Hall, 4.
12 "The reason": Rockwell, 45.
13 "jump from the lowest": Ibid., 80.
13 "We, the *Mitraille*": Chapman, 131.
13 "It is perfectly": Ibid., 121.
13 "There seems to be a fascination": McConnell, 13–14.
14 "All along": Ibid., 15.
15 "The aeroplane service": Baker in Sweetser, 34.
17 "swashbuckling explorer": *New York Times,* May 13, 2004, A3.
18 "It was borne": Bingham, 18.
18 "To keep myself": Boy Scouts of America, 14.
19 "An aviator is": U.S. House of Representatives, *Congressional Record*, July 14, 1917, 5137.
19 "When [a pilot]": U.S. Senate, *Congressional Record*, July 21, 1917, 5368.
19 "There is being attracted": U.S. House of Representatives, *Congressional Record*, July 14, 1917, 5134.
19 "there are many men": Ibid., 5122.
19 "No person": U.S. Congress, *Sixty-Fifth Congress, Session I* (1917), chap. 40, 243.

2. THE IVY LEAGUE AIR FORCE

21 "French Aviator Bags": *New York Times*, Feb. 8, 1916, 1.

21 "French Birdman": *Washington Post*, Feb. 8, 1916, 2.

22 "Does Marvels": *Washington Post*, July 2, 1916, A2.

22 "Two French Aviators": *Chicago Daily Tribune*, Aug. 5, 1916, 2.

22 "Guynemer flies alone": *New York Times*, Feb. 8, 1916, 1.

22 "American Aviators": *New York Times*, May 22, 1916, 2.

22 "Americans Bring Down": *New York Times*, May 27, 1916, 2.

23 "American Flier": *Chicago Daily Tribune*, June 25, 1916, 8.

23 "He was too courageous": Rockwell, 140.

24 "A flying corps is certainly": Lowell to Frazier Curtis, April 20, 1916, Harvard University Archives UAI 5.160, ser. 1914–1917, folder 178.

24 "I submitted your generous": Lowell to Godfrey L. Cabot, June 12, 1916, Harvard University Archives UAI 5.160, ser. 1914–1917, folder 178i.

25 "Harvard Aero Camp Gets Biplane": *Boston American*, July 13, 1916.

25 "As you know": Lowell to Roger Amory, July 14, 1916, Harvard University Archives, UAI 5, ser. 1914–1917, Folder 178, Military Training: Flying Corps.

25 "Harvard Leads in Air Preparedness": *New York Times*, July 16, 1916, 13.

25 "The Harvard Aero Corps a Reality": *Flying* 5, no. 9 (Oct. 1916): 379.

27 "the 'millionaire unit'": *New York Tribune*, March 25, 1917, 2.

29 "A fleet of twelve": *Daily Princetonian*, Nov. 20, 1916, 1.

30 "their flight in battle": "Twelve Aeroplanes Fly to Princeton," *Flying* 5, no. 11 (Dec. 1916).

31 "The colleges all closed": Campbell, *Cross & Cockade Journal*, 30.

31 "We did not join": Moseley, 8–9.

31 "What are you going to do": Fitzgerald, 150.

33 "The places of the three pilots": Carroll Winslow, 146.

33 "I know of no sound": McConnell, 87.

33 "the best and bravest": Ibid., 97.

33 "*too* brave if anything": Ibid., 133.

34 "Many, many thanks": Walcott, 8–9.

3. GOING

36 "War is practically inevitable": Walcott, 10.

39 "there were at least 50,000": Bingham, 50.

39 "The situation at that time": Pershing, 1:27.

39 "We could not have put": Ibid.

40 "Two or three of us": Campbell, *Cross & Cockade Journal*, 30.

40 "He gave us about ten minutes": Lee, 107.

41 "It was known": *Air Service Medical Manual*, 17.

42 "I don't believe": Theodore Roosevelt, *The Selected Letters of Theodore Roosevelt*, ed. H. W. Brands (New York: Cooper Square, 2001), 633.

42 "Many people": McMinnies, 1–2.

43 "There has been a decided": Office of the Chief Signal Officer to President, Harvard College, memorandum, Dec. 21, 1917, Harvard University Archives UAI 5.160, ser. 1917–1919, folder 1971.

43 "a service which can be recruited": Lowell to Major E. Z. Steever (Signal Corps), memorandum, Jan. 17, 1918, Harvard University Archives UAI 5.160, ser. 1917–1919, folder 1971.

44 "I think, en plus": Wright, 44.

44 "consist of a severe": Moseley, 21.

45 "I am going": Ibid., 18.

45 "Flying from my first impression": Walcott, 12.

45 "I was lying": Alan Winslow, Feb. 25, 1933, 8.

46 "Soon I had the answer": Ibid.

48 "This place is getting harder": Grider, 48–49.

48 "weed out those": Bingham, 47.

48 "It's going to be Hell": Grider, 49.

48 "There were more than 200": Sprague, Jan. 7, 1939, 15.

49 "the men who have been": George Hughes, in Vaughn, 16.

50 "The *Adriatic* is": Rowe, 2, 6.

51 "Dear Ruthie": Blodgett, 66.

52 *"Thursday, October 18"*: Coffin in Gilchrist, 5, 7.

52 "Q. sails on the same boat": Coolidge, 1.

53 "The attitude of the men": Rowe, 9.

53 "It is funny": Ibid., 9–10.

54 "Fellows are getting": Ibid., 9.

4. ABROAD I: FIRST IMPRESSIONS

55 "The principal streets": Rowe, 15.

56 "you see Tommies": Rogers, 60.

56 "for Paris": Rowe, 17.

56 "not nearly so attractive": Ibid.

56 "For real beauty": Ibid., 18.

56 "While everything": Ibid., 18–19.

57 "Women are wild": Heinrichs in Woolley, *First to the Front*, 19.

57 "all the unattached": Richardson, 5.

57 "Here I am": MacLeish, *Kenneth*, 25.

58 "I am very much": Blodgett, 68.

58 "This city": Ibid., 87.

58 "wild and full of pep": Conover, 46.

58 "During the morning": Moseley, 37.

59 "It is not the Paris": Roosevelt, 42.

60 "a Marquise": Coolidge, 8.

60 "Paris is wonderful": Ibid., 4, 9.

60 "It is a job": Ibid., 3.

60 *"Mon., Nov. 5"*: Coffin in Gilchrist, 8.

61 "It was a fine plan": Sprague, Jan. 7, 1919, 16.

62 "There are some 150": Walcott, 14.

63 "They are a very odd": Ibid., 57–58.

5. DRIVING THE MACHINE

65 "My first sortie": Walcott, 17–18.
67 "being sent to France": Ibid., 11.
67 "I went through": Mitchell, 121.
68 "All one has to do": Drew, 24.
68 "absolute flying classes": Ibid., 25, 24.
69 "Well, father": Ibid., 16.
69 "One gets into": Ibid., 25.
70 "clinging to": Ibid., 26.
70 "nothing but": Walcott, 29.
71 "Nothing to do": Ibid., 39.
71 "Coming back": Ibid., 40.
72 "There are nine": Conover, 154.
73 "The proper thing": Walcott, 32.
74 "In the meantime": Ibid., 37–38.
74 "a sea of gumbo": Roosevelt, 55.
74 "*Alors*": Walcott, 33.
76 "is absolutely unique": Nichols, 111.
76 "If you ever": Ibid., 123.
76 "But really": Rowe, 23–24.
77 "The air work": Woodward, 97.
77 "It's like the way": Nichols, 122.
77 "Curtis Munson": Moseley, 94.
78 "If you break": Drew, 16.
79 "Smashes are": Adams, 25.
79 "cussing like": Grider, 77.
79 "There has not been": Gates, 76.
80 "It's marvelous": Roosevelt, 80.
80 "hard luck's favorite": Hartney, 175.

6. THE PLEASURABLE SENSATION OF FLYING

83 "There's a great": Walcott, 31–32.
85 "Acrobacy used to be": Coolidge, 58.
86 "After a great many": Kinney, 27–28.
86 "to cling to in": Coolidge, 112.
87 "Well, I got around": MacLeish, *Price of Honor*, 70.
87 "I did not expect": Adams, 36–38.
87 "I can fly": Grider, 80.
88 "The driving": Gates, 90.
88 "flying a certain": Moseley, 103.
88 "In formation": Roosevelt, 108.
88 "I led a formation": Conover, 190.
89 "chases madly": Drew, 41–42.
89 "a fair approximation": Nichols, 192.
89 "An order came": Biddle, 33.
90 "the French were": Biddle in Fonck, ix.

90 "The only unpleasant": Roosevelt, 125.
91 "Leach went into": Avery, 207.
91 "Hagadorn pulled out": Ibid., 209.
91 "Hopkins went into": Ibid., 208.
91 "yesterday Philippauteaux": Ibid., 209.
91 "Cadet Whyte": Ibid., 210.
91 "Bieglow, of our": Ibid., 215.
91 "Who will be next?": Ibid., 208.
91 "*Jan. (?) 1918*": George Vaughn, 38, 41, 51, 48.
92 "*Saturday* it was foggy": Gates, 31.
93 "two fellows": Roosevelt, 111, 112.
94 "The spirits in camp": Conover, 176, 184.
95 "I believe that": MacLeish, *Kenneth*, 16.
95 "That's the way": Holden, 242.
95 "As far as being killed": Conover, 24.
96 "The aviators": Moseley, 42.
96 "You speak": Biddle, 19.

7. WAITING FOR THE WAR
98 "4 hours 15 minutes": Avery, 203.
98 "have done thirty hours": George Vaughn, 36.
98 "I have had about 40 hours": Richardson, 50.
98 "I have now been": Conover, 149.
98 "The number of hours": Holden, 235.
99 "In 1918 an R.F.C. trainee": George Vaughn, 57.
100 "We were given one tour": Irving, 78.
100 "Really I'm in no hurry": Nichols, 149.
100 "need not worry": Walcott, 64.
100 "Everyone's idea of heaven": Holden, 244.
100 "But I must confess": Drew, 55.
101 "I'm beginning to hear": Walcott, 54.
102 "There are two schools": Drew, 15.
102 "Only about 20%": Gates, 99.
102 "delightful": Roosevelt, 78–79.
102 "so fast": Woodward, 129.
102 "delicate": Coolidge, 34.
102 "small and graceful": Wright, 208.
102 "If a man is training": Drew, 15.
103 "I will probably get sent": Gates, 75.
103 "There is a chance": Ibid., 90.
103 "I'll bomb the place": Nichols, 112.
103 "I want to fly": Blodgett, 110.
104 "Some lunatic": Roosevelt, 84–85.
105 "So far as I could learn": Bingham, 82.
105 "Some change": Avery, 203.
106 "Take this plane": Dixon in George Vaughn, 83.

106 "It's as dangerous": Richardson, 52.

106 "I came here": Holden, 240.

108 *"April 7, 1918"*: Avery, 212.

108 "The rumor turned out": Holden, 242.

108 "we are not": Ibid., 244.

108 "There, just north": Ibid., 243.

109 "I hope some really great": Ibid., 245.

110 "for which I am": Roosevelt, 45.

110 "sweating the fat": Ibid., 82.

111 "non-payment": Heinrichs in Woolley, *First to the Front*, 48.

111 "In formation flying": Irving, 77.

112 "not feeling awfully well": Roosevelt, 132.

112 "I feel I owe it": Ibid., 96.

113 "after having thoroughly": Conover, 203.

114 "The fun was quite intense": MacLeish, *Price of Honor*, 88.

114 "but one must never": Coolidge in Roosevelt, 228.

114 "whisk it around": Ibid.

115 "The other day": Roosevelt, 138.

115 "Ham and I": Ibid., 141.

8. HOW TO FIGHT

118 "These notes": Rees, 1.

118 "Comparison of Pilots": Ibid.

120 "Our hunters": "Pursuit Work in a Single-Seater," 10.

122 "seconded by": Ibid., 13.

122 "I went out": Biddle, 99.

122 "bag at least": Ibid., 138.

122 "Attack ahead": "Pursuit Work in a Single-Seater," 2.

123 "The oldest and wisest": Ibid.

123 "Remember, however": Ibid., 8.

123 "Get very close": Ibid., 5.

123 "Most experienced pilots": Ibid., 4.

123 "It would always seem": Ibid.

124 "adopted for use": Hall and Nordhoff, 1:126.

124 "I had to undergo": Woodward, 137.

125 "Just what I expected": Rickenbacker, 9.

126 "as if somebody": Buffum, 217.

126 "It was the first time": Nichols, 182.

127 "Pursuit squadrons": Mitchell, 82.

127 "I'm a very poor gambler": Blodgett, 171.

9. THIS KILLING BUSINESS

128 "It's rather queer": Nichols, 175.

129 "After perhaps five": Ibid., 181.

129 "flying in a line": Ibid., 199.

130 "I saw my luminous": Ibid., 212.

131 "I didn't wait": Woodward, 147–48.
131 "I saw him slowly": Ibid., 148.
132 "I decided to take": Ibid., 148–49.
132 "It was very thrilling": Ibid., 149.
133 "poking around": Drew, 57.
133 "that delicate period": Rickenbacker, 82.
134 "and then pulled": Woodward, 153.
136 "Have you seen": Ibid., 178.
136 "please send all newspaper": Ibid., 179.
136 "The first of April": Ibid., 185.
137 "pilote de chasse": Ibid., 182.
137 "He told me": Ibid., 2.
137 "just nothing at all": Ibid., 12.
137 "Located Houston's grave": Ibid., 187.
138 "Talk about being": Blodgett, 145.
138 "So I went in": Ibid., 177.
139 "It's a great game": Ibid., 180.
140 "Dick Blodgett returning": Heinrichs in Woolley, *First to the Front*, 95.
140 "the American Ace of Aces": Rickenbacker, 93–94.
140 "Alert 8h 55 to 9h 34": *Gorrell's History*, ser. E, 12:184.
141 "Word came in": Lahm, 79.
142 "We had our losses": Mitchell, 193.
143 "I had asked Luf": Rickenbacker, 96–97.
143 "I doubt very much": Mitchell, 201.
144 "His encounter": Rickenbacker, 94.
144 "As I left": Mitchell, 199.
144 "A good pilot": Alan Winslow, March 11, 1933, 23.

10. ABROAD II: GETTING ACQUAINTED

147 "Lady Somebody's house": Grider, 64.
147 "jumping hedges": Taber, 84.
147 "we never had more fun": Skelton, *Callahan*, 5.
148 "There were just about": George Vaughn, 67.
148 "late 1400's": Campbell, *Let's Go*, 28.
148 "Yesterday Q. and I": Coolidge, 108.
149 "Lord and Lady Ostler": Grider, 74.
149 "the perfect example": Ibid., 83.
149 "I picked out": Ibid., 68.
149 "I have an awfully sweet girl": Ibid., 71.
149 "I had a wonderful party": Ibid., 72.
149 "made up of the best": Ibid., 83.
150 "Emma, I have had": Ibid., 78–79.
150 "Emma . . . at last": Ibid., 90.
151 "We are going": Ibid., 90–91.
151 "I wish you could see": Skelton, *Cross & Cockade Great Britain Journal*, 14.
152 "loafing, reading": Avery, 225.
153 "It has been great fun": Moseley, 37.

153 "I had a wonderful time": Gates, 102.
153 "Bernadine is only": Ibid., 128.
154 "who could not keep": Heinrichs in Woolley, *First to the Front*, 159.
154 "this wretched war": Ibid., 176.
154 "the Jazz Band": Conover, 172.
154 "It was too crowded": Gates, 68.
154 "This afternoon": Holden, 251.

11. IN PURSUIT

156 "They haven't even": Roosevelt, 113–14.
157 "This front": Moseley, 156.
157 "It seems absurd": Coolidge, 107.
157 "When we came back": Nichols, 217.
158 "All we heard": Ibid., 218.
159 "All the French balloons": Hall and Nordhoff, 1:309.
159 "We flew six hours": Ibid., 2:246.
161 "This offensive": Ibid., 1:309.
161 "I have been flying": Ordway, 225–26.
162 "We were peacefully": Nichols, 192.
163 "It had been": Holden, 253.
165 "I have been": Heinrichs in Woolley, *First to the Front*, 75.
166 "These high patrols": MacLeish, *Kenneth*, 75–76.
166 "Two planes sent out": *Gorrell's History*, ser. E, 12:177.
167 "It was a great war": Campbell, *Let's Go*, 55.
167 "For some reason": Ibid., 56–57.
169 "a nice looking fellow": Lahm, 59–60.
170 "Of course": Holden, 247.
171 "He was badly shaken": Alan Winslow, March 4, 1933, 24–25.
173 "He didn't crash": Grider, 104–5.
173 "Oh, it was a wonderful sight!": Hall and Nordhoff, 2:98.

12. LOOKING AT THE WAR

175 "How those devils": George Hughes in Vaughan, 139.
176 "Well, they simply": Ibid., 140.
177 "I heard a lot": Hart, *Cross & Cockade Journal*, 333.
178 "I motioned to go": Cole, 159.
179 "One time he": Crosby, 39–40.
181 "This is by far": Conover, 221.
181 "The sight is most magnificent": Ibid., 223.
182 "Wild eyed": Haslett, xiii.
182 "This is practically": Conover, 218.
182 "There I received": Ibid., 219.
183 "This Squadron": Crosby, 52.
184 "It might be explained": Morse, 25.

13. A SHORT HISTORY OF BOMBING

186 "The impression made": Prince, 18.
187 "got to be old hands": Ibid., 19.
187 "were highly complimentary": Ibid., 21.
187 "threw down with precision": "The War in the Air," *Flying* 4, no. 9 (Oct. 1915): 21.
190 "had been locked": Mitchell, 59.
190 "about six feet in height": Ibid., 104.
191 "Not only was the material": Ibid., 84.
193 "had seen the real": Ibid., 24.
193 "This is the most": MacLeish, *Price of Honor*, 127.
193 "I will be way down": Ibid., 127–28.
194 "In my wildest dreams": Ibid., 137–38.
194 "Today I learned": Ibid., 138.
195 "a great big project": Ibid., 160.
196 "Last night": Holden, 242.
197 "to clear the way": Nichols, 257.
198 "They came down": Mitchell, 212.
199 "It was the first": Ibid., 213.
199 *"July 10*—6 planes left": Hopper, pt. 4, p. 5.
200 "This may take some": Conover, 214.
201 "Our bombardment group": Mitchell, 241–42.

14. SUMMER: 1918

203 "I faced a big decision": Holden, 247–48.
204 "I feel like": Coolidge, 142–43.
204 "like the promised land": Buckley, 55.
204 "The map was being": Codman, 22.
205 "This is the queerest": Coolidge, 159.
205 "one of those white": Roosevelt, 161.
206 "We are in a sector": Holden, 248.
206 "We were patrolling": Sewall in Woolley, *First to the Front*, 123–24.
206 "These massed": Alan Winslow, March 18, 1933, 38.
206 "there must have been": George Hughes in Vaughan, 144.
207 *"Saturday.* Had my second": Avery, 223–24.
207 *"Aug. 5–19, 1918"*: Holden, 251.
208 "I heard a loud crashing": Campbell, *Let's Go*, 72–74.
208 "In three days": Holden, 251.
209 "Bursting shrapnel": Coolidge, 174.
209 "There is no use": Theodore Roosevelt, *The Letters of Theodore Roosevelt*, ed. Elting
      E. Morison (Cambridge, Mass.: Harvard University Press, 1951–54), 8:1363.
210 "I got my first": Roosevelt, 162.
210 "I got a Boche": Coolidge, 153.
210 "Day before yesterday": Avery, 222.
210 "I shall never forget": Coolidge, 153–54.
210 "now feel quite": George Vaughn, 89.
210 "you bet": Avery, 222.

210 "Ohioan Drops Foe Ace": Cleveland *Plain Dealer*, July 27, 1918, 1.

211 "the most famous": *Daily Mail* in Avery, 222.

211 "he bitterly complained": Mitchell, 213.

211 "Driving a big": *Boston Herald*, July 9, 1918, 1.

212 "I hasten to correct": Coolidge, 165–66.

212 "The magazines": Blodgett, 26.

212 "It seems to me": Holden, 252.

213 "Oh how unspeakably": Ibid., 257.

213 "Bertie Hall attacked": Rockwell, 128.

214 "supposedly": Hall and Nordhoff, 1:255.

214 "Fast Fighting": Bert Hall, "Fast Fighting and Narrow Escapes in the Air," *American Magazine*, Sept. 1918, 43–45, 102.

214 *"Date of Enlistment"*: Hall and Nordhoff, I:509.

215 "If you want to read": Richardson, 89–90.

215 "'Aviator' Fails": *Plane News*, Aug. 10, 1918, 22.

15. SEPTEMBER: ST. MIHIEL

217 "Rumor had it": Egbert, 277.

217 "When the attack": Holden, 252.

218 "rained in the night": Clapp, 40–50.

218 "It never ceased": Barth, 33.

219 "literally tore his hair": Gilchrist, 29.

219 "In the morning": Ibid., 34.

219 "by far the most eventful": Hart, *History of the 135th Aero Squadron*, 73.

220 "smelling the turbulent": Eastman, 81.

220 "flop and skid": Ibid., 82.

220 "Along in the trenches": Ibid.

220 "Strangest, from our point": Ibid., 83.

221 "like trying to recall": Coolidge, 189.

222 "Then the party": Ibid., 190.

222 "A Spad": Ibid., 191.

223 "We rolled out of bed": Holden, 253.

223 "Say! when my tracer": Ibid.

223 "I looked behind": Ibid.

224 "Shooting down balloons": Coolidge, 180–81.

224 "I fired at close range": Holden, 249.

225 "At last! At last": Ibid., 254–55.

226 "I was climbing": Littauer, 38.

227 "Planes #14, 20, 4": Hopper, pt. 4, p. 37.

227 "During the entire": Ibid., pt. 3, p. 99.

228 "Our air force": Mitchell, 245.

229 "leaving behind it": Ibid., 247.

229 "Most of the crews": Ibid., 248.

229 "our most tragic day": Clapp, 40.

230 "Our most disastrous raid": Karl C. Payne in Ticknor, 1:113.

230 "Out of the 9": Holden, 251.

231 "Our squadron has lost": Ibid., 252.

231 "Lots of friends": Ibid., 255.

231 "How can one help": Ibid.

231 "We were occupied": Conover, 223.

232 "Six of the fellows": Avery, 223.

232 "War flying": Rickenbacker, 334.

233 "Pursuit squadrons": Mitchell, 82.

233 "on account of dizziness": Avery, 219.

233 "It is queer": Holden, 255.

16. ABROAD III: END GAMES

236 "provided we haven't": George Vaughn, 136.

236 "There was no liquor": Knowles, 360.

237 "If you were scheduled": Ibid., 361.

237 "most enjoyable days": Conover, 224.

237 "At the officers' mess": Markham, 38.

238 "It never enters": Holden, 255.

238 "Generally speaking": Alan Winslow, March 11, 1933, 24.

239 "twelve dozen quarts": Lynd in Hart, *History of the 135th Aero Squadron*, 129.

239 "We're going into battle": Knowles, 358.

240 "The alcohol problem": *Air Service Medical Manual*, 106–7.

240 "The nervous": Ibid., 127.

241 "There is, therefore": Ibid.

243 "I am just like a kid": Sewall in Woolley, *First to the Front*, 116.

243 "There goes my Menkhoff": Avery, 227.

245 "I'm not sure": Sheets in Hart, *History of the 135th Aero Squadron*, 77–78.

17. THE LAST BATTLE

247 "On several occasions": Hart, *History of the 135th Aero Squadron*, 87.

247 "Went up, saw nothing": Richardson, 116.

248 "It was a pretty poor day": Gates, 154–64.

248 "Naturally, we felt": Morse, 52.

249 "received posthumously": Ibid., 51.

249 "This was also done": Knowles in Ticknor, 1:47.

249 "During the last few months": P. S. Rippon and E. G. Manuel, "Report on the Central Characteristics of Successful and Unsuccessful Aviators," *Lancet*, Sept. 28, 1918, 415.

250 "filling the skies": Rickenbacker, 314.

250 "Every plane": D'Olive, 7–8.

251 "I had shot a guy": Ibid., 8–9.

252 "until, while I was": Conover, 225.

254 "My companion": Coolidge, 208–9.

254 "Protection Patrol": *Gorrell's History*, ser. E, 12:257.

254 "We learned": Eastman, 117.

254 "apparently contrary minded": Ibid., 83.

255 "His scoreboard": Ibid., 117.

256 "I'm going out": MacLeish, *Price of Honor*, 226.

256 "Lieutenant MacLeish": Ibid., 227.

257 "Wouldn't you be tickled": Holden, 256.

257 "At last!": Ibid., 257.

259 "After having previously destroyed": *Medal of Honor Recipients*, 451–52.

259 *"October 2"*: Richardson, 119–23.

260 "Gosh, one doesn't know": Coolidge, 218.

260 "If Germany quits": Jerry Hughes in Vaughan, 174.

260 "Jack and I": Nichols, 173.

261 "Well, Mammy": Coolidge, 217.

18. NOVEMBER ELEVENTH

262 "This evening we have": Eastman, 121.

262 "One treads ground": Ibid.

263 "thinks we'll be": Ibid., 122.

263 "His idea is to have us": Ibid., 123.

263 "not much work was done": Littauer, 42.

264 "In the afternoon": Lindstrom, 126.

264 "Today was a beautiful day": Ibid.

264 "Well, thank heaven": Rowe, 131.

264 "No combats": *Gorrell's History*, ser. E, 18:305.

265 *"Tuesday, Nov. 5"*: Irvin, 21.

265 "There will be": Eastman, 128.

265 "They've signed": Ibid.

266 "This is probably": Gates, 171–72.

266 "All night long": Gilchrist, 125.

266 "to watch the excitement": George Vaughan, 141.

266 "which have been dimmed": Ibid., 142.

267 "in a fine hot bath": Holden, 257.

267 "An American uniform": Ibid.

267 "The news that the war": Moseley, 220–21.

268 "the French were mad": Eastman, 129.

268 "So this is France": Ibid.

19. AFTERWARDS

270 "I've never enjoyed": Rogers, 225.

270 "I've always maintained": Ibid., 217.

270 "fiendishly tempted": Eastman, 130.

270 "A fever for playing": Ibid., 131.

271 "I can't make out": Ibid., 98.

271 "It seems almost unbelievable": Ibid., 99.

271 "Still full of splendid ideas": Ibid., 124.

271 "fairly jumping": Ibid., 148.

272 "I was not unconscious": Ibid., 148.

273 "During the celebration": George Hughes in Vaughan, 189.
274 "It was a solemn party": Rogers, 223.
275 "We were just coming": Lahm, 157.
275 "He had orders": D'Olive, 13.
276 "He stunted": Crosby, 58–59.
277 "Thank Heaven": Gates, 173.
277 "Agreeable Surprise": *Out of Control*, Nov. 19, 1918, 10.
278 "You can't imagine": Holden, 258.
279 "Aviation Triumphant": *New York Times*, May 9, 1920, E2.
282 "because of its inaccessibility": Gorrell, *Measure*, vi.
285 "I hope that the reader": George Vaughn, preface.

BIBLIOGRAPHY

PRINCIPAL SOURCES
A list of the diaries, letters, and memoirs of pilots and other individuals that were the principal sources for this book.

Adams, Briggs Kilburn. *The American Spirit.* Boston: Atlantic Monthly Press, 1918.

Archibald, Norman. *Heaven High, Hell Deep, 1917–1918.* New York: Boni, 1935.

Avery, Walter. "The War Diaries and Letters of Walter L. Avery." Compiled by Robert B. Gill. *Over the Front* 1, no. 3 (Fall 1986): 201–29.

Biddle, Charles. *The Way of the Eagle.* New York: C. Scribner's Sons, 1919.

Bingham, Hiram. *An Explorer in the Air Service.* New Haven, Conn.: Yale University Press, 1920.

Block, Hyman C. "I Flew with the 89th Aero Squadron." *Cross & Cockade Journal* 9, no. 2 (Summer 1968): 124–33.

Blodgett, Richard Ashley. *Life and Letters.* Boston, 1920.

Buffum, Thomas B. "My Experiences with Escadrille SPAD 77." *Cross & Cockade Journal* 2, no. 3 (Autumn 1961): 215–23.

Campbell, Douglas. "Captain Douglas Campbell, 94th Aero Sqdn. USAS." *Cross & Cockade Journal* 6, no. 1 (Spring 1965): 30–42.

———. *Let's Go Where the Action Is!* Edited and annotated by Jack R. Eder. Knightstown, Ind.: JaaRE, 1984.

Chapman, Victor. *Victor Chapman's Letters from France, with Memoir by John Jay Chapman.* New York: Macmillan, 1917.

Codman, Charles R. *Contact.* Boston: Little, Brown, 1937.

Cole, Donald B. "Memoirs of Lt. Donald B. Cole, 135th Aero Squadron, USAS." *Cross & Cockade Journal* 6, no. 2 (Summer 1965): 153–63.

Conover, Harvey. *Diary of a WWI Pilot.* Spokane, Wash.: Conover-Patterson, 2004.

Coolidge, Hamilton. *Letters of an American Airman.* Boston: privately printed, 1919.

Crosby, Wilson G. *Fletcher Ladd McCordic, 1st Lieut. 88th Aero Squadron A.E.F.: A Tribute.* Chicago: privately printed, 1921.

Cunningham, Alfred A. *Marine Flyer in France.* Washington, D.C.: History and Museums Division, Headquarters, U.S. Marine Corps, 1974.

Davies, John. *The Legend of Hobey Baker.* Boston: Little, Brown, 1966.

D'Olive, Charles. "An Interview with Charles d'Olive." *Cross & Cockade Journal* 1, no. 1 (Spring 1960): 3–14.

Drew, Sidney Rankin. *Life and Letters.* Edited by Mrs. Sidney Drew. New York: Cheltenham, 1921.

Eastman, Joseph. Diary. Joseph Houston Eastman Papers, Hoover Institution Archives.

Egbert, Lester D. "Experiences of Lester D. Egbert." Edited by Paul Parker Jr. *Cross & Cockade Journal* 9, no. 3 (Autumn 1968): 269–82.

Gates, Percival. *An American Pilot in the Skies of France.* Dayton: Wright State University Press, 1992.

Grider, John MacGavock. *Marse John Goes to War.* Memphis: Davis, 1933.

Hall, Bert. *"En l'Air!"* New York: New Library, 1918.

Hall, James Norman. *High Adventure.* Boston: Houghton Mifflin, 1918.

Hart, Percival. "Observations from a D. H. 4." *Cross & Cockade Journal* 2, no. 4 (Winter 1961): 330–42.

Hartney, Harold E. *Up and at 'Em.* Garden City, N.Y.: Doubleday, 1971.

Haslett, Elmer. *Luck on the Wing.* New York: E. P. Dutton, 1920.

Holden, Lansing C., Jr. "The War Diary and Letters." Edited by Thomas E. Kullgren. *Over the Front* 1, no. 3 (Fall 1986): 230–60.

Irvin, Francis. *Francis L. "Spike" Irvin's War Diary and the History of the 148th Aero Squadron Aviation Section.* Compiled by W. P. Taylor and F. L. Irvin. Manhattan, Kans.: Aerospace Historian, 1974.

Irving, Livingston. "The War Experiences of Livingston G. Irving." *Cross & Cockade Journal* 1, no. 4 (Winter 1960): 75–84.

Joyce, Temple N. "An Ace with No Victories." From a taped interview with Temple N. Joyce, by John H. Tegler. *Cross & Cockade Journal* 3, no. 2 (Summer 1962): 95–106.

Kinney, Curtis. *I Flew a Camel.* With Dale M. Titler. Philadelphia: Dorrance, 1972.

Knowles, James. "Recollections of France and the 95th." *Cross & Cockade Journal* 10, no. 4 (Winter 1969): 355–65.

Lahm, Frank Purdy. *World War I Diary.* Maxwell AFB, Ala.: Historical Research Division, Aerospace Studies Institute, 1970.

Lee, Benjamin. *Benjamin Lee, 2d.* Boston: Cornhill, 1920.

Libby, Frederick. *Horses Don't Fly.* New York: Arcade, 2000.

Lindstrom, Gustaf. "Observations: The War Diary of Lt. Gustaf L. Lindstrom." Edited by Peter Kilduff. *Cross & Cockade Journal* 13, no. 2 (Summer 1972): 97–127.

Littauer, Kenneth. "Kenneth P. Littauer: From the Lafayette Flying Corps to the 88th Aero Squadron." *Cross & Cockade Journal* 13, no. 1 (Spring 1972): 22–43.

MacLeish, Kenneth. *Kenneth: A Collection of Letters.* Edited by his mother. Chicago: privately printed, 1919.

———. *The Price of Honor.* Edited by Geoffrey L. Rossano. Annapolis, Md.: Naval Institute Press, 1991.

Markham, Minor C. *Old Man . . . Mumbling / Survivor.* Privately printed, 1981.

McConnell, James R. *Flying for France.* Garden City, N.Y.: Doubleday, Page, 1917.

Mitchell, William. *Memoirs of World War I.* New York: Random House, 1960.

Moseley, George. *Extracts from the Letters of George Clark Moseley.* Privately printed, 1923.

Nichols, Alan. *Letters Home from the Lafayette Flying Corps.* San Francisco: J.D. Huff, 1993.

Ordway, Frederick. "A New Hampshire Pursuit Pilot." From a taped interview with F. I. Ordway of the Twenty-Seventh Aero Squadron, by John H. Tegler. *Cross & Cockade Journal* 4, no. 3 (1963): 217–38.

Pershing, John J. *My Experiences in the World War.* New York: Frederick A. Stokes, 1931.

Prince, Norman. *A Volunteer Who Died for the Cause He Loved, with Memoir by George F. Babbitt.* Boston: Houghton Mifflin, 1917.

Richardson, Roland W. *An American Pursuit Pilot in France.* Shippensburg, Pa.: White Mane, 1994.

Rickenbacker, Eddie. *Fighting the Flying Circus.* New York: Frederick A. Stokes, 1919.

Rockwell, Kiffin Yates. *War Letters of Kiffin Yates Rockwell.* Garden City, N.Y.: Country Life, 1925.

Rogers, Bogart. *A Yankee Ace in the RAF.* Lawrence: University Press of Kansas, 1996.

Roosevelt, Quentin. *Quentin Roosevelt: A Sketch with Letters.* Edited by Kermit Roosevelt. New York: C. Scribner's Sons, 1921.

Rowe, Josiah P., Jr. *Letters from a World War I Aviator.* Boston: Sinclaire, 1986.

Sheely, Irving Edward. *Sailor of the Air.* Tuscaloosa: University of Alabama Press, 1993.

Sprague, George E. "Flying Gobs." *Liberty,* Jan. 7, 1939, 14–16; Jan. 14, 1939, 24–28; Jan. 21, 1939, 51–52.

Taber, Sydney Richmond, comp. *Arthur Richmond Taber: A Memorial Record.* Princeton, N.J.: privately printed, 1920.

Vaughn, George A., Jr. *War Flying in France.* Manhattan, Kans.: Military Affairs/Aerospace Historian Publishing, 1980.

Walcott, Stuart. *Above the French Lines.* Princeton, N.J.: Princeton University Press, 1918.

Winslow, Alan. "No Parachutes." *Liberty,* Feb. 25, 1933, 6–11; March 4, 1933, 18–25; March 11, 1933, 20–29; March 18, 1933, 36–41; March 25, 1933, 44–49; April 1, 1933, 50–54.

Winslow, Carroll. *With the French Flying Corps.* New York: Scribner, 1917.

Woodward, Houston. *A Year for France.* New Haven, Conn.: Yale Publishing Association, 1919.

Wright, Jack Morris. *A Poet of the Air.* Boston: Houghton Mifflin, 1918.

OTHER SOURCES

Air Service Medical Manual. Washington, D.C.: GPO, 1918.

Aviation Medicine in the A.E.F. Washington, D.C.: GPO, 1920.

Barth, C. G. *History of the Twentieth Aero Squadron.* Winona, Minn.: Winona Labor News, n.d.

Bethell, John T. *Harvard Observed.* Cambridge, Mass.: Harvard University Press, 1998.

Boy Scouts of America. *The Official Handbook for Boys.* Garden City, N.Y.: Doubleday, Page, 1912.

Buckley, Harold. *Squadron 95.* Paris: Obelisk, 1933.

Clapp, Frederick Mortimer. *A History of the 17th Aero Squadron*. Garden City, N.Y.: Country Life, 1920.

Clark, Eugene Francis, ed. *War Record of Dartmouth College, 1917–1918*. Hanover, N.H., 1922.

Deullin, Albert. "La chasse en monoplane," and "Les patrouilles de chasse, novembre 1917." MSS, Service Historique de l'Armée de l'Air, Division Archives, France. The English translation used in this book is from "Pursuit Work in a Single-Seater," *Bulletin of the Information Section, Air Service, American E.F.* 6, no. 255 (1918). The name of the translator is not given, but the text is essentially the translation and additions prepared by Charles Biddle, which were reprinted as an appendix to Biddle's *Fighting Airman: The Way of the Eagle*, edited by Stanley M. Ulanoff (Garden City, N.Y.: Doubleday, 1968). Biddle's manuscript of the translation is in the San Diego Air & Space Museum Library & Archives.

Fitzgerald, F. Scott. *This Side of Paradise*. New York: C. Scribner's Sons, 1920.

Fonck, René. *Ace of Aces*. Edited by Stanley M. Ulanoff. Garden City, N.Y.: Doubleday, 1967.

Gilchrist, John W. Stuart. *The 104th Aero Squadron*. Privately printed, 1968.

Gordon, Dennis. *The Lafayette Flying Corps*. Atglen, Pa.: Schiffer, 2000.

Gorrell, Edgar S. *The Measure of America's World War Aeronautical Effort*. Burlington, Vt.: Lane, 1940.

———. "Why Riding Boots Sometimes Irritate an Aviator's Feet." *U.S. Air Services* 17 (Oct. 1932): 24–30.

Gorrell's History of the American Expeditionary Forces Air Service, 1917–1919. National Archives Micropublication NARA M990.

Hall, James Norman, and Charles Bernard Nordhoff, eds. *The Lafayette Flying Corps*. Boston: Houghton Mifflin, 1920.

Handy, Cortlandt W. *History of the U.S. School of Military Aeronautics at Princeton University, May, 1917–November 30, 1918*. N.p., 1919.

Hart, Percival Gray. *History of the 135th Aero Squadron*. Chicago, 1939.

Harvard's Military Record in the World War. Edited by Frederick S. Mead. Boston: Harvard Alumni Association, 1921.

Hopper, Bruce C. *When the Air Was Young: American Day Bombardment, A.E.F., France, 1917–1918*. N.p., 1944.

Howe, M. A. DeWolfe. *Memoirs of the Harvard Dead in the War Against Germany*. Cambridge, Mass.: Harvard University Press, 1920–24.

Jane's All the World's Aircraft. London: Sampson Low, Marston, 1916.

La Guardia, Fiorello H. *The Making of an Insurgent*. Philadelphia: J. B. Lippincott, 1948.

Maurer, Maurer, ed. *The U.S. Air Service in World War I*. Washington, D.C.: Office of Air Force History, 1978–79.

McMinnies, William Gordon. *Practical Flying*. New York: George H. Doran, 1918.

Medal of Honor Recipients, 1863–1973. Washington, D.C.: GPO, 1973.

Morse, Daniel P., Jr. *The History of the 50th Aero Squadron*. New York: Blanchard, 1920.

Paine, Ralph D. *The First Yale Unit*. Cambridge, Mass.: Riverside, 1925.

Princeton in the World War. Princeton, N.J.: Princeton University, 1932.

"Pursuit Work in a Single-Seater." *Bulletin of the Information Section, Air Service, American E.F.* 6, no. 255 (1918).

Rees, L.W.B. *Fighting in the Air*. Washington, D.C.: Gibson, 1917.

Skelton, Marvin L. *Callahan, the Last War Bird*. Manhattan, Kans.: Military Affairs/ Aerospace Historian Publishing, 1980.

———. "John McGavock Grider—War Bird." *Cross & Cockade Great Britain Journal* 11, no. 1 (Spring 1980): 8–20.

———. "More on John McGavock Grider of 'War Birds.'" *Cross & Cockade Journal* 20, no. 3 (Autumn 1979): 259–68.

Sloan, James J., Jr. *Wings of Honor: American Airmen in World War I*. Atglen, Pa.: Schiffer, 1994.

Sweetser, Arthur. *The American Air Service*. New York: Appleton, 1919.

Taber Scrapbook. Scrapbook Collection, Seeley G. Mudd Manuscript Library, Princeton University.

Ticknor, Caroline, ed. *New England Aviators, 1914–1918: Their Portraits and Their Records*. Boston: Houghton Mifflin, 1919.

Van Wyen, Adrian O. *Naval Aviation in World War I*. Washington, D.C.: Chief of Naval Operations, 1969.

Vaughan, David K. *Flying for the Air Service: The Hughes Brothers in World War I*. Bowling Green, Ohio: Bowling Green State University Popular Press, 1998.

Vaughn, David. "Watcher of the Sky: The World War I Flying Experiences of George A. Vaughn Jr." MS, n.d.

Woolley, Charles. *First to the Front: The Aerial Adventures of 1st Lt. Waldo Heinrichs and the 95th Aero Squadron*. Atglen, Pa.: Schiffer, 1999.

———. *The Hat in the Ring Gang: The Combat History of the 94th Aero Squadron in World War I*. Atglen, Pa.: Schiffer, 2001.

Wortman, Marc. *The Millionaires' Unit*. New York: Public Affairs, 2006.

ACKNOWLEDGMENTS

Here, at the end of a book that has been long in the making, I must look back and thank the many individuals and institutions that have helped me along the way. First, the individuals—old friends and strangers, pilots, historians of war, librarians, compilers of pilots' stories. I thank Tom Danaher, Bill Deane, George Grabone, the late Dominic Hibberd, Bob Holland, Don Macaulay, John Nolan, Anthony Preston, Julian Putkowski, James Salter, Richard Snow, David, George, and James Vaughn, Geoffrey Ward, Bob Wohl, Charles and Nancy Woolley, and my capable and patient editors, Alex Star and Laird Gallagher. And two special individuals, my daughters, Joanna Hynes and Miranda Preston, who not only have borne the burden of a writer-father all their lives, but have helped him.

Among institutions I owe most to the patient staff members of Princeton University's Firestone Library and Seeley G. Mudd Manuscript Library. I am also indebted to the Harvard University Archives and to two of its archivists, Andrea B. Goldstein and Barbara S. Meloni; to Ronald Bulatoff of the Hoover Institution Archives at Stanford University; to Paul Oelkrug of the McDermott Library at the University of Texas; to Sarah Hartwell of the Dartmouth College Library; to the Yale University archives; to the staff of the U.S. Army Heritage and Education Center, U.S. Army Military History Institute, Carlisle Barracks; to the Maine Maritime Museum Library; to the Raymond Mander and Joe Mitchenson Theatre Collection, now in the archives of the University of Bristol Theatre Collection; and to Connie Houchins of the Andalusia Foundation.

INDEX

Page numbers in *italics* refer to illustrations.